International Building Exhibition Berlin 1987
Examples of a New Architecture

GW00506597

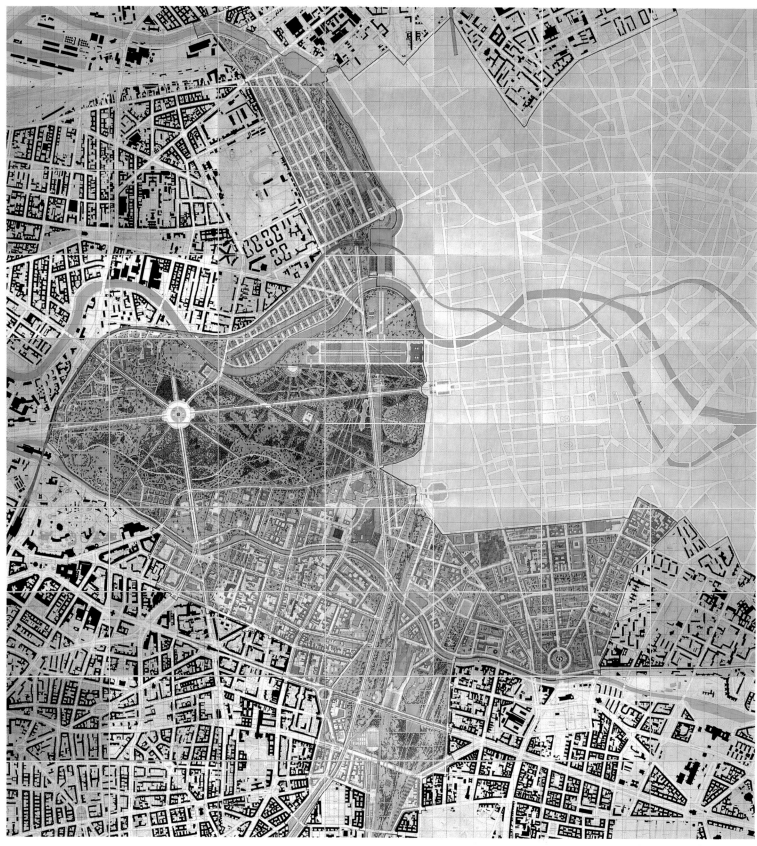

Overall urban development plan to show IBA sectors designated for new building work (southern Friedrichstadt, southern Tiergarten) in context (from the exhibition "Idea, Process, Result")
Josef Paul Kleihues
with Mirko Baum, Ludger Brands, Walther Stepp
70 maps of Berlin, 1:1000 with additions in ink and felt colour.
Single sheet: 60.0 x 80.0 cm. Overall dimensions: 6.0 x 5.6 m.

"Urban development is always part of a political process and of a planning process, and results when small projects are wedded to ideas of wider scope. In the downtown demonstration areas of the new building sector the IBA as planning process has led to various kinds of compromise and also to an isolated approach to problems of limited relevance. The plan reproduced here shows the most important of the IBA projects evolved over the last five years, and in particular those where decisions have already been taken. In addition, it illustrates the possibilities of a long-term urbanistic process in the IBA areas, and shows the context in terms of city development, especially as regards the so-called central area. It is intended to stimulate discussion, and not just for the duration of the International Building Exhibition."

INTERNATIONAL BUILDING EXHIBITION BERLIN 1987

Examples of a New Architecture

ACADEMY EDITIONS, LONDON

Edited by Josef P. Kleihues and Heinrich Klotz

Coordinator: Peter Schwarz
Catalogue editors: Annegret Burg, Detlef Mallwitz, Peter Schwarz and
Monika Taeger (urban renewal)
Design: Rolf Brenner, Annegret Burg and Detlef Mallwitz
Production: Rolf Brenner
Editorial supervision: Michael Maegraith
Plan photography: Udo Hesse (new urban building)

Translated by Ian Robson

Published on behalf of the Culture and Leisure Department, Municipal Science
and Arts Office, Frankfurt am Main

Acknowledgements
All picture rights by the architects except:
Luftbildtechnik: p. 129 (ri.)
Borsig-Archiv, Berlin: p. 15 (le.)
Ullstein Bilderdienst, Berlin: p. 129 (le.)
Landesbildstelle Berlin: p. 15 (ce. and ri.), p. 43 (le.),
p. 57 (ce.), p. 129 (ce.)
Uwe Rau, Berlin: p. 43 (ri.), p. 57 (le. and ri.)

Jacket:
Aldo Rossi,
Gianni Braghieri, Milan
Perspective with superimposed
ground plan and façade sketches
Felt pen and crayon on blueprint
71.8 x 109.5 cm

Of related interest:
ARCHITECTURE IN PROGRESS
Internationale Bauausstellung
Berlin 1984
An "*Architectural Design*" Profile
The first special presentation of
extensive projects from the
International Bauausstellung Berlin
for the Pragerplatz including
contributions by Josef P. Kleihues,
Vittorio Magnago Lampugnani,
Hardt-Waltherr Hämer and an important
commentary by Colin Rowe.
Published by Academy Editions,
London
278 x 222 mm, 129 pages,
over 200 illustrations with 32 pages in
colour
ISBN 0-85670-813-5

Published in Great Britain in 1986 by
ACADEMY EDITIONS
7 Holland Street, London W8

ISBN 0-85670-896-8

© 1986 DAM, Frankfurt am Main, and Ernst Klett Verlage GmbH
und Co. KG, Stuttgart
Verlagsgemeinschaft Ernst Klett – J. G. Cotta'sche Buchhandlung
Nachfolger GmbH, Stuttgart.
All rights reserved
No parts of the contents of this book may be reproduced without the written
permission of the publishers

Printed and bound in the Federal Republic of Germany

Contents

The present catalogue to the IBA Exhibition in the German Museum of Architecture, Frankfurt, is wholly devoted to the graphic illustration of a broad selection of IBA projects. A detailed account of the objectives, techniques and results will follow in special publications of the IBA. In the series "Documents and Projects" the following volumes are due to appear in 1986/87: Friedrichstadt South Side (Vol. III), Tiergarten District South Side (Vol. IV), Prager Platz (Vol. V), Tegel (Vol. VI). A comprehensive project volume will conclude the series.

Preface

The series of exhibitions scheduled to be held in 1987 to mark the 750th anniversary of Berlin will raise this venture, after a decade of preparatory work, to its rightful status: the *International Building Exhibition, Berlin.*

As prelude to the event, Frankfurt is offering an initial comprehensive panorama of what we can expect to see on location in Berlin. The presentation of the project drawings shows what work was in fact carried out; but we are also reminded of those projects which did not get beyond the drawing-board stage, which only exist as concepts.

The presentation of the International Building Exhibition (IBA) in Frankfurt was envisaged as an appropriate tribute to *the* architectural event of the eighties; but there was another factor, too, namely the special situation of Frankfurt, which makes it so-to-speak the main gateway to West Berlin – Frankfurt is the principal point of departure for flights to Berlin, and it is a switchboard for contacts of all sorts between the island city and the rest of the world.

There is yet another consideration to justify this partnership between the two cities: Berlin and Frankfurt are exemplary focus-points for endeavours in the advancement of contemporary architecture; looking at them in conjunction, we can get an idea of what architecture can achieve today in the Federal Republic of Germany, in fields ranging from housing to urban development. It would appear to be no exaggeration to say that what is being done here constitutes a major contribution to present-day international architecture.

Heinrich Klotz

Examples of a New Architecture

"One cannot sufficiently praise the effect of proportion, which is foundation for the glory of architecture, the beauty of the work created, and the miracle of the artist's vocation."
Daniele Barbaro

"The grandness or beauty of forms derives entirely from the associations of thought they provoke in us, or from the qualities they express."
Archibald Alison

To make it clear right from the start: as an isolated event, the Frankfurt exhibition of selected architectural examples from the International Building Exhibition Berlin 1987 ought to be incomprehensible, really. But from the outset it was planned as the first part of a cycle of three exhibitions on the IBA, one of whose purposes is to show that there is no dominating trend in architecture today, and that the IBA has endeavoured to give the various theoretical and artistic attitudes a chance.

In spring of 1987, on March 21, a second exhibition will be opened in the New National Gallery, Berlin. Its title: "750 Years of Architecture and Urban Development in Berlin". The aim of this project is to show how the International Building Exhibition sees itself as a contemporary constituent of the architectural history of Berlin. It is only against the background of this history that the goals and methods, the process and the results of the IBA can be understood.

Then, on May 15 1987, the exhibition proper of information on the IBA will be opened in the former Merkur departmentstore on Lindenstrasse, in conjunction with "IBA On Site". The informational exhibition will show the demonstration areas IBA urban renewal and IBA new urban building, and also the proverbial two sides of the coin via a thematic presentation of the planning problems and planning results of the two sections; the "On Site" segment will show what has been realized where and how.

A totally different approach was adopted for Frankfurt: the artificial isolation of some of the resultant projects from the complex and, in reality, inseparable context.

The image of a city as a whole, the image of its architecture, cannot be a true one unless it includes those aspects that an image can only reflect in an abbreviated way, so to speak: ground-plan, site development, structural design and – if we expand our horizon somewhat further – socio-cultural factors and the historical context in which the language of architecture evolves.

This we know, as visitors to other towns and as residents of our "own" little world of buildings. But how often do we speak of visual impressions, of the image of the architectural manifestation of a town or city?

However we gather these images and assimilate the impressions, whether we employ strict yardsticks of proportion like Daniele Barbaro, for whom the Villa Maser was built, or Archibald Alison, the early exponent of reception theory, or whether we lay more weight on participation, like the more modern school of process orientation, when the sketches and drawings of architects stand alone, in isolation, they reveal something more or something different, compared with a presentation along didactic lines, arranged according to themes and processes.

The architects should speak for themselves, by way of sketch, technical drawing or elaborate graphic presentation: that was the object of this exhibition. The catalogue contains only a selection of the plans displayed. The spell of the image, of the appearance is preserved here: much remains concealed in that which purports to be visible, but sometimes, too, the mask will fall away, for him who has eyes to see.

Josef Paul Kleihues

Interview on the IBA Exhibition

Heinrich Klotz: The International Building Exhibition, Berlin, was planned at a time when it was becoming generally evident in the western half of the world that new trends were making their mark on architecture. So the IBA also came to be a forum of dialogue between an old and a new architecture. There have been not only open-minded discussions but also very polemical controversies. The IBA started off under an aura of controversy, though that wasn't really the objective. Is that a fair statement?

Josef Paul Kleihues: Yes, I would say so, basically. The actual controversy, however, revolved in the first instance around the policy of Hämer and myself: though our views and our projects differed in many respects, we had a common goal right from the start, namely to put an end to the unfeelingness and routine that to a large extent characterized housing projects and urban development in the sixties, particularly, and continuing into the seventies. In view of this it is not surprising that our urbanistic and architectonic objectives gave rise to discussion, and indeed polemical disputes, though the latter have since died a natural death.

HK: Well, it was only to be expected that Berlin would prove to be fertile ground for controversy. Way back in 1974 in the International Design Centre, and then again a year later, I organized one-week conferences in which we were already discussing new architecture, for instance concepts like "urban repair" and "integrative architecture". Robert Venturi and Aldo Rossi both came to Berlin; a year later there were O. M. Ungers and Charles Moore, who took part in a public debate, and who had drafted model projects. All these impulses and concepts were new at the time, and initially they were tossed around like catchwords. It then fell to the IBA, via these exchanges, to produce proof for what had up to then only been theory and preliminary discussion, i. e. to endow these concepts with reality. We could compare recent architectural developments in Frankfurt with the IBA, for it is these two cities that most clearly manifest the new trends in architec-

ture. But in Frankfurt they didn't have years of discussions – they adopted a very ad hoc policy. And that was the difference between a municipal building programme and an IBA.

JPK: That's only partially correct. In Berlin, for instance, the central issue was, right from the start, the "restoration" of architecture and urban development, but the concept of "urban repair" didn't emerge until '76 or '77. It's my belief that, more than anything else, the political decision to hold an International Building Exhibition was prompted by a different consideration, namely the realization that modernism, degenerating into apolitical technicism, and a transport policy that strongly promoted the dominant role of individual modes of transport, were key causes of destruction and alienation in the city. It was this background that convinced the politicians of the need to think along other lines, to subject political, architectural and town planning attitudes to a *metà noeîte*.

HK: But you have to admit that these very Berlin politicians were not always so idealistic as regards the IBA, they didn't only endorse and support its objects, they also tried to throw spanners in the works – no way could you call it unanimous approval. The various district administrations in Berlin, for instance, had their eyes on local interests and repeatedly set up obstacles for the IBA, which was supposed to draw up planning programmes for the whole of Berlin, and was subsidized by Bonn for this reason.

JPK: Well, that's a problem that I'm sure Berlin didn't just encounter in connection with the IBA. The district administrations have always been very involved in questions of city planning and architectural development, and have quite often been in conflict with the city senate's policies in these matters. But to return to the events leading up to the IBA: it was quite a shock for me to learn that the original idea was to stage the International Building Exhibition at an isolated location adjacent to the Tiergarten park, although – or maybe it was in fact because – certain symposia had been held at which questions of architectural theory were discussed more or less in an ivory tower, remote from the realities of

everyday life. I well remember a very early meeting (somewhere around 1975) called by the then chief architect of the senate, Hans-Christian Müller, at which I was the only one to raise doubts about this idea, or more precisely about the justification for such an idea. In the first instance, however, I had no opportunity to convince the others and the chief architect that there must be no repetition of the 1957 Interbau. It was not until the *Morgenpost* newspaper published the series "Models for a City", which I initiated together with Wolf Jobst Siedler – the first instalment appeared as a four-page supplement in January 1977 – that the ice was broken. This first report called for the repair of the destroyed city and for a programme for an integrated building exhibition, and was the stimulus for further series and lengthy discussion; it helped to mobilize politicians and architects, and finally led to a process of rethinking. But it wasn't just this *Morgenpost* series (for which you, Wolfgang Pehn and others wrote, and which even at that early date had contributions by architects such as Carlo Aymonino, Jim Stirling, Aldo Rossi, and Charles Moore), there was also a number of political meetings. Thus we had talks with the chief architect and the mayor in office at that time, and with other politicians, and we were eventually able to persuade them to plan for an integrated building exhibition, even though the other proposal was already more or less signed, sealed and delivered. It was this rethinking that generated the themes urban renewal and new urban building, themes on the face of it poles apart, but in the final analysis complementary: thus we have on the one hand the preservation and tactful renovation of the Luisenstadt and SO 36 districts, to which no one had given a kind thought for years, and on the other hand a critical reconstruction of the city, which takes courage – especially in the southern Friedrichstadt area, but also of course Prager Platz and the south side of the Tiergarten quarter.

HK: I have to point out here that the IDC symposia of 1974 and especially 1975 also called for a building exhibition that would not be held "in the middle of nowhere". The concept of "integrative architecture" had already been created. But what were the obstacles met with in the realization of the IBA? For example, there has always been the problem that when somebody wants to build a house he is only too eager to claim the sudsidy from Bonn, but then he wants his old idea implemented, minimal architecture to save expense; what was supposed to be new architecture, that he doesn't want.

JPK: A lot of people seem to think that, but I would disagree. The problems we had with the clients were far less serious than those relating to zoning and building regulations. The disputes we had with the local administrations and officials of the senate building department were often far more of a headache than the effort involved in putting our ideas across to the various clients, whether community housing associations or private investors.

HK: These years in which the IBA was taking shape saw many architects from all over the world coming to Berlin, including the very top names, and also architects of the up-and-coming generation. What were the criteria of selection? Why do we find a particular architect represented in this vast panorama of different architectural styles, and another one absent?

JPK: That's a good question and in fact quite easy to answer. We can observe how, since the early seventies, the different theories of architecture have become more articulate than used to be the case, though we must also admit that in effect different theoretical systems in architecture began to evolve and take more definite shape way back in the Age of Enlightenment, i. e. the end of the 18th century; still, there has virtually never been a time like the present that saw these various contemporaneous tendencies manifest themselves with such clarity. Today, in contrast with, say, the twenties, we cannot speak of the dominance of *one* theoretical school, of *one* tendency in architecture. In the twenties, concepts like functionalism, *neue sachlichkeit* or the new functionalism, and rationalism were grouped together under the designation "international style"; despite their differences, the architects of the day aspired to a common political and artistic outlook, which was to find its documentation in an internationally accepted style. Today, we can no longer identify aspi-

rations of this nature – various trends exist contemporaneously, each with a will of its own. Thus, even among young architects, we find a nostalgic revival of interest in the theoretical tradition of classicism …

HK: You mean Schinkel …

JPK: Yes, but it goes back before Schinkel's time, this interest, and it encompasses post-Schinkel developments, too. Then again, we cannot ignore the renewed discussion of rationalism, which for me at least offers more perspectives for the future. And finally, regional cultural development is very much in the spotlight, as exemplified by the great interest being shown in traditionalism as a trend in architecture. I could mention other theoretical constructs in architecture. In awareness of the existence of these various tendencies and philosophies we sought to bring the protagonists of different theories to Berlin, not just to hold discussions with them, but to let them get to grips with the history of the city, the requirements of modern life, and the social, technical and economic conditions of the city. We invited them to submit entries for competitions, and in individual cases arranged direct commissions for the design of a house.

HK: To take up the theme of regionalism, is it possible to transplant an Italian like Grassi to Berlin, just like that? I mean, he is very much influenced by a tradition of architecture strongly defined by the special characteristics of Italy. Can one for example build such stark structures as Rossi and, particularly, Grassi have designed under northern skies, can one erect buildings like these where the Italian sun does not shine?

JPK: I have always been intrigued by this question. It seems to me now that the two architects you mention create in Berlin a different type of building from in Italy. But the work of many other architects also reveals definite echoes of the influence of Berlin; most of them, after all, possess a high level of intellectual curiosity and are highly sensitive to the cultural evolution of other places. Of course Grassi will build a house that corresponds to *his* theoretical objectives, which are deeply rooted in realism, as you know: a window is a window, a

house is a house, etc. But it is interesting to note that he does in fact discover the Berlin window and incorporate it in his house; he grasps the recalcitrant, no-nonsense attitude of the Berliners, a legacy of Prussian thriftiness that has left its mark on their character. In this respect his house on Rauchstrasse is virtually a revelation of the better Prussian tradition, and at the same time establishes a historical relationship to the simplicity of the architecture and the landscape of Italy. Speaking of Aldo Rossi, I remember him visiting Berlin in the mid-seventies: we went to have a look at Block 270 in Wedding, a project of mine that had just been completed. For Aldo Rossi, that was a Berlin house: the stone, the block look, the simplicity of the architecture. Later, when he was commissioned to do some work in Berlin, he said: "When I think of Berlin, two materials interest me especially – red brick without plaster finish and, alongside it, the steel structure". We can see the results in his house on Rauchstrasse and, even more so, in his designs for Wilhelmstrasse, which are just starting to go up. So Rossi and Grassi are just two instances that show that when architects design buildings for Berlin they by no means abandon their theoretical and artistic ideals, they rather enrich and concretize them through the dialectical confrontation with the cultural evolution of Berlin. This I find to be an interesting and commendable effect.

HK: We spoke of the various trends in contemporary architecture. One trend that seems to me to be rather under-represented is American postmodernism. True, Charles Moore can be seen in the Tegel quarter, but there is no Venturi. Why not?

JPK: First, I have to stress that "postmodernism" is not a very eloquent designation. There have been many attempts to define this term in relation to architecture, philosophy, literature, music, film, but, at least for the layman, they confuse the issue more than anything else, they often tend to lump everything together – a good deal more thinking needs to be done here. What strikes me about postmodernism is above all its tendency to look back, as is clearly evidenced by present-day historicism. In this respect I would consider Rob Krier's work to be perhaps especially typical of postmodernistic thinking in architecture. This type of historicism is really very nostalgic and conservative; it is a trend that is heavily impregnated with resignation, and manifests little hope or faith in the future; it is problematical because as regards life and thus social considerations it calls for an orientation on the past that is not viable. I will gladly endorse the call for a recultivation of craftsman skills *alongside* industrial development, but we surely don't want to go back to tilling the fields with horse-drawn plough.

HK: Yet Rob Krier was given a great opportunity by the IBA to realize his ideas on a large scale, but not Venturi.

JPK: Let me point out that Bob Venturi – as opposed to Bohigas, OMA, Rossi, Eisenman, Abraham, Reichlin and Reinhart, etc. – was the only foreign architect not to submit a scheme for the restricted competition Koch/Friedrichstrasse. Rob Krier, on the other hand, entered for the open international competition Rauchstrasse and was awarded the first prize by the jury under the then chairmanship of Gottfried Böhm. But the Rauchstrasse project is, like nearly all IBA projects, an example of the custom of asking several architects of different outlooks to take part in the practical realization. The eight buildings here were executed by seven different architects, namely Rob Krier himself, Hollein, Rossi and Grassi, along with the younger architects Valentini/Herrmann, Brenner/Tonon and Nielebock.

HK: Not forgetting Jim Stirling…

JPK: Yes, but he wasn't involved in the housing schemes on Rauchstrasse, he's building the science centre next door to the Cultural Forum, which is already structurally more or less completed.

HK: The IBA is by and large an exhibition of grant-aided housing developments. Public-sector buildings, as featured in Frankfurt, play very much a subordinate role in the scenario, take Stirling's project for instance.

JPK: The IBA programme does foresee the planning of public parks, the degrading of thoroughfares, and the erection of a number of public buildings. I might mention the phosphate elimination plant in Tegel, a technical project designed by Gustav Peichl; there will be Charles Moore's library at Tegel docks; we already mentioned Jim Stirling's science centre. Two schools and three kindergartens will be built in southern Friedrichstadt. Two kindergartens are being built in the southern Tiergarten quarter on IBA plans, and they'll no doubt shortly commence the redevelopment of the Cultural Forum to Hans Hollein's plans.

HK: This exhibition gathers a large number of plans and projects under one roof. The criteria for selection were strict. And through this selection we wanted to make a statement of policy. We don't pretend to have accorded everyone his due. The exhibition also includes projects which were not carried out; many second and third prizewinners and highly commendeds are to be seen. So it is our intention to show just the pick of the bunch or those projects that have been realized, but as far as possible to provide a comprehensive review of the multiplicity of ideas, whether or not they have led to concrete entities.

JPK: That's right. This is basically an exhibition that deliberately isolates the architectural aspect of the International Building Exhibition from its many other aspects, which nevertheless intangibly permeate the whole show. For there can be no architecture that does not reflect social, political, economic and many other factors. What the International Building Exhibition has produced is inseparably bound up with the programme of urban renewal under Hämer's aegis and of new urban building, which has been in my charge since 1979. This will be clearly set out in the big information exhibition due to open early May in the old Merkur department-store.

HK: We have been unable to include many of the projects for restoration, renovation and revitalization. Yet hasn't real life always produced examples of friction between the restorers and the advocates of new building? Isn't this inevitable? Would it be wrong to assume that conflicts arose between you, who wanted to erect a new building, and your colleague, who wanted to retain the old one?

JPK: That's what people generally assume; maybe even they would like it to be so. But the fact is that Hämer and I look upon the two sectors of the IBA as two sides of a coin. We both seek to find solutions for very disparate problems and to do very different jobs with equal commitment. On the one hand there is the conservation and careful renovation of existing structures, on the other hand it's a question of proceeding tactfully and with great care with the integration of kindergartens, schools and also new housing developments into the existing organism which is the city. Houses by Siza and Baller are examples of this. "Two sides of a coin" is, I believe, the best way of expressing the situation: there is not one IBA isolated from the other IBA, there is only one IBA comprising both old and new buildings. This double programme is to be found in many other cities. We know how interested other countries are in the IBA – look at what they are doing in Madrid, Barcelona, Rome, Vienna, or Paris: everywhere projects are being planned that are clearly oriented on the International Building Exhibition. What Oriol Bohigas has accomplished in Barcelona was inspired by the IBA just as much as were the "Models for a New Community Housing Policy" in Vienna. This programme for living accommodation of quality and dignity in Vienna is virtually a mini IBA. All these projects represent a break with the partially abstract, partially technocratic and overregulated methods of housing and urban development. The rediscovery and revitalization of the idea that architecture is inseparable from urban development, which was a primary goal of the IBA, constitutes a major advance in the campaign to make the city a place worth living in again.

New Urban Building

**Demonstration Area
Tegel**

Tegel

Lakes and woods,
Humboldt and Borsig,
IBA on the outskirts of town

"One cannot very well imagine Paris without Versailles, London without Windsor, or Berlin without Charllottenburg, or indeed without Tegel, the gourmet might say."   Theodor Fontane

"The dictum of the physician Hippocrates still holds good: if one drinks water that has not been purified, but is heavy and does not taste good, one will have a hot and swollen belly."
                              Leon Battista Alberti

The Tegel Woods, the broad vista of the lake dotted with green islands under a sky of looming clouds, radiant sunshine, or starry night; the white shimmer of Humboldt House, and close by the Borsig works, the "industrial archaeology" of this suburb on the northwestern edge of Berlin. Fontane knew what he was talking about, and the people of Berlin fully appreciate their Tegel. "Round up the kids and jump in the car, we're off to Tegel, hurrah hurrah!" – a rhyme something like this springs to the Berliner's lips when he thinks of this part of town. A century ago it was just as popular for an afternoon out as it is today: the entire city treasures this location with its lakes and its woods.
But the Berliners know that Tegel Lake ceased to be a fountain of youth years ago: you might not get a "swollen belly" just from swimming in it, but the water is definitely not recommended for drinking, though Berlin's lakes are in fact the reservoir for the city's drinking water supply.
In its capacity as demonstration area for the International Building Exhibition, Tegel has mistakenly been thought of as a high-class project, especially when compared with the very problematical planning areas of Kreuzberg.
But Berlin is made up of many districts, and Tegel is an important Berlin district, important too for southern Friedrichstadt and SO 36. Which is why Tegel must retain its identity, it must not lose the regional advantages of its rural situation, unspoilt by the metropolis Berlin: there needs to be an impression of mutual solidarity among the different localities of Berlin, and this impression would suffer if Tegel, a land-scape and leisure area serving the entire city, were not a part of the Building Exhibition.
What the IBA seeks to demonstrate in Tegel is characterized in the main by two themes and areas:
firstly
redesigning the dock area, which long ago ceased to serve its original function. Here, Charles Moore's outline plan for the development of the area forms the basis of an extensive residential, cultural and leisure complex, at present under construction.
secondly
a projected phosphate elimination plant by the North Canal: apart from its technical function in the service of the environment, this will pay homage to the tradition of industrial architecture so typical of Berlin. Our demonstration programme also calls for new buildings on the Linse site between the phosphate plant and the dock basin, and on the south aspect of Street 7. Gustav Peichl and Thomas Herzog have submitted plans for the Linse site, the realization of which will be commenced in the IBA year 1987.
Let us first take a look at Tegel docks. At the point where the old part of Tegel borders on the nature area a new locality will be created, which will serve to retain the specific character of Tegel for the people who live there, and also, avoiding any drastic measures, to make it more attractive for daytrippers and holidaymakers.
Back in 1980, the international competition for a residential, cultural and leisure centre was organized in close collaboration with the district administration of Reinickendorf and various citizens' action groups; in autumn of that year the jury chaired by Harald Deilmann awarded the prizes.
Volume II of our series "Documents and Projects – Areas of New Building" details the results of this restricted competition for the planning of an urban site, in which nine architects took part. Some of these projects are highlighted in the German Museum of Architecture. Two of these schemes not only gave the jury a difficult time, but are still the subject of heated discussions today: Charles Moore's urban landscape, winner of the first prize, and the "little town on the waterfront" by Leon Krier, which was specially commended. Memories of ancient cities – theatre, library, gymnasium and other public institu-tions firmly embodied in the urban ground-plan and enhanced by piazza and street perspectives – this is the idealistic concept that has for years characterized Leon Krier's drawings with their historical emphasis and nostalgia. Krier has commented on his project as follows:
"The public buildings must be constructed to the highest standards of craftsmanship and technology. Classical architecture found the definitive answer to all problems in this field. Not only did we employ a scale that gives an urban district a pleasant and familiar atmosphere, we also tried to give the buildings that special imprint which alone makes a location into a real, unique locality."
Charles Moore also speaks of the "unique locality":
"Admittedly, we have designed the cultural institutions, leisure facilities and dwelling-houses as individual buildings, but through their arrangement on the site they constitute parts of a whole, relating to each other and enhancing each other. Walking through one of the components we get glimpses of the rest of the site that stimulate our perceptions. The urban areas where we live, and which we remember, are localities defined by the interaction of the individual elements building, water, and landscape. Within the entire planning area water is the connecting element between the parts."
In later stages of the planning process Charles Moore revised parts of his design. But the basic idea remains untouched as constituent of the urban development plan, which is now under construction, and is binding on all architects involved.
Thus, this project of the International Building Exhibition also fulfils the objective of commissioning individual designs to enrich the image of a precisely laid down and binding outline urban development plan. Work started on these projects last year after definitive plans had been produced, but the phosphate elimination plant has already been completed. The purpose of this plant is to improve the quality of the water in Tegel Lake, and thus make a small contribution toward restoring the ecological balance of our planet. The technical specifications were already finalized in 1979 when we initiated our programme, so it was not easy for the IBA to get a hearing for its proposed planning commission; this

Gate of former Borsig works in Tegel, photographed in 1950.

Aerial view of Tegel Lake with Tegel Docks (1969).

Tegel Manor (country seat of Wilhelm von Humboldt), c. 1875. Built 1821–23 to a design by Karl Friedrich Schinkel. Steel engraving by Johann Poppel after L. Rohbock.

eventually bore fruit in Gustav Peichl's design.

Building should involve more than the purely technical meeting of a need, yet this maxim is neglected in many fields. In the recent history of architecture there have been few fields so dominated by organizational and logistical criteria as that of industrial architecture and so-called technical structures.

On the other hand, Berlin can boast a tradition of industrial architecture of more than merely local significance. Many individual examples, not least the constructions of Behrens and Hertlein for AEG and Siemens, enjoy an international reputation. Gustav Peichl is an architect who has always taken a particular interest and pleasure in the technical side of architecture and in buildings generously endowed with technical paraphernalia. He puts heart and soul into his designs for the necessary technology, sets it off with imaginative touches, and thus relativizes its abstractness. Thus, the phosphate elimination plant, though a technical instrument, is of more than purely ecological significance, it has the chance of becoming a social symbol of the symbiosis of art and technology. Le Corbusier remarks in *The Modulor*: "The physics of the universe is reflected by technical processes. They are conquests deriving from the astuteness and cunning of man, who refuses to kow-tow before the unfeeling and inexorable happenings in nature and the cosmos." The Tegel projects of the IBA, however, must be seen as an index of our changing relationship to nature (*physis*) and art (*téchnē*). Where there once was a naive ambition to be the mas-

ter of creation, and a belief that phenomena of nature could be subjugated by merely concentrating on or even analytically delineating particular functions, we now see a readiness to appreciate things as the Greeks did: as *cosmos*, that is, a complex world structure in which man experiences truth and boundless creativity through contact with the forces of nature. Many people today see in technology a danger, and rightly so; but shouldn't we go a step further and see technology as *the* danger? – namely, the danger threatening man when he abandons himself to a functional interpretation of that which exists, thereby giving up his own ontological self, i. e. the openness of "world". This would mean that the urge to master nature, fuelled by mechanical rationality, is not a contingency but a condition of human existence. If this is the case, though, there would be no point in trying to escape from the industrial way of life via regression. And it is this flight into an illusionary world of theatrical scenery, as practised by "postmodernism", "neoclassicism" and "neoromanticism", which is in fact the capitulation Le Corbusier warned against. It would be more appropriate for us to remind ourselves of the double function of *techne* that inspired the ancient Greeks: skill/art, an instrument of rationality and, at the same time, imaginative emancipation, the expression of *poiesis*, the creative urge that gives itself form and relevance.

This complex and closely defined sense of *téchnē* forms the basis of a concept of architecture that for some years now we have been trying to clarify and expound as a "poetic rationalism". Postmodernism is

just a spectacular but futile form of the step that will lead us out of the cul-de-sac in which the alternatives of the modern movement ended. But what is not wanted is the restoration of a representative historicism that exhausts itself in quotations, ironical allusions or nostalgic clichés; rather, architecture needs to be reinstated in what the Greeks called "the world": a world where man is participant in a "game", a world that reveals itself in this game by showing up the differences between *poïesis* and *lógos* (reason), metaphor and function, existential insecurity and institutional form. An International Building Exhibition can provide examples of this, but it must also come to terms with the fact that the participating architects have adopted points of view that often differ greatly. This, too, quite possibly one of its most interesting aspects, comes to light in the Frankfurt exhibition.   Josef Paul Kleihues

15

**International Planning Survey
Residential and Recreational Facilities
at Tegeler Hafen (Tegel Docks), 1980**

**First Prize
Charles Moore
John Ruble
Buzz Yudell, Santa Monica, California**

with Andra Georges, Phing Kwee, Peter
Zingg, Bill Hersey (graphic presentation),
Robert Flock and Jason Balinbin (model)

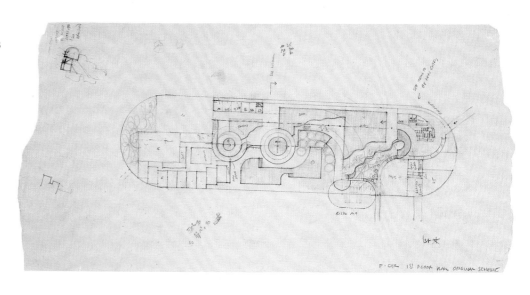

1
Leisure area, 1st. floor plan
Pencil and crayon on yellow tracing paper
29.7 x 61 cm
Signed: F. CiR 1st. floor plan
Original scheme

2
General perspective
Crayon on transparent Xerox copy
60.4 x 126.3 cm
Signed: Hersey

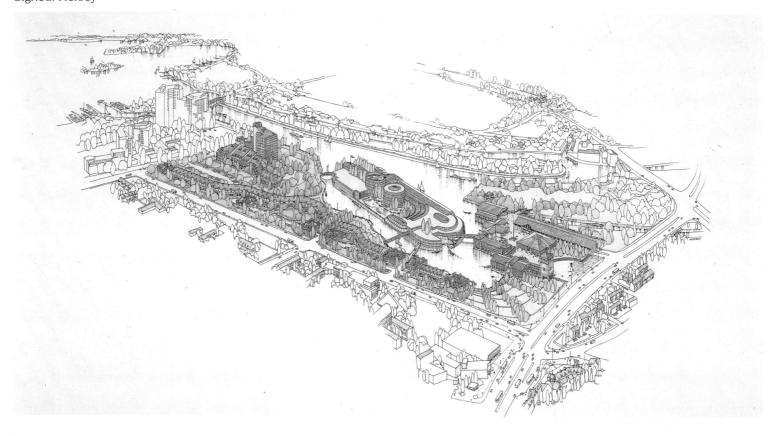

3
Interior perspective of leisure area
India ink on transparent paper
61 x 60.9 cm
Signed: Hersey

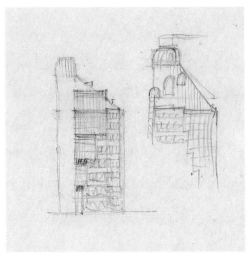

4
Sketch
Pencil on yellow tracing paper
30.4 x 31.6 cm
Signed: "Housing tower elevation"

5
Perspective of the embankment, toward
Neptun & Nixe
India ink on transparent paper
61 x 61 cm
Signed: Hersey

**International Planning Survey
Residential and Recreational Facilities
at Tegeler Hafen, 1980
"The New Dock Quarter"**

**Special Prize
Leon Krier, London**

with Francisco Sanin

6
Overall plan, scale 1 : 2000
Crayon on paper
36.9 x 60 cm
Signed: Design 1980
Drawing: Leon Krier 1983

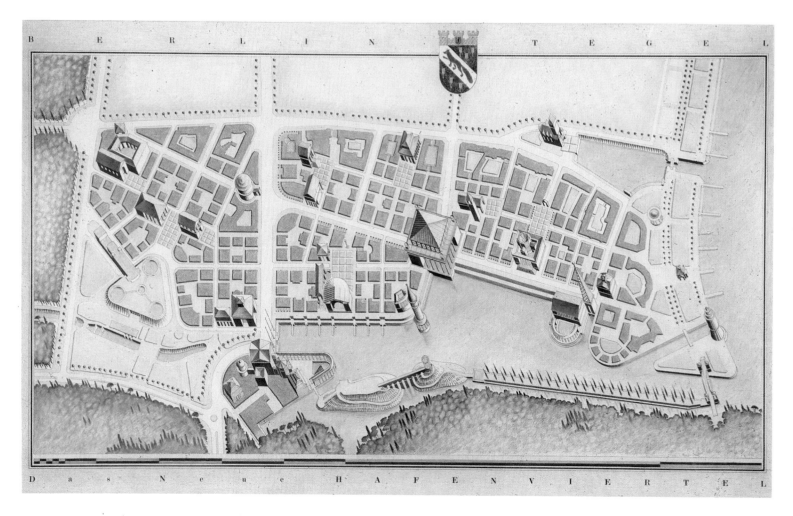

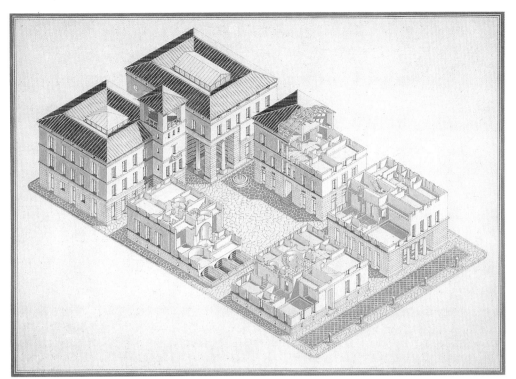

7
Insula Tegeliensis – axonometric drawing,
scale 1 : 200
Coloured pencil on paper
38.3 x 53.6 cm
Signed: Design 1980
Drawing: Leon Krier 1982

8
Insula Tegeliensis –
Perspective of courtyard
Sepia ink on paper
22.8 x 22.6 cm
Signed: Design 1980
Drawing: Leon Krier 1982

**International Planning Survey
Residential and Recreational Facilities
at Tegeler Hafen, 1980**

**Third Prize
Arata Isozaki & Associates, Tokyo**

Mamoru Kawaguchi, Walter Liebender,
Hajime Yatsuka, Makoto Kikuchi, Naoki
Inagawa, Eisaku Ushida, Masahiro Horiuchi,
Itsuro Shimoki, Hideo Matsuura, Tadashi
Murai, Takashi Ito, Shuichi Fujie, Jun Aoki,
Yoshiko Amiya, Arata Isozaki

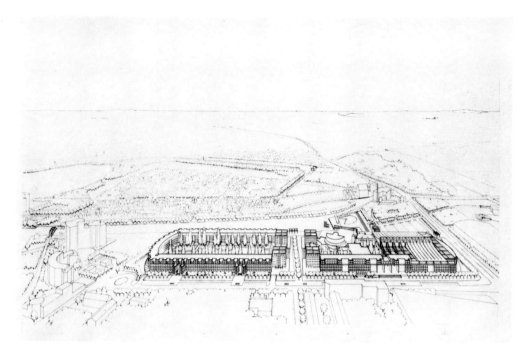

10
Perspective view of the Tegel
Harbour development
India ink on transparent paper
84 x 151.2 cm

9
Aerial view from the south
Photographic reproduction
88 x 134 cm

**International Planning Survey
Residential and Recreational Facilities
at Tegeler Hafen, 1980**

**Second Prize
Stavoprojekt Liberec, Studio 2, ČSSR**

John Eisler, Emil Přikryl, Martin Rajniš, Jiri
Suchomel, Dalibor Vokač

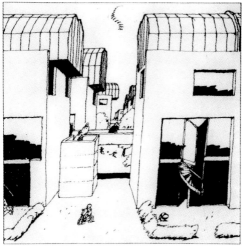

11–13
Perspectives
India ink on transparent paper
Originals lost

14
Perspective towards south
India ink on transparent paper
90 x 181 cm

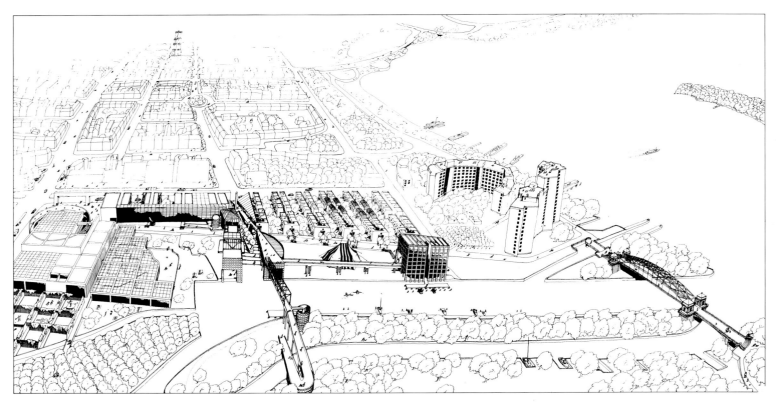

21

**Residential and Recreational Facilities
at Tegeler Hafen
First Revised Version, 1981**

**Charles Moore
John Ruble
Buzz Yudell, Santa Monica, California**

with Maya Reiner, Jörg Weber, Kai Haag,
Christiane Haag

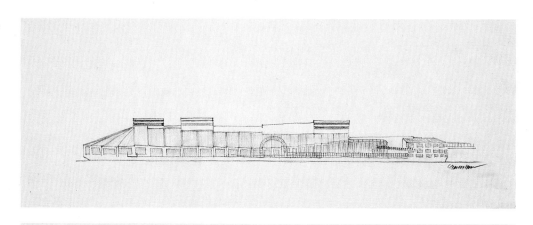

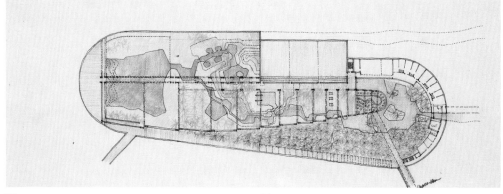

17
General perspective of Tegel Harbour
Transparent Xerox copy, crayon backed
61.2 x 175 cm
Signed: March 1981

15
Sketch, view of leisure area
Pencil and crayon on yellow tracing paper
31.6 x 52.7 cm
Signed: Charles Moore

16
Plan of leisure area
India ink and crayon on yellow
tracing paper
30.5 x 55.1 cm
Signed: Charles Moore

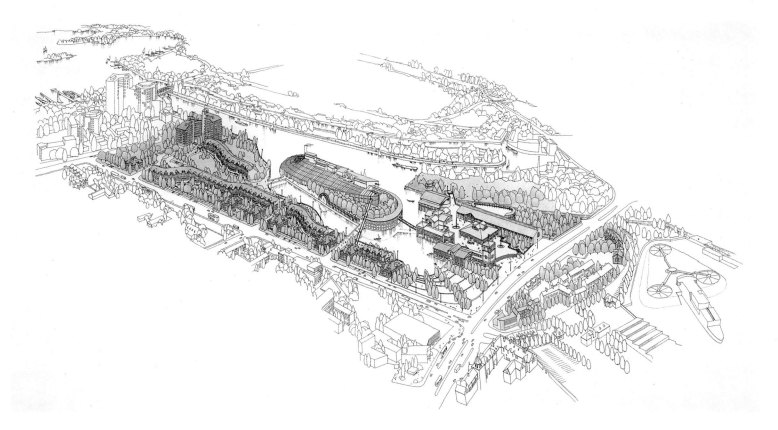

**Residential and Recreational Facilities
at Tegeler Hafen
Overall Concept with Residential
Development, Municipal Library,
Reconstruction of Tegel Dock Basin
with Leisure Island, Promenade and
Bridge Structure
Planning since 1982
Under construction since 1985**

**Charles Moore
John Ruble
Buzz Yudell
Thomas Nagel, Santa Monica,
California**

with Leon Glodt, Eileen Liebman, Regina
Maria Pizzinini, Renzo Zecchetto
Colour design: Tina Beebe
Garden design: Cornelia Müller, Elmar
Knippschild, Jan Wehberg, Berlin

18
Perspective sketch
Felt tip on yellow tracing paper
45.8 x 54 cm

19
Study of façade, scale 1:100
Pencil on yellow tracing paper
61 x 51 cm

20
Rough sketch, elevation
Pencil on yellow tracing paper
61 x 57 cm (detail)

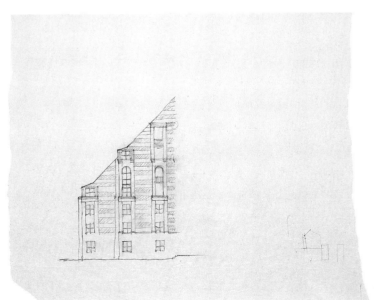

Residential Development "Tegeler Hafen"
Urban Villa, House 18
Planning since 1985

Charles Moore
John Ruble
Buzz Yudell
Thomas Nagel, Santa Monica, California

with Leon Glodt

OSTANSICHT

21a
Villa Moore
East elevation, scale 1 : 100
Crayon on photocopy
23 x 26 cm (detail)

21b
Villa Moore
South elevation, scale 1 : 100
Crayon on photocopy
24 x 24 cm (detail)

21c
Villa Moore
North elevation, scale 1 : 100
Crayon on photocopy
24 x 24 cm (detail)

Municipal Library "Tegeler Hafen"
Planning since 1984

Charles Moore
John Ruble
Buzz Yudell
Thomas Nagel, Santa Monica,
California

with Regina Maria Pizzinini, Leon Glodt,
Renzo Zecchetto
Colour design: Tina Beebe

22
Partial view of façade, library interior
Elevation with bookshelves, scale 1 : 25
Silkscreen, watercolour on Capa board
61 x 91.5 cm

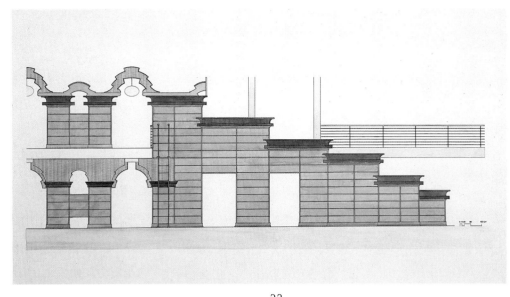

23
Perspective section
Library interior
Photocopy
76.4 x 107.4 cm

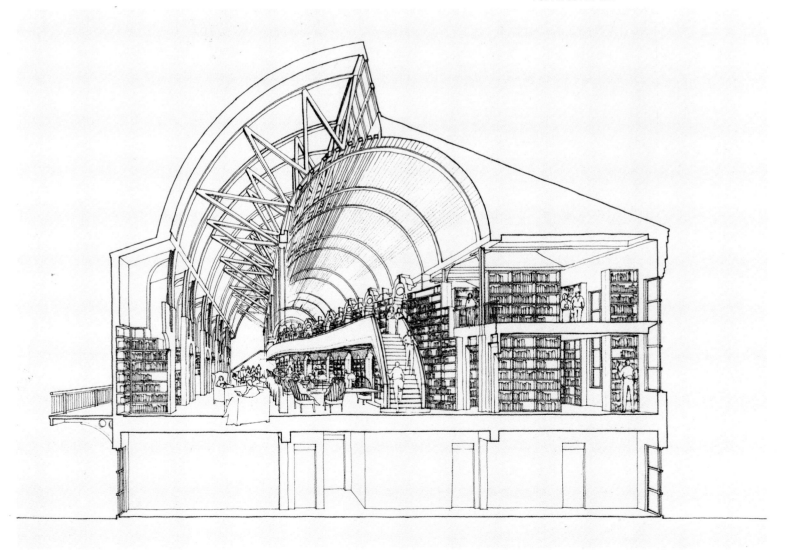

Residential Development "Tegeler Hafen"
Urban Villa, House 16 A
Planning since 1985

Antoine Grumbach, Paris

with Didier Gallard

24
Elevation, scale 1 : 50
Crayon on transparent paper
29.7 x 42 cm

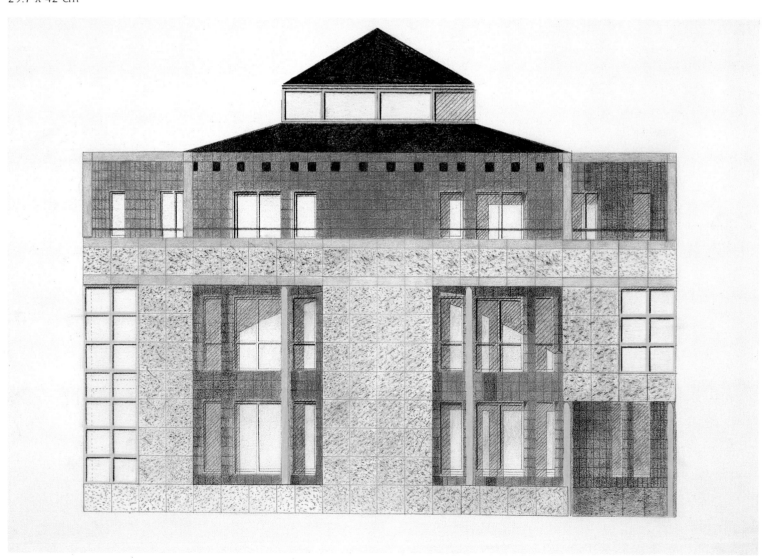

Residential Development "Tegeler Hafen"
Urban Villa, House 16 D
Planning since 1985

Robert A. M. Stern
Graham S. Wyatt, New York

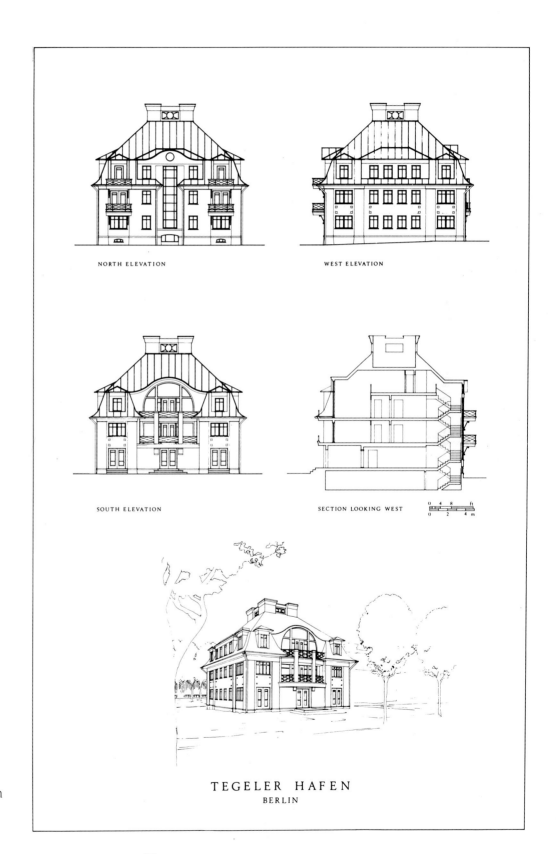

NORTH ELEVATION

WEST ELEVATION

SOUTH ELEVATION

SECTION LOOKING WEST

TEGELER HAFEN
BERLIN

25
North, west and south elevations, section
and perspective, scale 1:100
91.6 x 61 cm

Residential Development "Tegeler Hafen"
Urban Villa, House 16 C
Planning since 1985

Stanley Tigerman
Robert Fugman
McCurry, Chicago

with Frederick Wilson, Carlos Martinez

26
Sketches
India ink on paper
13.4 x 21 cm
Signed: Tegel Harbour
Stanley 85, Berlin

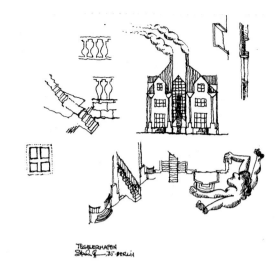

27
Pencil, crayon, spray technique
on cardboard
49.5 x 61.5 cm

28–33
Cross sections, elevations, perspectives,
scale 1:50
Pencil, crayon, spray technique
on cardboard
49.5 x 61.5 cm

29

Residential Development "Tegeler Hafen"
Urban Villa, House 16 B
Planning since 1985

Paolo Portoghesi, Rome

34
Perspective view, scale 1 : 50
Photocopy
45.2 x 45.4 cm

35–37
Sketches
Ink on paper
Three sketchbook pages
23 x 17 cm

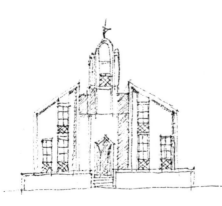

Residential Development "Tegeler Hafen"
House 17
Planning since 1985

Regina Poly
Karl-Heinz D. Steinebach
Friedrich Weber, Berlin

with Hans Dieter Brandt, Karl Heinz Ahlborn

38
Perspective of House No. 17
Coloured photocopy
62.3 x 96.4 cm
Signed: C. Schlesinger '86

Residential Development "Tegeler Hafen"
Urban Villa, House 16
Planning since 1985

John Hejduk, New York

40
Sketches on a letter from Moore, Ruble, Yudell, in which the planned footprint for the villas is explained
India ink on paper
29.7 x 21 cm

39
Sketches on a sheet of writing-paper
by John Hejduk
India ink on paper
28 x 21.6 cm
Signed: John Hejduk, Architect
(letterhead)

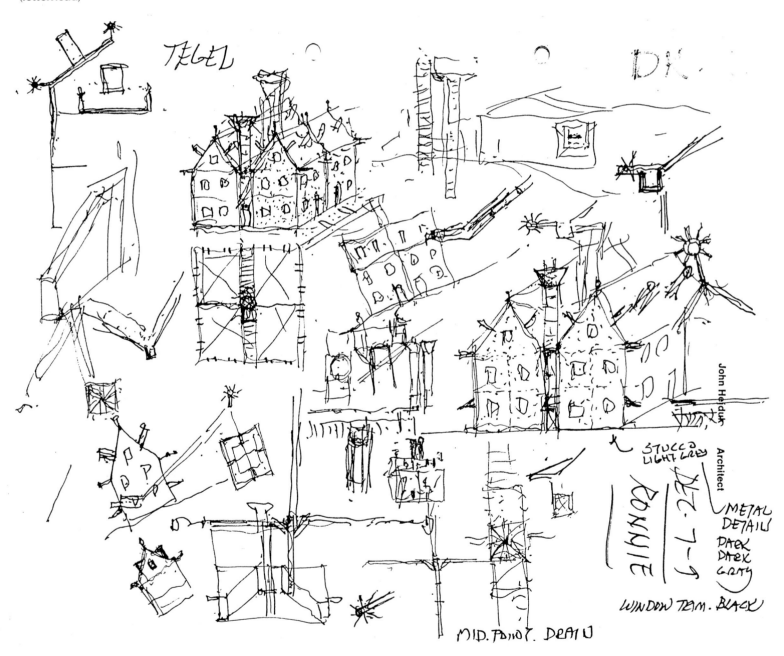

Moore Ruble Yudell
Architects & Planners
1640 Nineteenth Street
Santa Monica, California
90404
213 829·9923

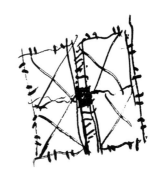

TEGEL VILLA DESIGN GUIDELINES

GENERAL: Within the urban design scheme for Tegel Harbor, the villas play a special role as free-standing, four-square, <u>foreground</u> buildings. Together, they define a kind of chorus line front for the housing area along 7th Street, while separately and in pairs they mark corners and entrances leading to the harbor and promenade.

ENVELOPE: The 16 x 16m footprint may not be exceeded. Projections (dormers, chimneys, loggias, etc.) beyond the roof plane are possible, as long as their total volume does not exceed 7% of the volume of the envelope. Maximum height will be 16m.

Charles Moore
John Ruble
Buzz Yudell
MRY

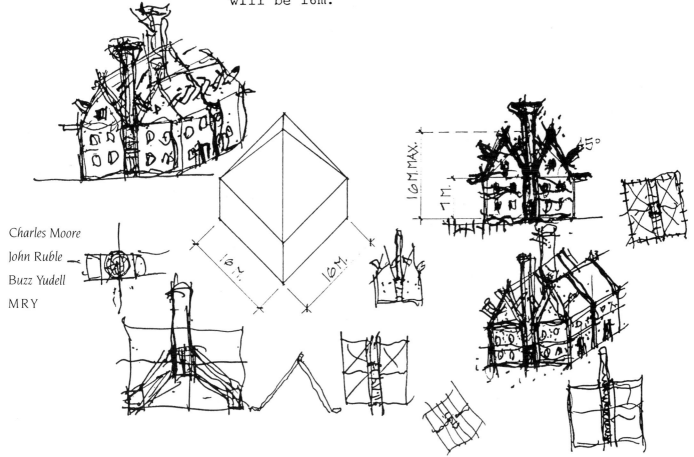

**Urban Survey and Preliminary
Designs, Karolinenstrasse
Planning 1983–1985**

Thoms Herzog, Munich

with Michael Bunge, Regina Streckebach,
Manfred Elsner, Farahbod Nakhaei

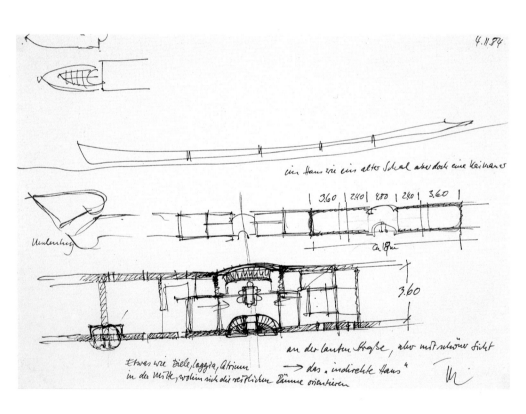

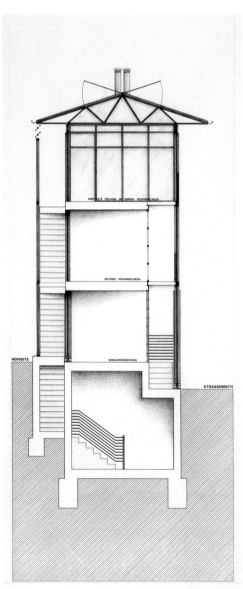

41
"A house like an old scarf, but nevertheless
a jetty wall" (sketch)
Pen, felt pen and crayon on paper
20.1 x 29.7 cm
Signed: 4.11.84 sign.

42
Section, scale 1 : 33.3
Crayon on Xerox copy
81.1 x 35.5 cm

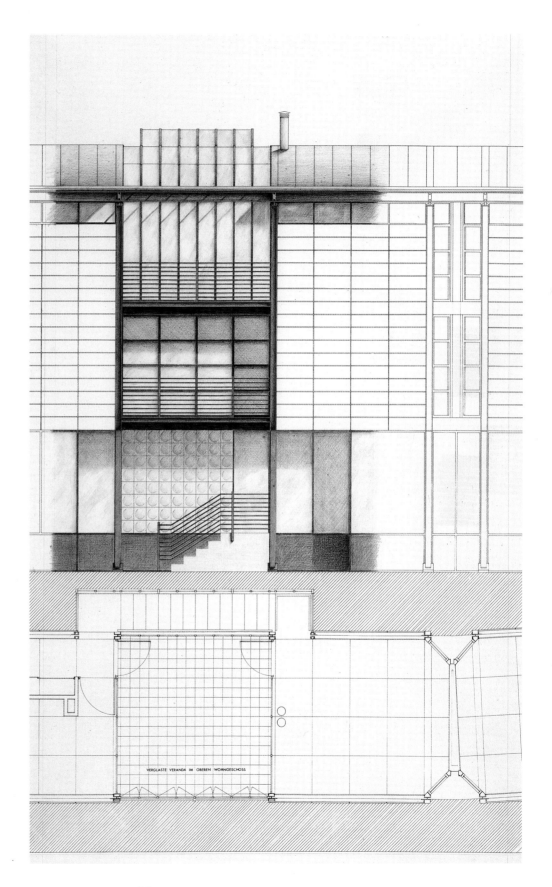

43
Plan and partial elevation with stairs,
scale 1 : 33.3
Crayon on Xerox copy
81.1 x 50 cm

VERGLASTE VERANDA IM OBEREN WOHNGESCHOSS

Survey and Design Entered for Competition for Phosphate Elimination Plant in Tegel, Berlin, 1980

Gustav Peichl, Vienna

with Peter Nigst, Peter Kugelstätter, Rudolf Weber, Franco Fonatti
(subsequently commissioned to build plant)

44
Sketch
Front view with clearing ponds
Pencil and crayon on paper
30 x 42 cm

45
Sketch
Bird's-eye view of the factory development and of the three circular clearing ponds of the filter tract
Pencil and crayon on paper
30 x 48.8 cm

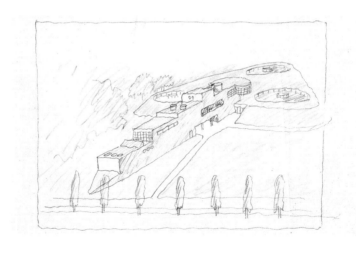

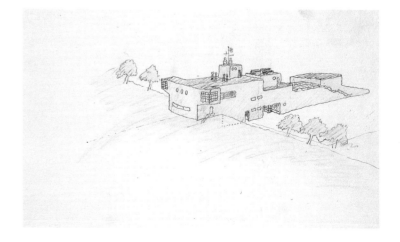

46
A sketch of the factory development
Pencil and crayon on transparent paper
29.7 x 46.8 cm
Signed: PEA Berlin 1980 Peichl

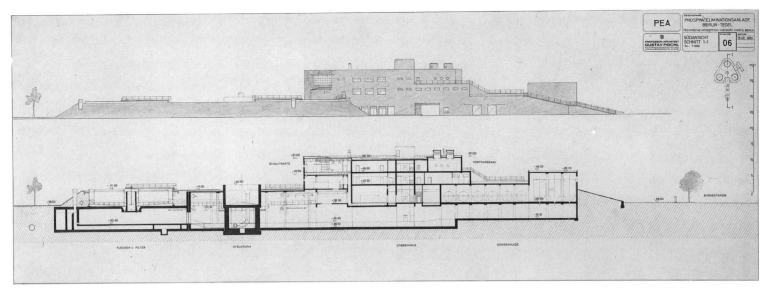

47
South elevation with longitudinal section,
scale 1 : 200
Coloured blueprint
44.9 x 125.1 cm
Signed: Plan No. 06, 15.02.80

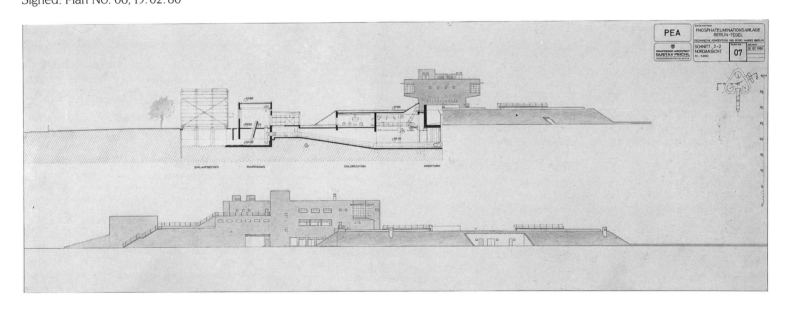

48
Section of entire plant and north elevation
of control building, scale 1 : 200
Coloured blueprint
44.7 x 124.9 cm
Signed: Plan No. 07, 15.02.80

**Phosphate Elimination Plant in Tegel,
Berlin
Planning 1980–1985
Completed 1985**

Gustav Peichl, Vienna

with Peter Nigst, Peter Kugelstätter, Rudolf
Weber, Franco Fonatti

50
Façade drawing of the factory
development
Side elevation, north, scale 1 : 100
Pencil and crayon on transparent paper
30 x 86.7 cm

49
Cross section of the factory development,
scale 1 : 100
Pencil and crayon on transparent paper
29.7 x 41.8 cm
Signed: Vienna, 23. 7. 80 F.F.

51
Cross section of the factory development,
scale 1 : 100
Pencil and crayon on transparent paper
30 x 42 cm
Signed: Vienna, 23. 7. 80 F.F.

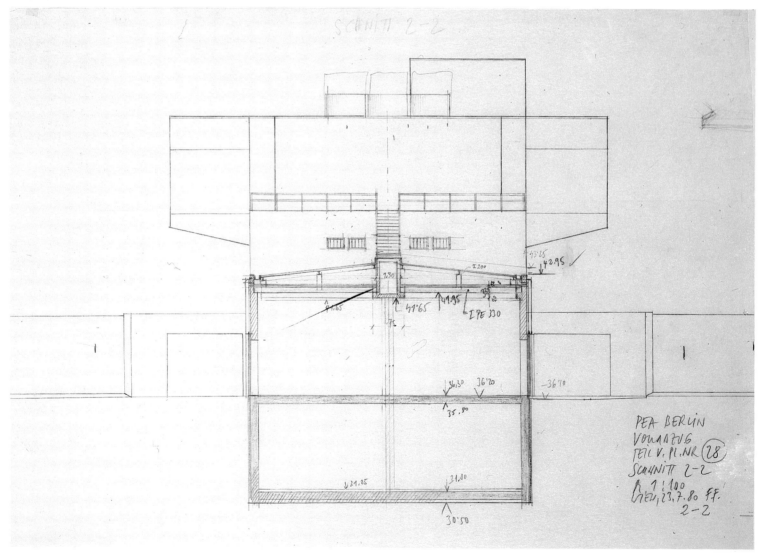

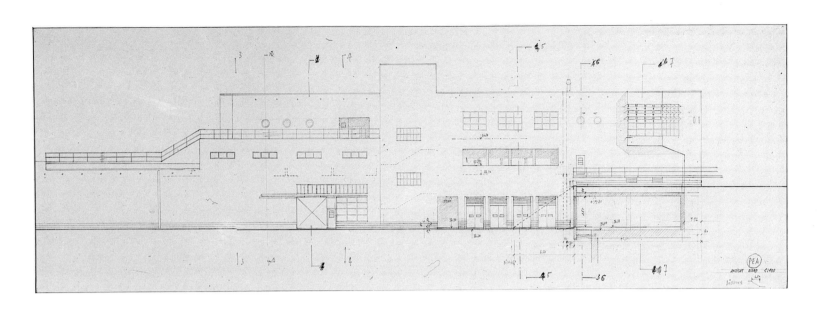

SCHNITT 6-6

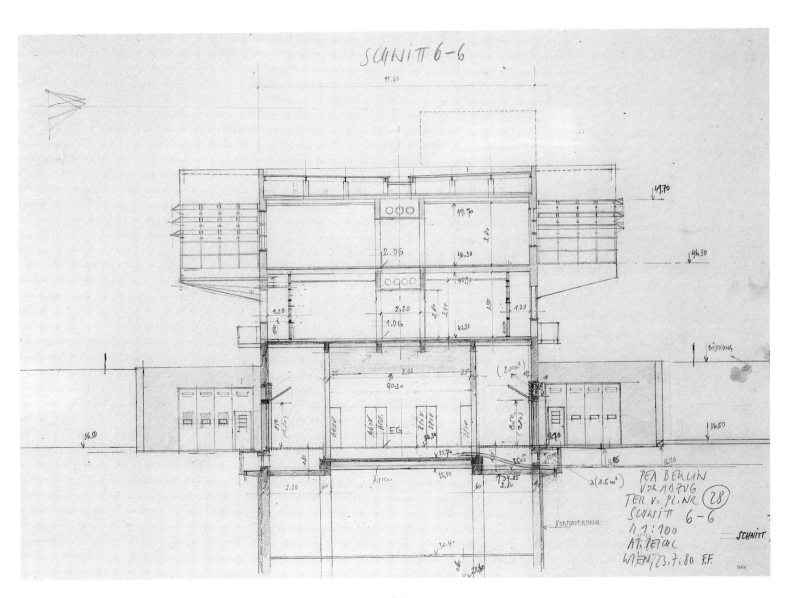

PEA BERLIN
VORABZUG
TEIL V. PL.NR. ⑤
SCHNITT 6-6
n. 1:100
A.T. PETAL
WIEN, 23.7.80 F.F.

39

**Residential Development Schloss-strasse 19
Planning since 1983**

Gustav Peichl, Vienna

with Peter Nigst, Franco Fonatti

52
Corner perspective of housing development, left: the PEA
Pencil on transparent paper
30 x 57 cm

53
Front perspective
India ink on paper
29.9 x 41.9 cm
Signed: Pea/3, Berlin 1983

54
Sketch
Ground floor plan, scale 1:500
Pencil and crayon on paper
30 x 52 cm

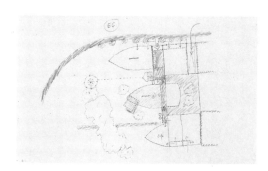

55
Preliminary study
Front elevation, scale 1:100
Pencil, India ink and crayon
on paper
30 x 56.4 cm
Signed: F.F. 2.3.84

New Urban Building

**Demonstration Area
Prager Platz**

Prager Platz

Frills and trappings laid waste
Aggressive emptiness
Historical collage

"There came a period when the charm radiated by old towns was not so harmless, for it might lead one to believe that the architect's ambitions did not go beyond the decorative aspect, that a picturesque backdrop was all that was needed."
Fritz Schumacher

If we remind people what Prager Platz used to look like before it was destroyed, a testimony to the prestige-consciousness of the bourgeoisie, we notice how their eyes light up in wonderment, only to be followed by resignation and moans about the present day being incapable of producing such achievements in architecture and town planning. Recalling the square as it once was, sadness and nostalgia conjure up happy memories of the good old days, for that is what they were in the eyes of many people, the years leading up to the outbreak of the First World War.

Yet the glittering image is deceptive, it reflects only one side of its epoch: that of the frills and trappings, the ornamental feathers fluttering on hats and helmets. No doubt about it, it made a proud picture: the decorative circle of green, the oval shape of the square, set off by seven monumental cornerstones, not counting the oriel turrets. Motley awnings, motley life. And the streetcar loop, for a time the terminus of the line to Gendarmenmarkt: the umbilical cord to the centre of the one-time capital of the Reich.

Wide pavements and relatively small-sized blocks, urban compactness and variety of uses, these would no doubt have gone a long way toward fulfilling Jane Jacobs' criteria for urban structures to promote communication, and Kevin Lynch would also have been likely to find this setting a good example for the balanced integration of striking visual elements.

In its time, all of this – and the architecture, too – was in keeping with the then fashion of using historical allusions in architecture to underline a conviction of self-importance: a new century was beginning, and there was a strong awareness that nothing could stand in the way of Berlin's progress toward the status of European metropolis.

But what was the reality behind this architectural historicism of the dawn of a new century? In his critical review of historicism, which he contributed in 1984 to the exhibition catalogue "The Adventure of Ideas: Architecture and Philosophy since the Industrial Revolution", Winfried Nerdinger made the point that from about 1840 on architecture entered the "phase of dogmatic or archaeological historicism". "This historicism stemming from a historical education ... led to textbooks and pattern books for all styles and to learned reconstructions of the entire architecture of ancient times, it dominated the training of architects and sparked off the endless arguments of those decades as to the right style. Starting from a scientific reconstruction of the historical development of the various styles and of their principles of construction, the aim was to determine which style could be used anew or developed further in view of its country of origin, its process of development or its constructional possibilities."

Few remnants of this scientific meticulousness were to be seen at the beginning of the twentieth century. The stereotype elements were mass-produced for Kurfürstendamm and Prager Platz. Nerdinger was right when he said that, even with serious "attempts to find a scientific basis for historical design", the problem was that "historical education was not anchored in a relevance to life, and, in particular, the question of style was usually obscured by ideological or political considerations".

Thus, a lot of architecture drew a veil over the realities of everyday life, and Prager Platz was undoubtedly one of the late examples meant to camouflage the scandal of the tenement blocks of Berlin.

Yet precisely this was, in the opinion of the more well-to-do citizens, no longer really necessary at the beginning of the twentieth century, for, as Werner Hegemann points out, "after the 1870 war the 'educated classes' in Germany also began to accept the tenement, which Berlin the victorious presented to them as the modern type of city dwelling".

It was all the more true for Prager Platz when in 1907, as it began to take shape, Muthesius complained that "everywhere the cheapest kind of surrogate swindle is blooming unhindered". He goes on: "The only thing that counts is to use luxurious

trappings to make an impression on those who have no judgement of their own. The typical apartment occupying one floor of a building is provided by the least educated elements of the populace and accepted by the best educated. Had not German taste sunk to practically rock-bottom level, were there not a total erosion of the feeling for the most elementary requirements of good taste, quiet respectability and upper-class reserve, no cultured person could possibly bear to live in apartments of this nature, just as he would never consent to wear ill-fitting clothes of shabby materials which have been got up to give a superficially pretentious air. The German citizen of today has not yet learnt to apply the most elementary rules of quality and unobtrusive good taste to his dwelling-place and furniture."

That is one side of the coin; looking at the other side, no one today would dream of questioning our duty to preserve such testimonies to the architecture and urban history of Berlin, after many years of missed opportunities. Nor, unfortunately, is there any question that we have failed to provide a new model to contrast at least with the areas and volumes of housing at the turn of the century – we are hampered by the regulations for the subsidization of council housing, which, though well meant, are restrictive in character and effects. Highly significant is the trend for architects, of all people, to prefer the oft-criticized stupidity of the ground-plan of the Berlin tenement to the functional sophistication of their own housing projects.

But there was nothing to be salvaged from Prager Platz after the second wave of destruction. After the wounds inflicted by the Second World War, the oft-criticized reconstruction mania removed what was left of the ruins standing on Prager Platz, as elsewhere. Plenty has been said about this act of blind destructiveness. Today, we can only be thankful that none of the schemes put forward in the fifties, sixties, and even early seventies was realized.

There must have been some sort of spell cast by the urban ground-plan (which can still be traced) that prevented the worst from happening.

This gave us the opportunity, in 1976, to include Prager Platz as a demonstration project in the series "Models for a City". "Models for a City" was the title of a series

Prager Platz as it was in 1926

Prager Platz with Hormocenta building, seen in 1980

of articles suggested and edited by Wolf Jobst Siedler and myself, and published in the *Berliner Morgenpost* newspaper, in which we launched the idea of an International Building Exhibition whose goal would be a critical reconstruction of the city that had suffered such devastation during the war and the postwar years. We asked Carlo Aymonino and Rob Krier – starting from the historical ground-plan of the city and the urban space – to make a tentative suggestion as to how a locality with a new character could be created, with an image and utility spectrum that, respecting the traces of history, mediated the future. These target plans were published in 1977; in the autumn of 1979 Gottfried Böhm and Rob Krier tried to give them more concrete shape and presented detailed designs for the reconstruction of Prager Platz on townplanning principles and for its architectonic remodelling. One of the first decisions of the IBA was to stipulate that all future concepts should follow Gottfried Böhm's overall urbanistic plan.

Unlike Rob Krier, who in accordance with his first concept proposed a more strongly introverted realization of the site, Gottfried Böhm followed the historical urban plan literally and suggested a modern interpretation as a solution for the monumental corner figuration.

In the course of lengthy discussions the urban ground-plan, the geometric contour of the buildings and the principal construction materials were designated on the above lines. More information on this planning process and a detailed presentation can be found in Volume VI of our series "Documents and Projects – New Urban Building".

In Frankfurt, considering the special objective of this exhibition, we are showing a series of sketches, plans and models which on the one hand give an idea of the evolution of the planning, but above all provide an impression of the future countenance of Prager Platz, the way it will one day look to its residents and users. The sketches also make clear how firmly the three architects participating in the realization of the project adhere to their theoretical interpretation of architecture, even within the framework of a prescribed planimetric and stereometric outline. This in fact was one of the basic ideas of the new buildings section of the International Building Exhibition: to work out fundamental definitions in the realm of urban development as a binding scheme for the realization of individual projects, definitions which will be appropriate to differing theoretical and artistic attitudes.

The concept of history as a "path toward knowledge of our own condition", a thesis mooted by Savigny in the journal for historical jurisprudence in 1815, entails both cool and objective research and dynamic interpretation from the point of view of the pragmatic artist. From the word go, the dialectic of these two factors provided the stimulus for the International Building Exhibition Berlin 1987 to investigate the history of architecture in Berlin. The IBA has attempted to rediscover a tradition which the modern movement for a time failed to understand.

The daredevil flirtation of the modernists with "design without limitations" (Werner Hofmann) led to excesses and finally fizzled out in the trivial grid schemes of timid planning rationality; the attempt to reestablish the links with history can be seen as a reaction to this, but it is very much a tightrope walk. On the one side we have the distorted and sensational showpieces of eclectic impresarios, as evidenced in Paris (Ricardo Bofill), on the other we have the reticent, conceptually executed work of "critical reconstruction". An exposition of this term on the basis of a strict grammatical system will have to be postponed for the time being: suffice it to say that the idea of "critical reconstruction" embodies a dialectic – between "separation" and "restoration", demarcation lines and lines of reference that respect no demarcations, creativity in design and bonds with tradition. The concept of time and history

immanent in this dialectic also had a key role in Freud's metapsychology, when he defined the triad of moments involved in transmission: "repetition", "remembrance" and the liberating and separating process of "working through". It should not be forgotten, though, that Freud's model had been anticipated in Schelling's philosophy of history.

The current tendency of the language of architecture to adopt historical features can, or perhaps must, be interpreted as an attempt at transmission. The projects envisaged for Prager Platz, too – with their aspects of repetition, charged with feeling, unemotional retracing of the vestiges of remembrance, and modern reworking – have differing relationships to the strands of time that relate the past to the future. The object of the transmission is, to put it in a nutshell: emancipation on new terms. An interest in the past, in antecedent models and idealizing projection, is not an end in itself in the scheme of critical reconstruction, it is a condition of more profound self-experience: an experience, though, that only comes about when the ego does not lose itself in romanticizing repetition and the endless threads of remembrance and reflection, but incorporates itself into the differential of forces that holds between the three moments of "transmission".   Josef Paul Kleihues

**Urbanistic Survey Prager Platz (1978)
and Subsequent Planning of Buildings
for Northern and Western Perimeter**

Gottfried Böhm, Cologne

with Hans Linder, Harald Thomä, Friedrich
Steinigeweg, Corinna Schaade, Klaus
Bölkow, Franz Kilian, Georg Adolphi

56
Perspective of Prager Platz and
the projected development
Pencil on transparent paper
91.6 x 139.5 cm

57
Perspective, Prager Platz
Copy on transparent paper
65.2 x 150 cm
Signed: Prager Platz Berlin 136/9
142/45 Sept. 78

58
Northwest development, elevation with
perspective view of entrance to the
swimming pool, scale 1 : 100
Copy on transparent paper
33.6 x 49.8 cm
Signed: G. B. 81

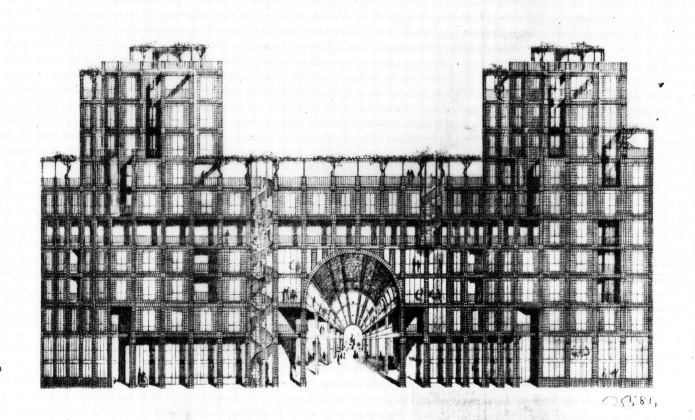

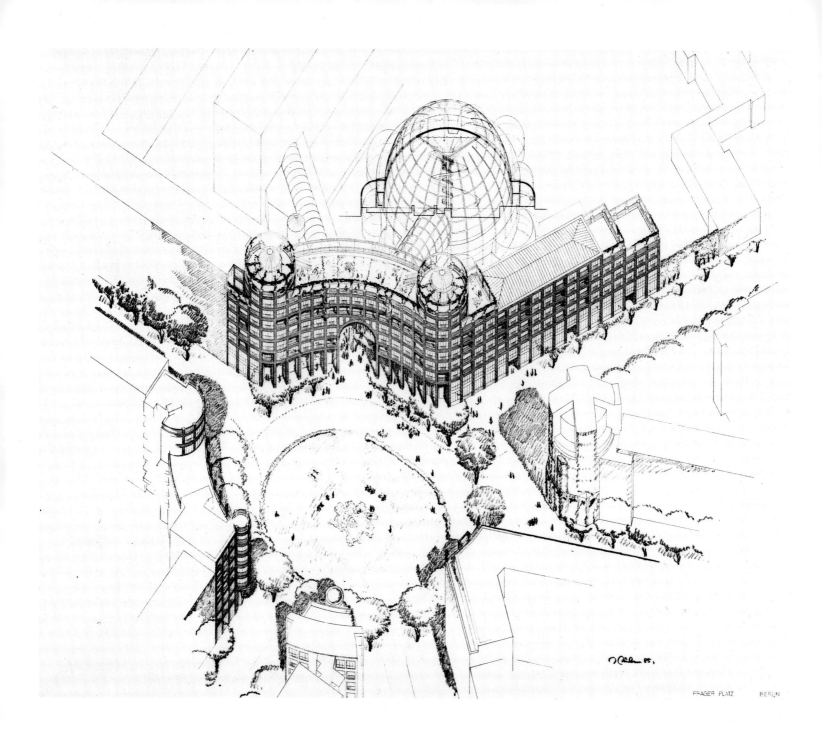

PRAGER PLATZ   BERLIN

59
Axonometric drawing, scale 1:200
Copy on transparent paper
89.5 x 109.4 cm
Signed: G. Böhm 85
Prager Platz Berlin Isometrie 223/2 105/95

**Façade Configuration for Existing
Prewar House
Prager Platz 6
Planning since 1983**

Gottfried Böhm, Cologne

60
Elevation, sketch, scale 1 : 100
Photocopy
43.6 x 35.5 cm
Signed: 15. 10. 83 GB

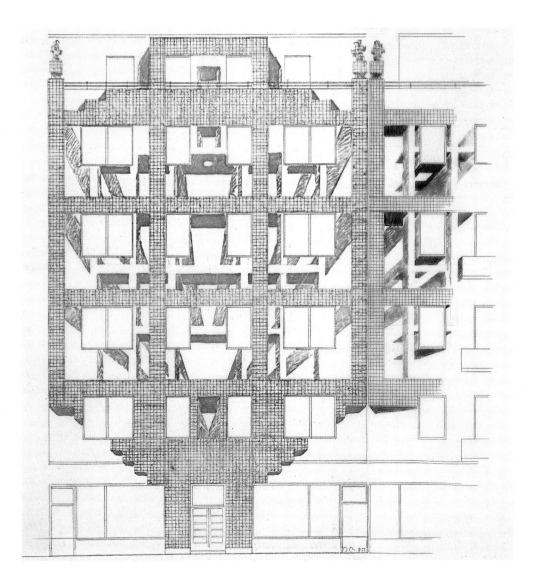

61
Elevation, scale 1 : 50
Left: copy on transparent paper;
Right: pencil and crayon on transparent
paper
51.4 x 49.3 cm
Signed: GB 851

Urbanistic Survey Prager Platz, 1978

Rob Krier, Vienna

62
Square plan, scale 1 : 500
a) Street plan around the Prager Platz
b) Existing buildings
c) Survey with square walls completed
d) Final proposal
Oil crayon on blueprint
40 x 60 cm

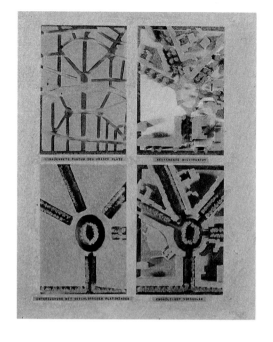

63
Axonometric drawing, scale 1 : 200
Sepia crayon on transparent paper
90 x 120 cm
Signed: 1978 Krier

**Apartment House Prager Platz, Corner
of Motzstrasse and Prager Strasse
Planning since 1981**

Rob Krier, Vienna

64
Elevation, scale 1 : 100 (detail)
Pencil and watercolour on
watercolour board
71.5 x 52 cm (full size)

65
Sketch
Perspective of Prager Platz
Pencil and crayon on transparent paper
65.8 x 64.1 cm
Signed: 20.8.81 Krier

49

Prager Platz
Project for Berliner Morgenpost Series
"Models for a City", 1976/77

Carlo Aymonino, Rome

3 Sketches

66
Elevations, plans, axonometric drawings
India ink on paper
21.6 x 12.2 cm

67
Perspectives, axonometric drawings, plans
India ink on paper
23.8 x 10.5 cm

68
Axonometric drawings
India ink on paper
21.4 x 11.5 cm
Signed: Prager Platz X 76

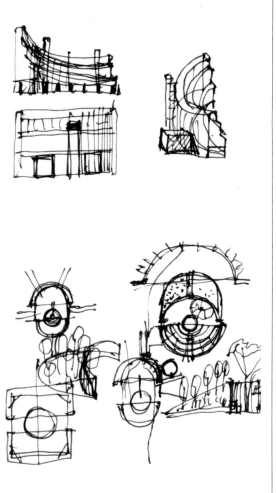

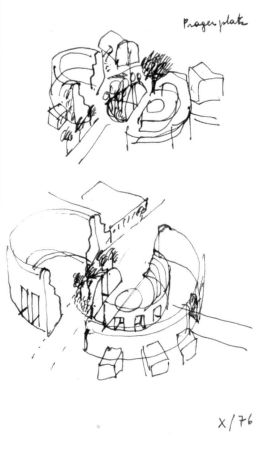

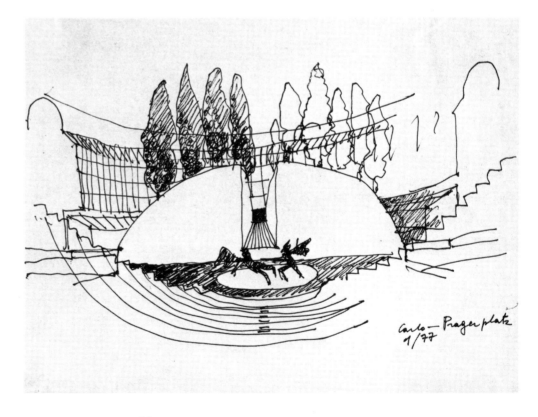

69
Perspective study of the square with
neighbouring development in background
India ink on paper
22 x 28 cm
Signed: Carlo – Prager Platz 1/77

70
Sketch
Perspective view of the square and
neighbouring development in background
India ink on yellow paper
24 x 31.8 cm
Signed: Carlo – Prager Platz 1/77

**Residential Development Prager Platz,
Corner of Prinzregentenstrasse and
Aschaffenburger Strasse
Design 1981/82**

**Carlo Aymonino
Aldo Aymonino
M. Luisa Tugnoli, Rome**

with Michael Peterek

71
Sketches
Axonometric drawing plan, side elevation
and schematic section
India ink on transparent paper
28.8 x 21.1 cm
Signed: 7/1/81

72a + b
Sketches
a) Corner view and plan of the building
with sketch of the Prager Platz
India ink on paper
22.7 x 14.8 cm
Signed: Berlino 28/XII/80

b) Plan, scale 1 : 200
India ink on paper
22.7 x 18.5 cm
Signed: Pragerplatz 1/81, scale 1 : 200

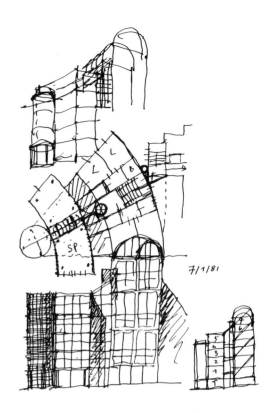

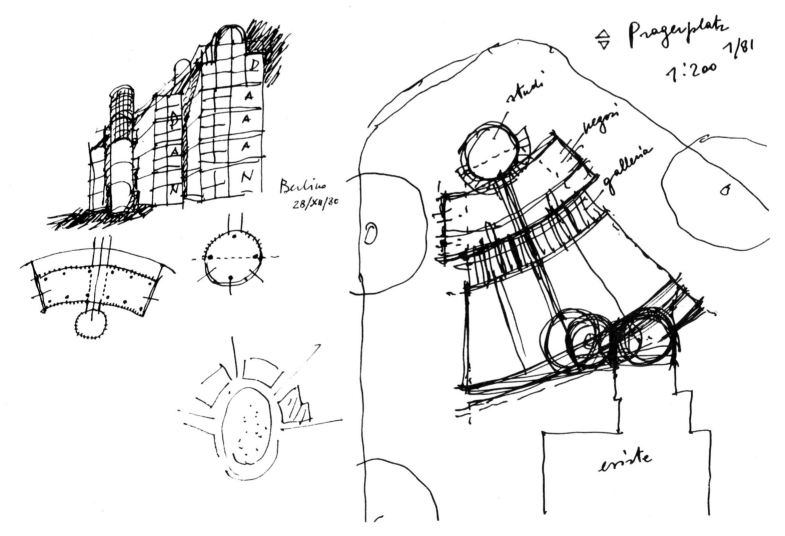

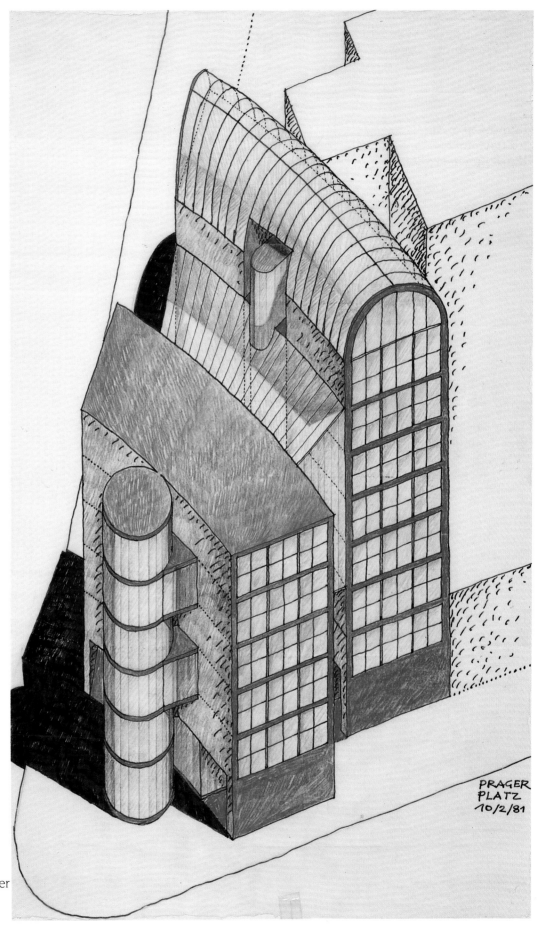

73
Axonometric drawing
India ink and crayon on transparent paper
60.3 x 35.5 cm
Signed: Prager Platz 10/2/81

**Residential Development Prager Platz,
Corner of Prinzregentenstrasse and
Aschaffenburger Strasse
Working drawings in preparation
since 1985
Construction commenced recently**

**Carlo Aymonino
Aldo Aymonino, Rome
Klaus Kammann, Berlin**

with Barbara Wilkens

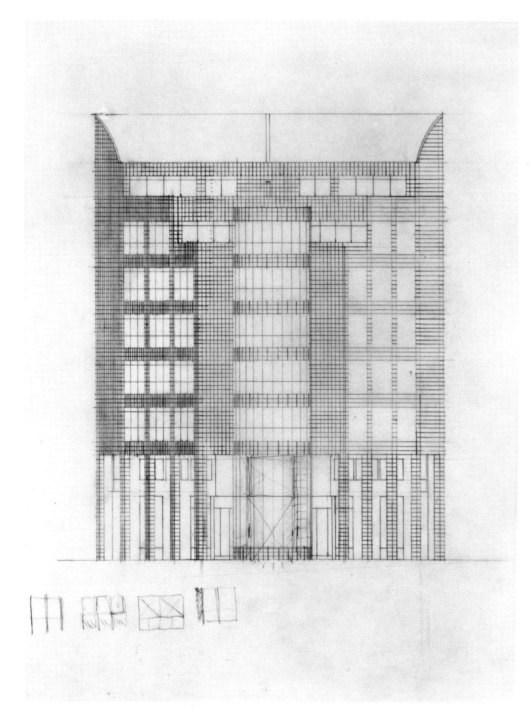

74
Front elevation, scale 1:100 (study)
Pencil on transparent paper
52.7 x 33 cm

75
Side elevation, scale 1:100 (study)
Pencil on transparent paper
54 x 33 cm

New Urban Building

**Demonstration Area
Southern Tiergarten District**

Southern Tiergarten District

Garden and urban area
Solitary examples of modern architecture
Future as a forum

"A sense of form is the blind and, at the same time, binding reflexion of the object in itself, on which it must rely: the self-impenetrable objectivity falling to the subjective power of mimesis, which in its turn gains strength from its antagonist, rational design."

Theodor W. Adorno

First, a few general observations on the premises of and approaches to urbanism in the new urban building sector of the IBA in this district.

Together with southern Friedrichstadt, with which it has strong urbanistic and topographic connections, the southern Tiergarten district has with its complex problems the makings of a demonstration ground for the International Building Exhibition which will be of key significance for the entire city. "Southern Tiergarten district" is the designation conventionally applied to the so-called diplomatic quarter between the zoo and Kemperplatz. In terms of the International Building Exhibition it covers a demonstration ground extended southward beyond the Landwehr Canal as far as Kurfürstenstrasse: a fascinating area with its variety of uses and neighbourhoods. Here, on the southern edge of the Tiergarten, Berlin's great inter-city park and recreation ground, covering over 200 ha, is where they originally planned to hold the International Building Exhibition of the eighties, a sort of rehash of the 1957 Interbau. The current programme of the 1984 International Building Exhibition was arrived at after intensive discussions, and is characterized by a much greater diversity of themes and by inclusion of several urban districts: the diplomatic quarter will now serve principally as an overspill for the Tiergarten park, which in summer can hardly cope with the crowds of recreation seekers.

To trace the progressive urban development of this area with its complex user structure and rich variety of aspects we have to go back to the eighteenth century. In Philipp Gerlach's urban extension plans of 1735 we can get a foretaste of future developments from the delineation of the western city limits. With the end of the eighteenth century, artists and, above all, wealthy burghers began to take up residence in the neighbourhood of Tiergartenstrasse. Sophisticated villas began to spring up around St Matthew's church square in the first half of the nineteenth century. The Tiergarten was designed by Peter Joseph Lenné as a peripheral landscaped park (later to become a downtown park); it was earmarked by Hobrecht for special attention as an integrated component of his plans for Berlin (1858–62), the first vision of metropolitan magnitude. While the villa character of the residential area between the edge of the Tiergarten and the Landwehr Canal was maintained well into the present century (expansion westward taking place from 1936 onward with the development of the diplomatic quarter via low-density building), the Hobrecht plan resulted in high-density block building in the adjacent district south of the Landwehr Canal.

It is this urbanistic contradiction that makes it especially challenging today, after wartime devastation and the totally new concept of rebuilding work around St Matthew's church square (Cultural Forum on Kemperplatz), to take all these factors into account in seeking meaningful solutions and an appropriate overall structure for the concrete planning and architectural objectives in this district.

The Cultural Forum, however, which was conceived and described in glowing terms as an open composition of demonstrative monuments to illustrate the roles within the cultural scheme of the various institutions, has for years had the sorry appearance of a stopgap embodiment of an idealistic project. Let us make no bones about it, this project in fact entailed the sacrificing of what was left of an urban area that was once notable for its small-scale architectural entities, we might even say cameos.

The solitary monumental edifices of Philharmonic Hall, National Gallery and National Library combine with Stüler's delicate church of St Matthew to produce a highly heterogeneous urbanistic picture which leaves a negative, cold impression on the visitor.

Yet the incomplete construction site of the Cultural Forum has long since evinced a function as effective excentric magnet, pulling toward the cultural bond of the Spree river. And, looking into the future, we can see a good chance of the establishment of a living area of more than transitory validity right here on the axis of the two city centres. But first, let us take a look at the four very different neighbourhoods that delineate this district.

The *first area*, from the western edge of the railway triangle to Lützowplatz, that is, south of the Landwehr Canal, is as far as we are concerned substantially an area of urban renewal.

Here, the IBA has so far left its mark only in a small way, though the imprint is clearly to be seen. Antoine Grumbach's corner house is one example. Other projects, such as the redesigning of Magdeburger Platz, came to nothing. Nor was it possible, unfortunately, to realize Richard Meier's project, which called for the opening of Potsdamer Strasse to the Cultural Forum. As regards Lützowplatz, we have in mind a radical cutback of thoroughfares without impairing traffic or functional requirements. We believe – and the Senators for Urban Development and the Environment, and for Building and Housing, agree – that it will be possible to extend the profile of Hofjägerallee in a southward direction too, retaining its stark geometric contour, but setting it off with different types of buildings and plantings. Thus, we are not just interested in new peripheral structures. It is in fact planned to increase the area of Lützowplatz by 5000–6000 m^2, and so make it into an attractive city square with its new look, open to the Tiergarten.

The necessary downgrading of streets, however, will probably have to wait until after the end of the International Building Exhibition. The first of the projected buildings for the eastern side of the square are now going up, and Vittorio Gregotti's peripheral development of Lützowstrasse is also under way; the "gatehouse" for the early townhouse rows of the IBA has been completed.

The *second area* is the erstwhile diplomatic quarter, whose western extremity with the well-liked development on Rauchstrasse marks the beginning of the demonstration area southern Tiergarten district. It is not planned to do any great building work in the core of the diplomatic quarter, between

Southern Tiergarten district,
Cultural Forum, as it was in 1984.

Bellevuestrasse seen from Potsdamer
Platz, c. 1910.

The former diplomatic quarter was originally envisaged as the site of the IBA, but
will now remain undeveloped as a buffer
for the Tiergarten park and as a reserve
development area. This is how it looked in
1982.

Klingelhöferstrasse and the Cultural Forum.
The idea is to safeguard a few suitable and
imposing pieces of land, so that once Berlin is no longer a divided city sites will be
available for the erection of important edifices of national, European, or international
significance.

We are thus proposing the provisional use
of substantial portions of this quarter for
an inner city park, a green space that
would make provision for leisure activities
we should not like to see in Berlin's central
garden, the Tiergarten.

Which brings us to the *third area*, the Tiergarten itself, that incomparable downtown
park by Peter Joseph Lenné. It is our desire
to restore this city park (except for the
area between Reichstag and Congress Hall)
to its former glory, to attempt the reconstruction of Lenné's garden as a historic
entity, though we are all conscious of the
fact that there have been discrepancies
between planning and reality.

The *fourth area*, also directly bordering on
the Cultural Forum, but now outside the
IBA precinct, is the cleared site of the one-
time Potsdamer railway station with the
adjacent Potsdamer Platz – it is still called
Potsdamer Platz today, though of course it
no longer exists as such. Understandably
enough, if you visit this quarter, if you
examine it on a map of the city, if you
study the contexts of urban layout and
also of national politics, you will be temp-
ted to heave a sigh of resignation and

abandon all thoughts of planning activities
in the foreseeable future. Yet, in contrast to
the diplomatic quarter and the Spree
curve, this is an area entrusted with a mission: the simple fact that it is situated in
the Western Sector of the divided city
defines this mission – to establish at last a
continuous, tangible relationship to the
adjacent districts in the Eastern Sector,
i. e. a link running via the Friedrich suburb,
southern Friedrichstadt and Luisenstadt
out to SO 36 and Neukölln.

Problems of urban development – not of
town planning – have always been neglected. Thus, many observers of the IBA in
context, with its terms of reference prima-
rily in the field of urban development, have
come away with a false impression, right
up to the present day. But from the beginning of our work onward it has been a different story: we have attracted attention
with individual specimens of architecture,
but what involved the most time and effort
was the preparatory work on problems of
urban development. But we will have more
to say about this in the Berlin exhibitions
and the source publications of our series
"Documents and Projects".

In their dialogue with the Cultural Forum
the neighbouring districts and especially
the central area have an array of planning
ideas and architectural schemes to discuss,
some of them poles apart. Material decisions, however, have still to be taken. The
danger of an isolated decision on an indi-

vidual project is greater here than probably
anywhere else in the city. At the very least,
an urban ground-plan needs to be laid
down. It was Berlin that wanted finally to
take the plunge and approve a plan which
went beyond functional-rational aspects
and a minimum quota of open spaces to
take account of the artistic questions of
town planning.

Architecture and town planning just cannot
be reduced to the denominator of functionalism and rationalism. Wherever they are
permitted to operate as incipient and
adventurous art they combine constructive
rationality with the power of the poetic,
they become what Hölderlin called a trans-
cendent design of man abiding in his merit
and in his spirit of poetry.

Josef Paul Kleihues

Residential Complex on Lützowplatz
Wichmannstrasse/Lützowplatz
Lützow Embankment
Planning 1979–81
Completed 1983

Oswald Mathias Ungers, Cologne

with Karl-Lothar Dietzsch, Georg
Hagemann, Burkhard Meyer, Barbara Taha,
Bernd Wippler

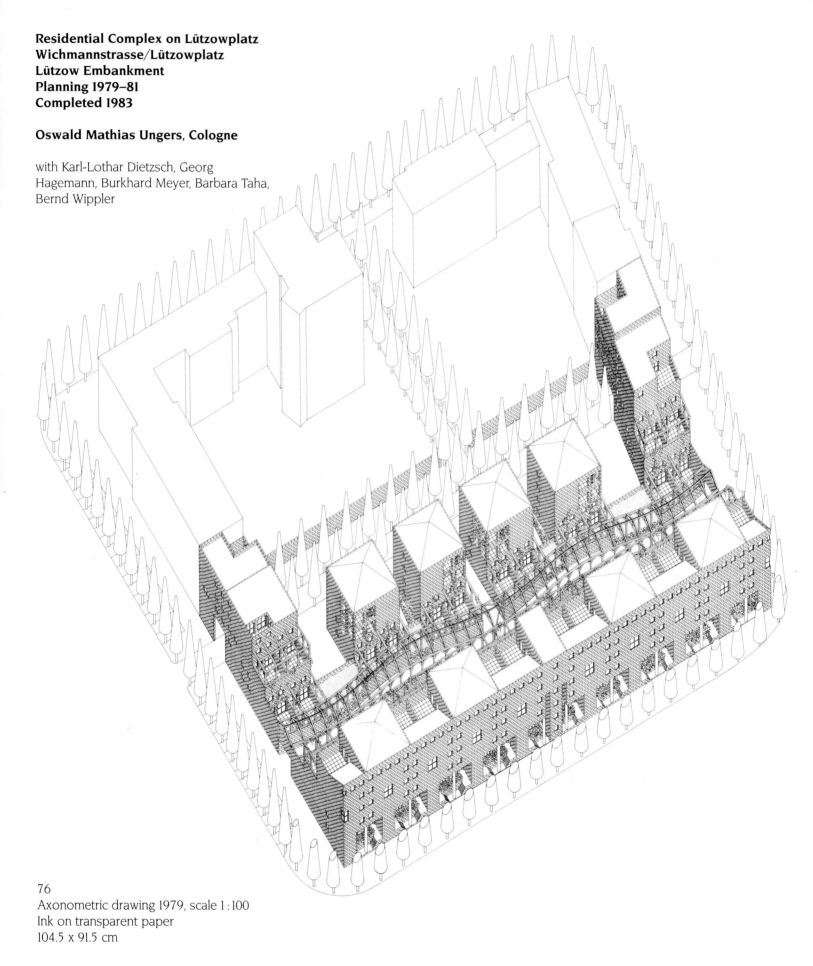

76
Axonometric drawing 1979, scale 1:100
Ink on transparent paper
104.5 x 91.5 cm

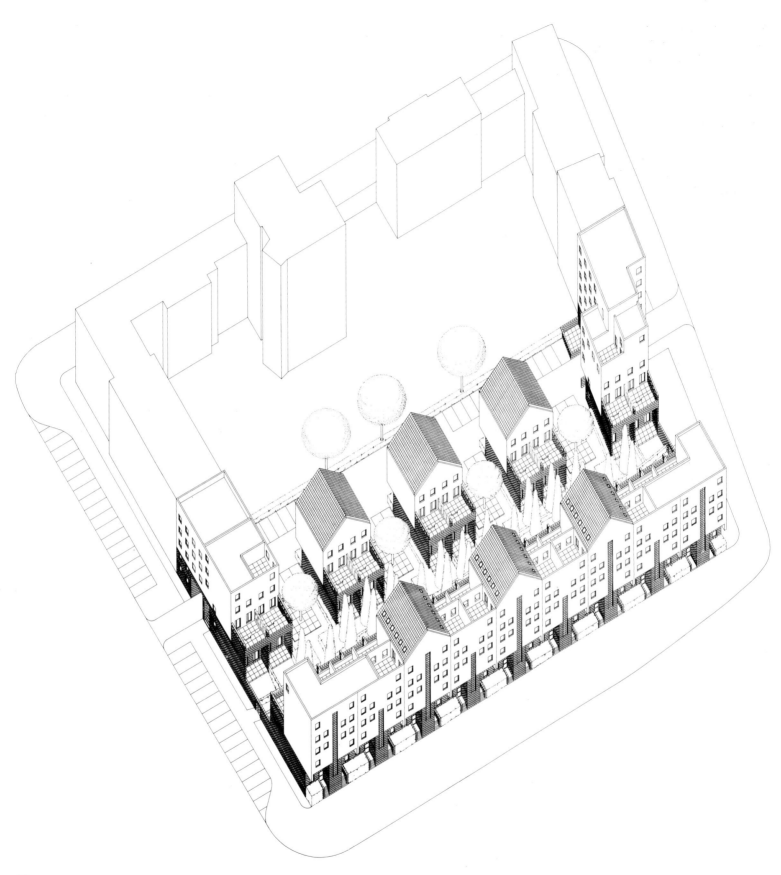

77
Axonometric drawing, scale 1:100
Ink on transparent paper
104 x 103.5 cm

**Façade Design for Hotel Berlin
Lützowplatz/Einemstrasse
Kurfürstenstrasse
Planning 1985/86**

**Klaus Theo Brenner
Benedict Tonon, Berlin**

with Peter Pütz

78
Axonometric drawing of the corner façade
Schillerstrasse/Lützowplatz
India ink on transparent paper
60 x 80 cm

79
Axonometric drawing of the corner façade
Kurfürstenstrasse/Einemstrasse
India ink on transparent paper
60 x 80 cm

80
Axonometric drawing of the corner façade
Lützowplatz/Einemstrasse
India ink on transparent paper
60 x 80 cm

81
Superimposition of site plan, elevation and
axonometric drawing
Pencil and crayon on yellow tracing paper
30 x 67 cm

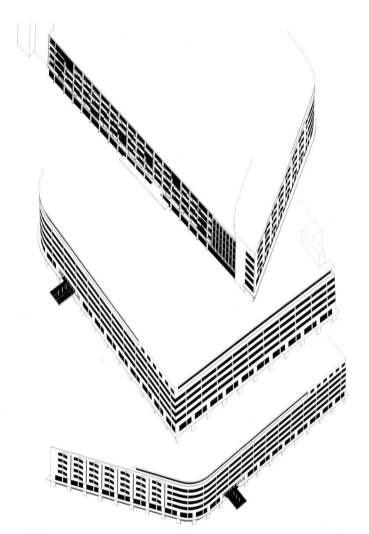

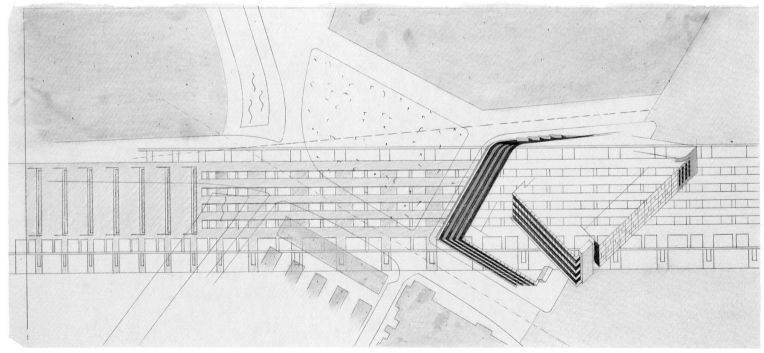

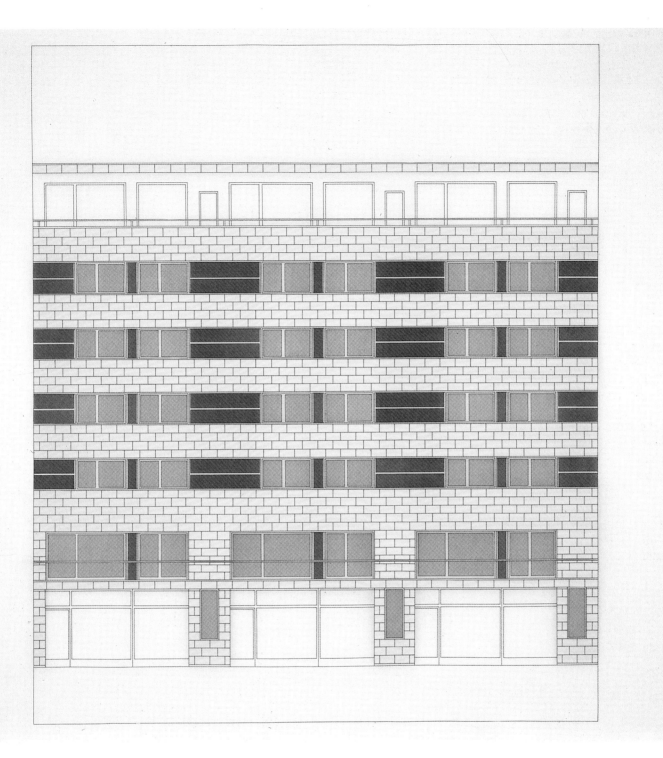

82
Partial view of façade, scale 1:50
India ink, grid film and crayon
on transparent paper
60 x 75 cm

**Urban Villa, Kurfürstenstrasse 60
Planning since 1982**

**Ante Josip von Kostelac,
Seeheim-Malchen**

with Hans Bezzenberger, Ludger Kilian

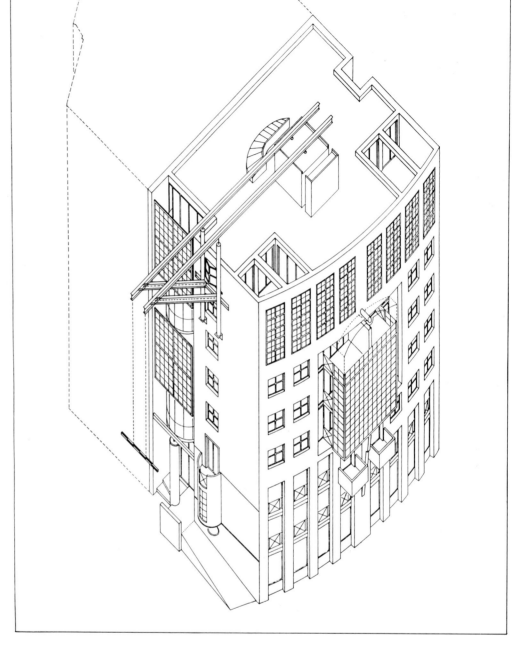

83
Axonometric drawing, scale 1:100
Ink on tracing paper
142 x 100 cm

84
Axonometric sketch
Pen on grafting paper
20.5 x 14.5 cm
Signed: 8. X. 1985 Kustrasse 60

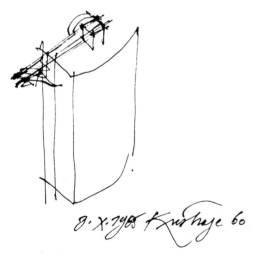

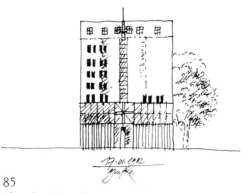

85
Sketch of façade
Pen on watercolour paper
16.5 x 12 cm
Signed: 17. VI. 1982 A. J. v. Ko.

86
Sketch of façade
Pen on watercolour paper
16.5 x 12 cm
Signed: 29. VII. 1982

Urban Villa, Kurfürstenstrasse 59
Planning since 1982

Heinz Hilmer
Christoph Sattler, Munich

88
Perspective elevation (south side),
scale 1 : 50
India ink on transparent paper
65.4 x 68.1 cm

87
Perspective Kurfürstenstrasse 59
elevation; in the background:
Kurfürstenstrasse 60
Photocopy
42 x 29 cm

**International Competition
Residential Park by Lützowplatz, 1981**

**Highly Commended
Adalberto Del Bo
Giorgio Grassi
Edoardo Guazzoni
Agostino Renna, Milan**

with Christian Herdel, Fabio Mantovani,
Davide Tedesi

89–92
4 municipal development studies

Sketch 1
Pencil, crayon and felt pen
on transparent paper
20.8 x 21.8 cm

Sketch 2
Felt pen on transparent paper
21.2 x 22 cm

Sketch 3
Pencil and felt pen on transparent paper
21.3 x 21.9 cm

Sketch 4
Pencil and felt pen on transparent paper
21.2 x 21.8 cm

All signed: GG '80

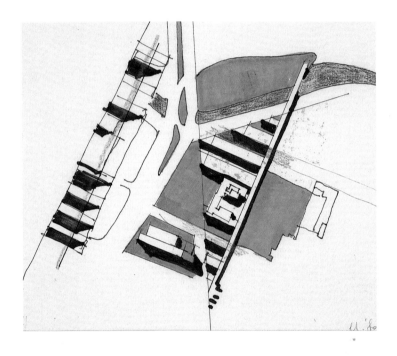

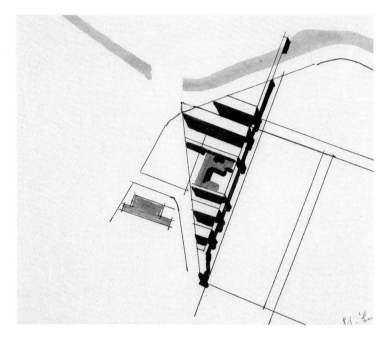

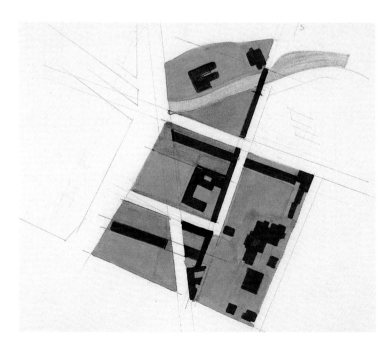

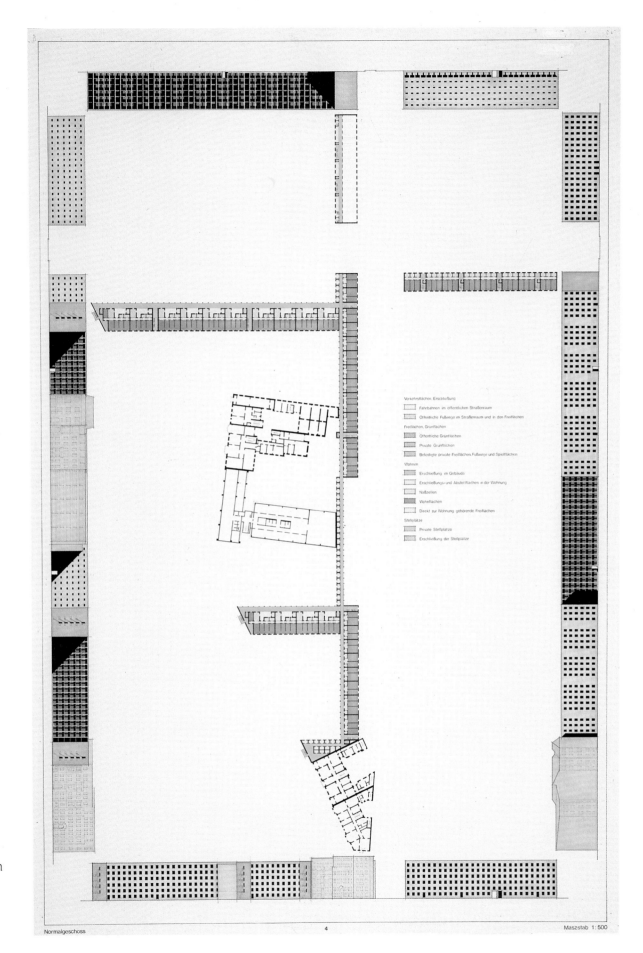

93
Standard floor plan with
elevations,
scale 1:500
Felt pen on blueprint
88.2 x 66 cm

Normalgeschoss

4

Maszstab 1:500

94
Partial façade elevations, scale 1:100
Pencil and felt pen on the reverse side of
a Giorgio Grassi poster
64.6 x 67.5 cm
Signed: Giorgio Grassi, 1981

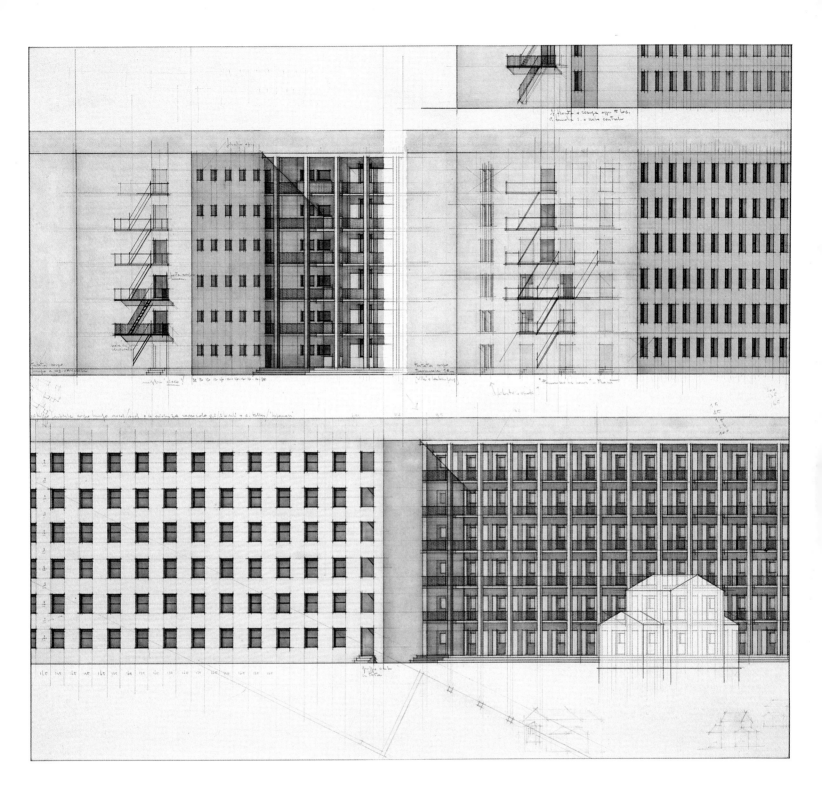

95
Partial façade elevations, scale 1:100
Pencil and felt pen on the reverse side of
a Giorgio Grassi poster
64.6 x 70.8 cm

Residential Park by Lützowplatz,
Lützowstrasse 64 B
Planning 1985/86
Under construction since 1986

Siegfried Gergs, Stuttgart

97
Lützowstrasse elevation and ground floor
plan, scale 1:50
Pencil and crayon on cardboard
89.6 x 65.1 cm
Signed: Stuttgart, May 1985

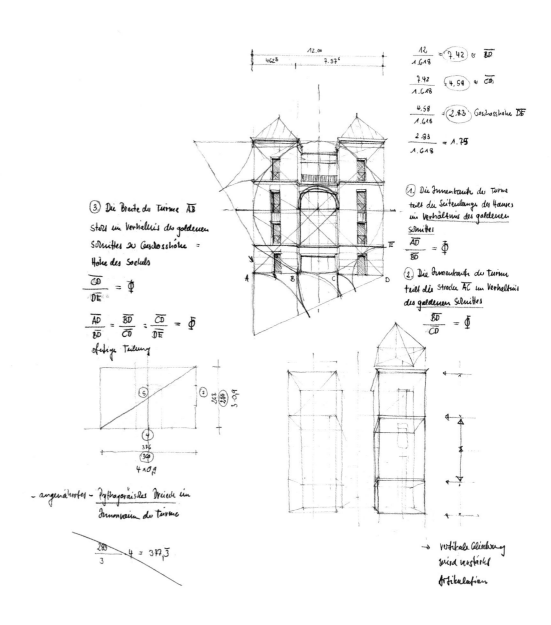

96
Sketches
Pencil on paper
30 x 23 cm (46 cm open)
Signed: Stuttgart, 26. August 1985

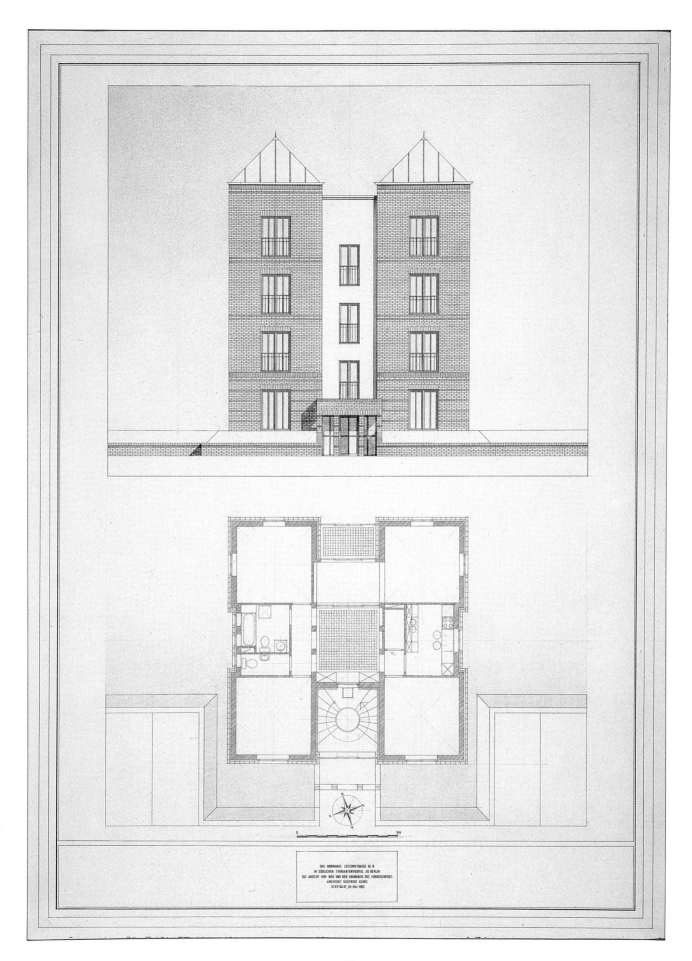

DAS WOHNHAUS LÜTZOWSTRASSE 64 B
IM SÜDLICHEN TIERGARTENVIERTEL ZU BERLIN
DIE ANSICHT VOM WEG UND DER GRUNDRISS DES ERDGESCHOSSES
ARCHITEKT SIEGFRIED GEBGS
STUTTGART, IM MAI 1985

**Residential Park by Lützowplatz
Apartment House Lützowstrasse,
Corner of Lützowplatz
Planning since 1985**

Mario Botta, Lugano

with Mischa Groh

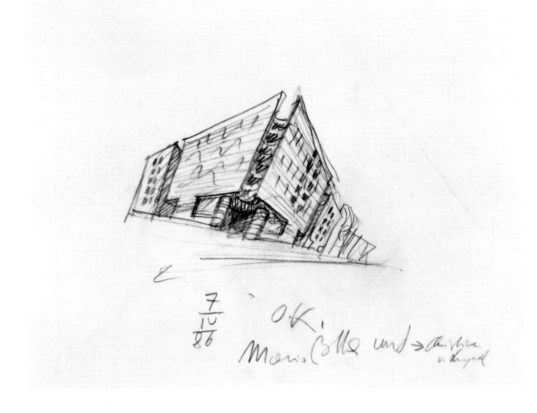

98
Sketch, perspective of Lützowstrasse/
corner of Lützowplatz
Pencil on transparent paper
31.3 x 38.5 cm
Signed: 7/IV/86 O.K. Mario Botta
and Christine von Strempel

99
Elevation Lützowstrasse, scale 1:100
Pencil on paper
39.2 x 52 cm

**Residential and Commercial Premises
Lützowplatz 5
Planning since 1985**

**Dietrich Bangert
Bernd Jansen
Stefan Scholz
Axel Schultes, Berlin**

with Maude Kohlhardt, Andreas Wolf,
Andreas Voigt

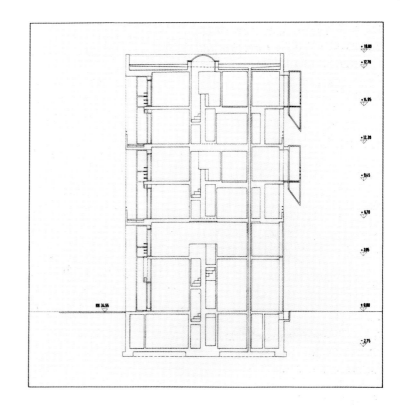

100
Section of shops/maisonettes, scale 1 : 100
Pencil on transparent paper
42 x 29.7 cm

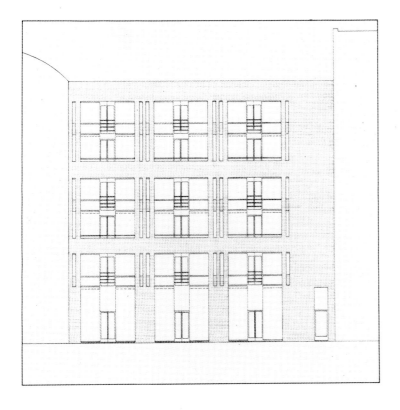

101
View of Lützowplatz, scale 1 : 100
Pencil on transparent paper
42 x 29.7 cm

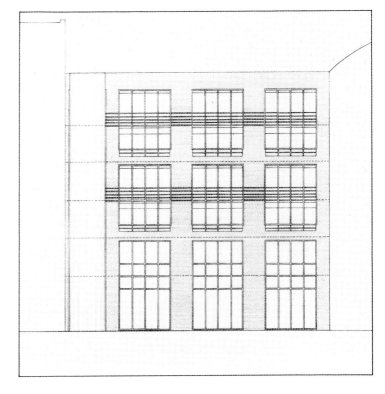

102
View of courtyard (alternative in brick),
scale 1 : 100
Pencil on transparent paper
42 x 29.7 cm

Residential Park by Lützowplatz
Apartment House Lützowplatz 3
Planning since 1985

Peter Cook, Christine Hawley, London

with Rosemary Latter, C. J. Lim

103
View of Lützowplatz, relief image, scale 1 : 50
Mixed media collage
42 x 59.4 cm

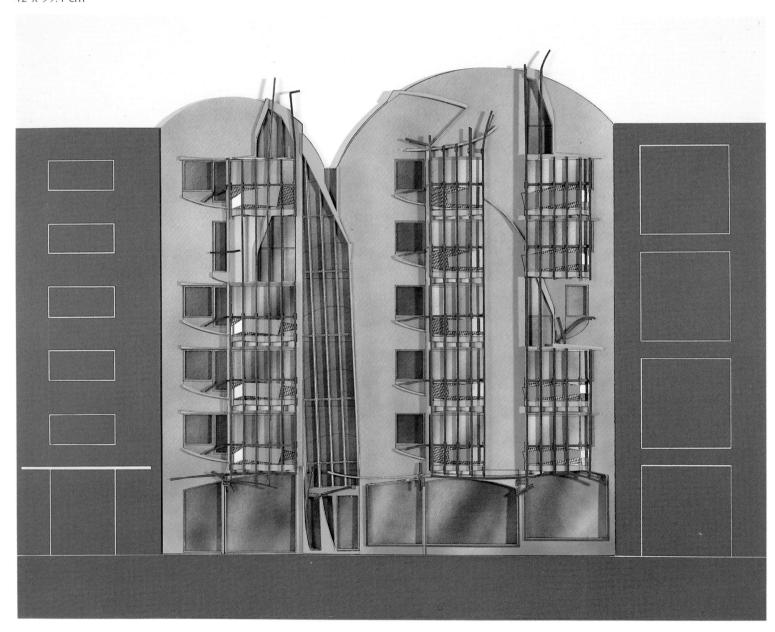

104
View of courtyard, scale 1:50
Blueprint on Capa board, coloured by air-
brush
42 x 59.4 cm
Signed: LPB/A2 Berlin IBA
Lützowplatz Ost Architects
Peter Cook and Christine Hawley

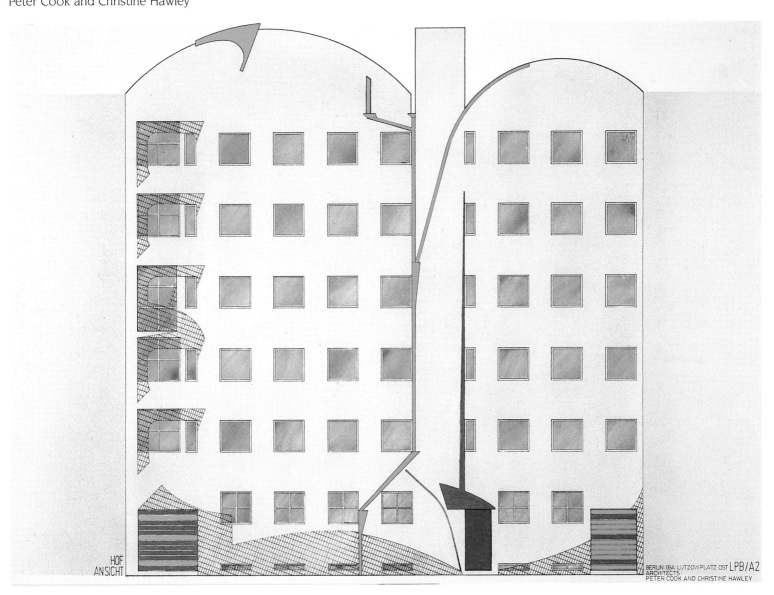

Residential Park by Lützowplatz,
Lützowstrasse 60
Planning since 1985

Christian de Portzamparc

with Jean-François Limet

105
Sketch
Pencil on paper

106
Sketch
Pencil on paper

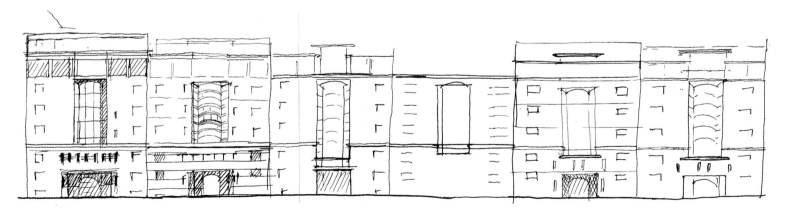

**Residential and Commercial Premises,
Corner of Lützowstrasse and Kluck-
strasse
Planning 1984
Completed 1985**

Antoine Grumbach, Paris

with Didier Gallard, Pierre Caillot

107
Detail, corner study
Chalk on transparent grafting paper
64.7 x 49.8 cm

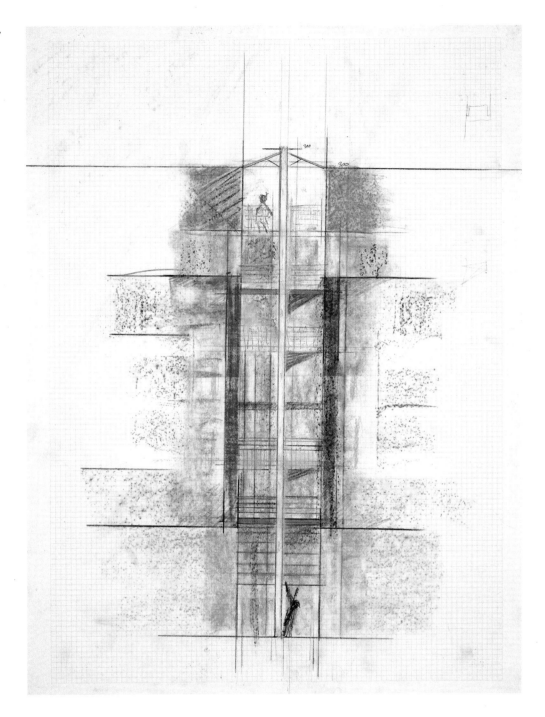

108
Axonometric sketch, elevation
Lützowstrasse
Felt pen on cardboard
23.8 x 32.9 cm

109
Sketch
Felt pen and crayon on cardboard
23.8 x 32.8 cm
Signed: 3 initials and date (unreadable)

110
Sketch for the spatial completion of
the block corners
Pen and crayon on cardboard
23.8 x 32.8 cm

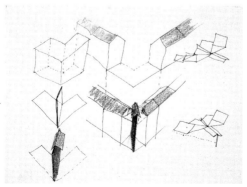

**Restricted International Competition
Magdeburger Platz, 1981**

**First Prize
Henry Nielebock, Berlin
Johannes Grützke (sculptor), Berlin**

with Axel Finkeldey, Siggi Hein, Klaus Meier,
Martin Voss
Landscape architects: Müller/Heinze/
Wehberg/Knippschild, Berlin

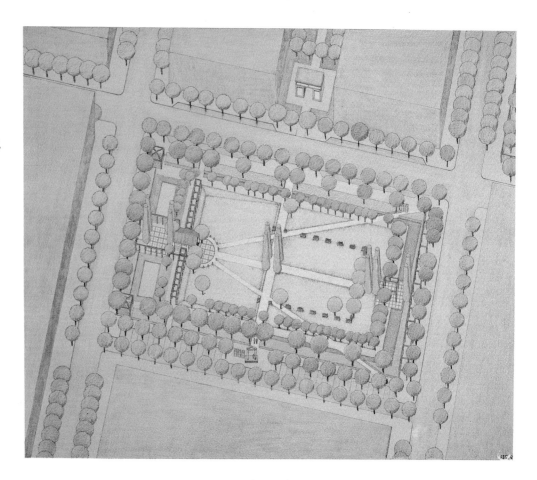

111
Tree planting scheme for the square
Axonometric view, scale 1:200
Blueprint, coloured
87.2 x 102 cm

112
Johannes Grützke
Perspective view of the axis of the square
Chalk and crayon on kraft paper
100 x 100 cm

Apartment House Pohlstrasse 77
Planning since 1985

Hans-Busso von Busse, Munich

with Ulrich Budning

113
Sketch
Felt pen on Lufthansa boarding pass
22 x 16.8 cm
Signed: IBA Pohlstr. 23. 7. 85

114
General representation of the project
Plan, elevation Pohlstrasse 77; section
perspective of Pohlstrasse; scale 1 : 200,
façade detail
Pencil and crayon on blueprint
75.5 x 124.2 cm

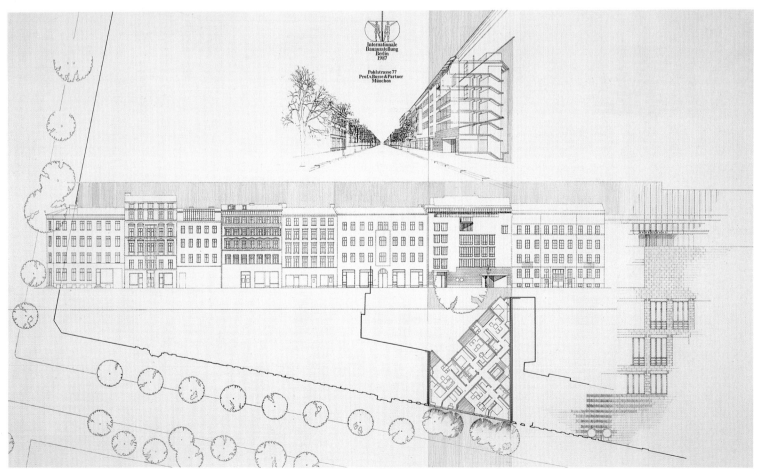

**Restricted International Competition
Lützowstrasse, 1981**

**Second Prize
Gregotti Associati, Milan
Pierluigi Cerri
Vittorio Gregotti
Hiromichi Matsui**

with Spartaco Azzola, Renzo Brandolini,
Klaus Theo Brenner, Vera Casanova,
Christina Castello, Raffaelo Cecchi, Graziella
Clerici, Camilla Fronzoni, Emilio Puglielli
(A 1st Prize was not awarded)

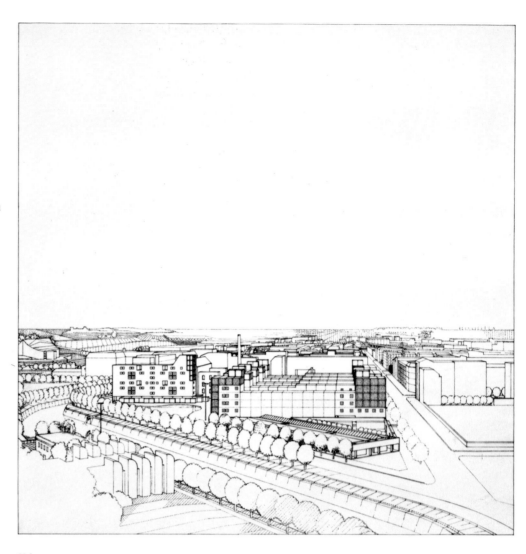

115
Aerial view, eastwards over
the Landwehr Canal and the proposed
development
India ink on transparent paper
73 x 53.6 cm

116
Study of the façade, scale 1 : 200,
with sketches
Pencil and India ink on transparent paper,
coloured
32.5 x 109.6 cm

Peripheral Block Development
Lützowstrasse 46–51
Planning 1981–85
Completed 1986

Gregotti Associati, Milan
Augusto Cagnardi
Pierluigi Cerri
Vittorio Gregotti
Hiromichi Matsui

with Spartaco Azzola, Walter Noebel,
Peter Salomon

117
Partial elevation Lützowstrasse
Façade study for colour scheme,
scale 1:50
Crayon on blueprint
68.5 x 66.4 cm

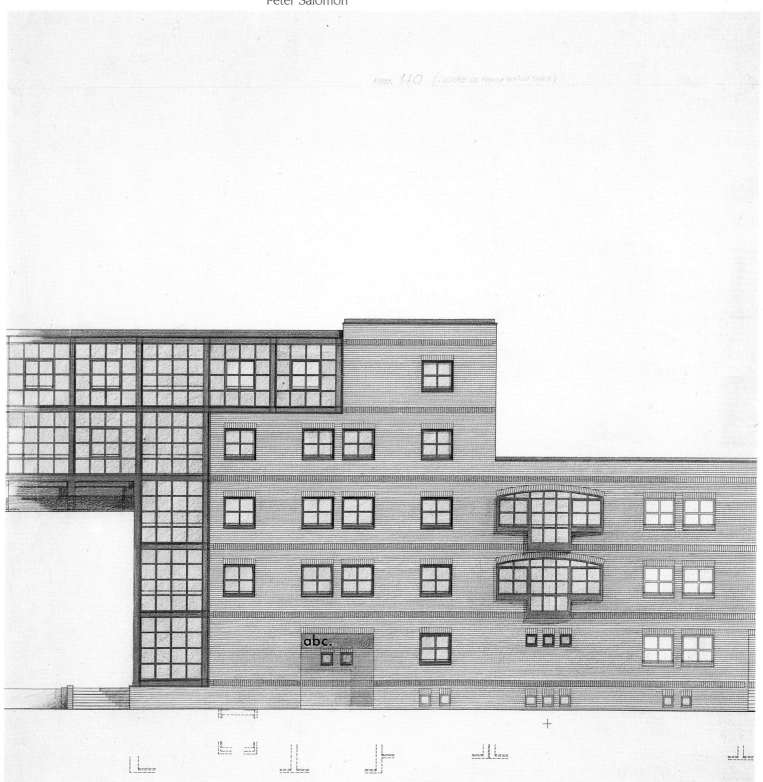

117

Patio House Lützowstrasse 43–44
Planning 1984/85

Gregotti Associati, Milan
Augusto Cagnardi
Pierluigi Cerri
Vittorio Gregotti

with Walter Noebel, Michele Reginaldi,
Peter Salomon

118
Sketch of inner courtyard, elevation,
scale 1:100, room, designs in perspective
Felt pen, crayon and pencil
on transparent paper
32.8 x 44.8 cm

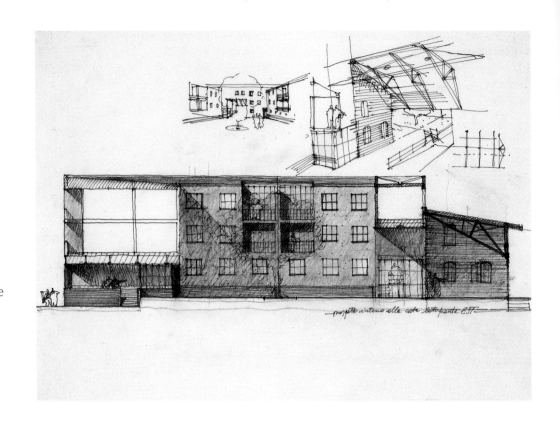

119
Sketches
Spatial representation: perspectives,
elevations, top view
India ink on transparent paper
33 x 45 cm

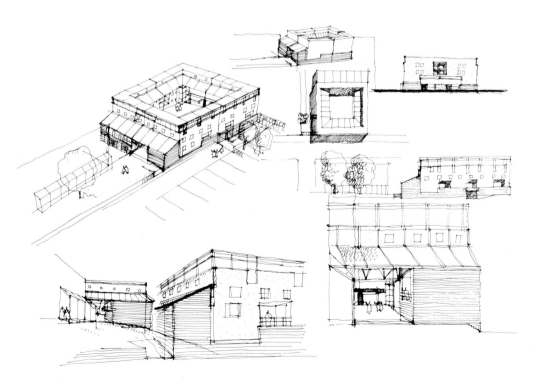

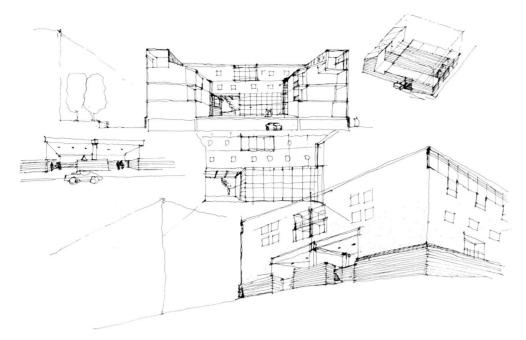

120
Sketches, perspectives
India ink on transparent paper
33.1 x 45 cm

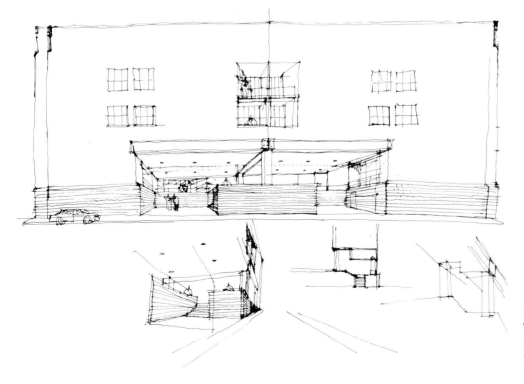

121
Sketches
Top view of Lützowstrasse, detail sketches
India ink on transparent paper
33 x 45 cm

**Restricted International Competition
Lützowstrasse, 1981**

**Third Prize
Office for Metropolitan Architecture,
OMA, London
Rem Koolhaas, Elia Zenghelis and
Ron Steiner**

with Omri Eytan, Batsheva Rouen and
Norman Chang, Katarina Galani, Andreas
Kourkoulas, Ricardo Simonini, Alex Wall

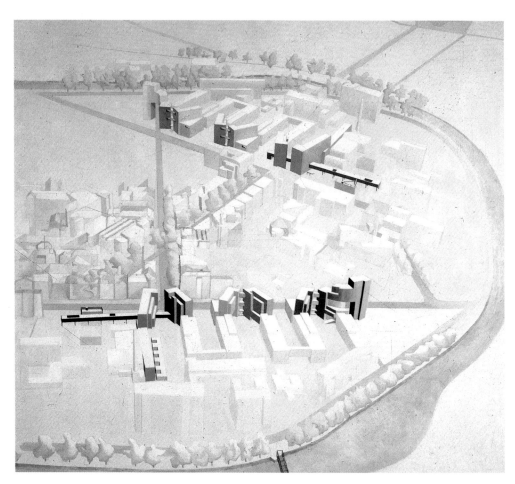

122
Axonometric overall view of proposed
development with Landwehr Canal.
Exaggerated representation showing the
smooth transition of the elevation from the
south (top) to the elevation from the north
(bottom)

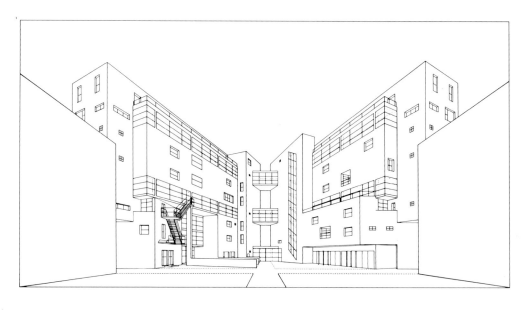

123
Courtyard perspective
(detail)

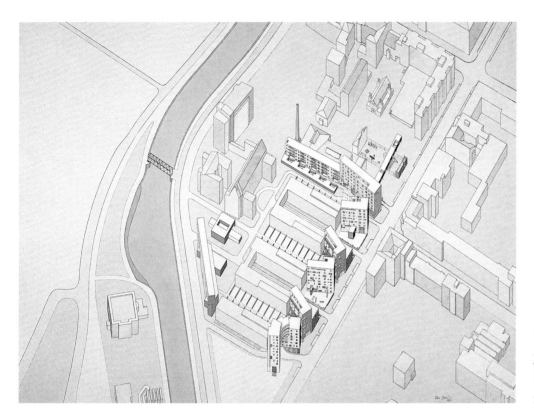

124
Axonometric drawing, scale 1 : 500
Tempera on cardboard, photocopy
74.4 x 99 cm
Signed: sign. Elia Zenghelis, 1981

125
Fringe development Lützowstrasse
East perspective
India ink on transparent paper
75 x 75 cm

**Restricted International Competition
Lützowstrasse, 1981**

Alison and Peter Smithson, London

126
Ground floor plan and west elevation
Blueprint, coloured
59.3 x 84.1 cm

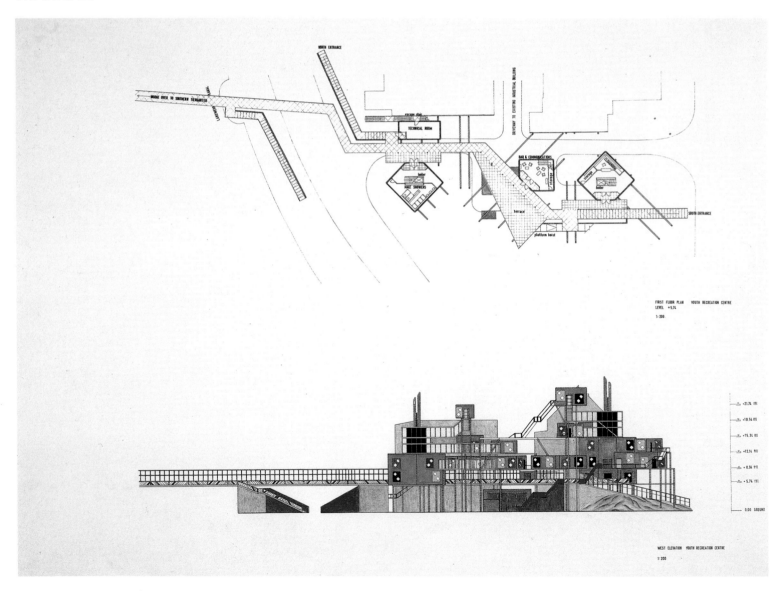

**Survey for Youth Recreation Centre
and Cultural Facilities
Conversion of Old Pumping Station VII
Lützowstrasse 1983**

**Coop Himmelblau
Wolf D. Prix
Helmut Swiczinsky, Vienna**

with Joe Kolleger, Frank Stepper

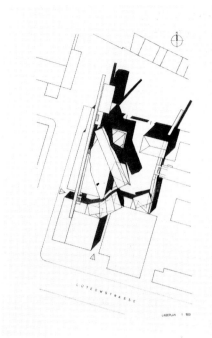

128
Sketch *Open Building Berlin*
Youth centre
Pencil on paper
42 x 30 cm
Signed: Berlin Coop Himmelblau 83

127
Site plan, scale 1 : 500
Copy on transparent paper
70.4 x 64.5 cm

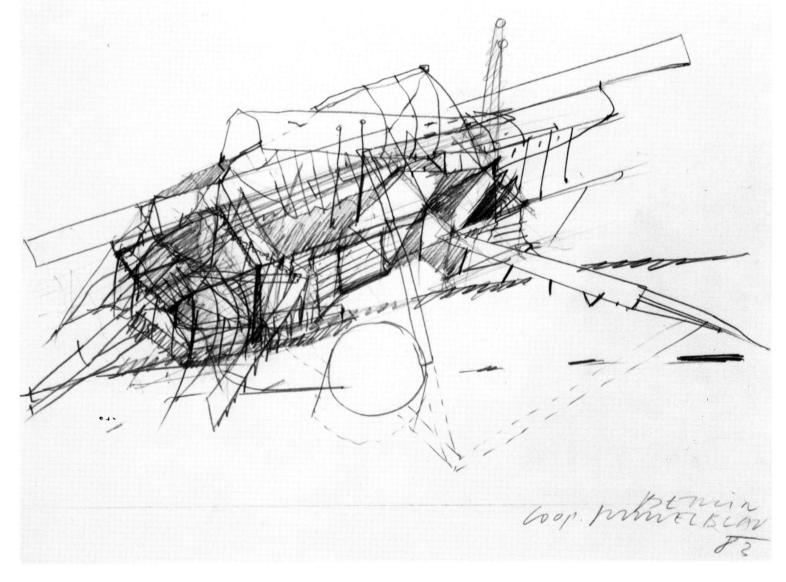

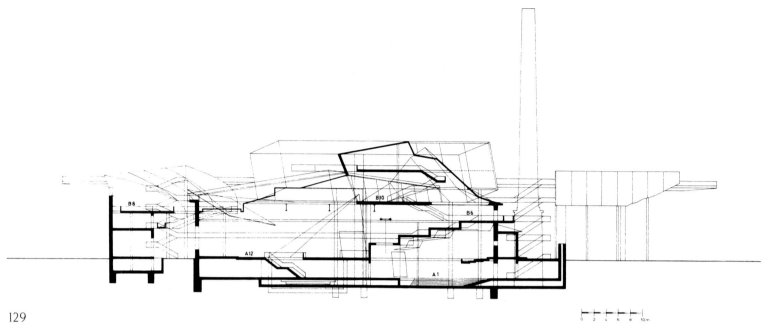

129
Section A-A, scale 1:200
Transparent copy
48.4 x 72.8 cm

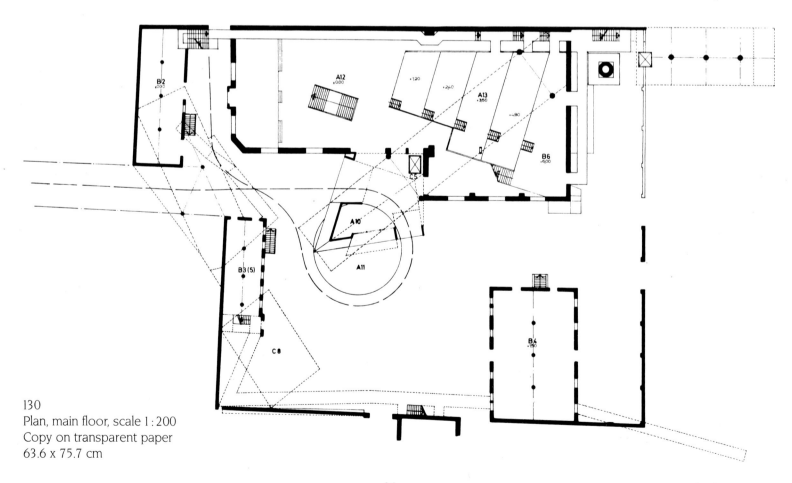

130
Plan, main floor, scale 1:200
Copy on transparent paper
63.6 x 75.7 cm

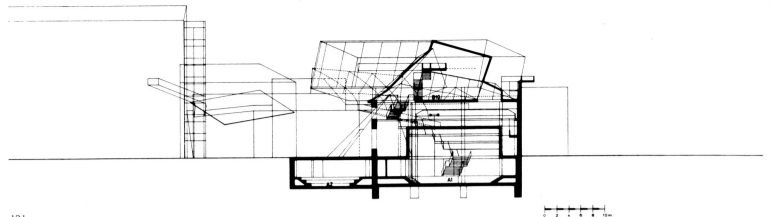

131
Section B-B, scale 1 : 200
Copy on transparent paper
51.2 x 76.6 cm

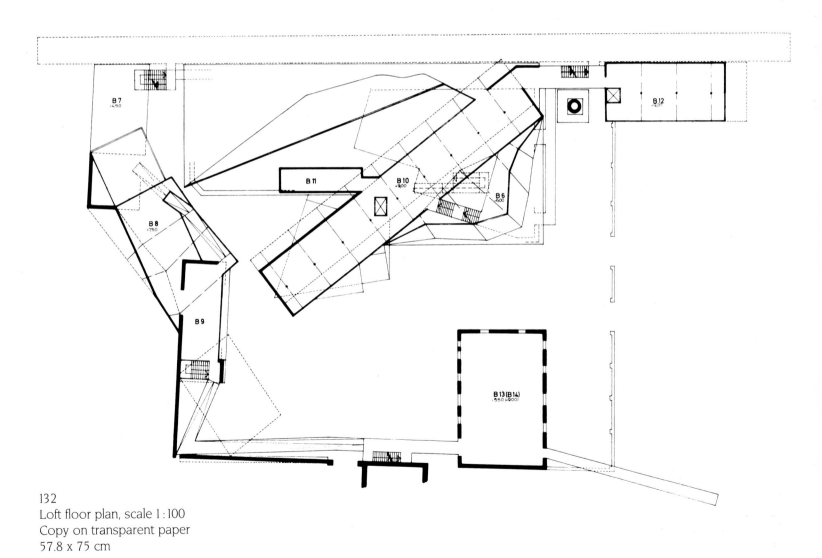

132
Loft floor plan, scale 1 : 100
Copy on transparent paper
57.8 x 75 cm

**Kindergarten Lützowstrasse
Planning 1983/84**

**Jasper Halfmann
Klaus Zillich, Berlin**

with Konrad Möckel, Holger Siegel,
Robert Witzgall

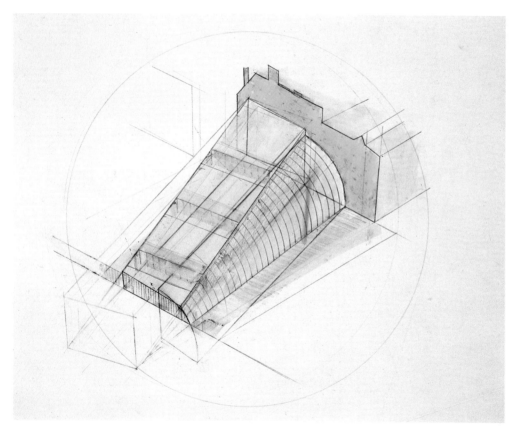

133a
Detail of 133
Axonometric study, scale 1:200

133
General representation of the project
in elevations, sectionals, plan, roof view,
scale 1:100, and axonometric study
India ink, pencil, crayon, chalk and felt
pen on transparent paper, mounted on
paperboard
190 x 79.7 cm

Kindergarten Lützowstrasse, 1983

Aldo van Eyck, Amsterdam

134
Site plan sketch with text 3 A
Felt pen on transparent paper
57.5 x 59.7 cm
Signed: 3 A, sign. "Aldo"

falls " Einklemmen" auch für Kinder erwünscht ist, so ist... the "other" Aldo the man you're looking for.! If you want something "good". However, which means something "reasonable & nothing else", then I'll take the Job. Signed: "Aldo"

Kopf B als dominant zurück liegend und

aberts orientiert.

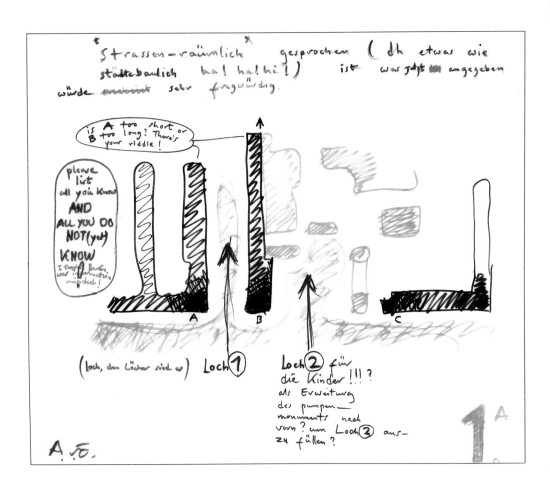

135
Site plan sketch with text 1 A
Felt pen on transparent paper
52.3 x 59.8 cm
Signed: 1 A, sign. A.f.E.

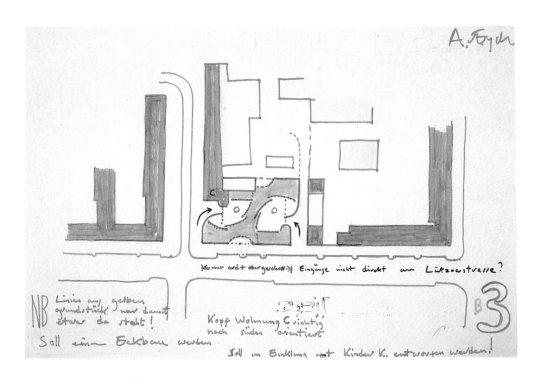

136
Site plan sketch, scale 1:500
Felt pen on transparent paper
39.5 x 59.6 cm
Signed: 3 B gez. A. v. Eyck

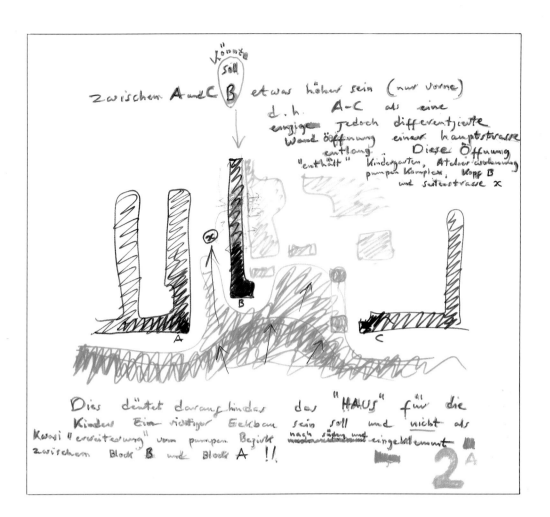

137
Site plan sketch with text 2 A
Felt pen on transparent paper
55 x 59.8 cm
Signed: 2 A

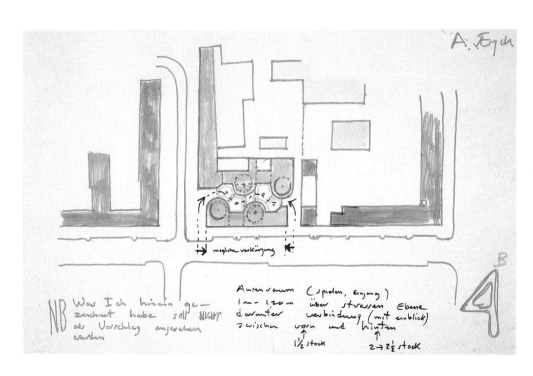

138
Site plan sketch, scale 1 : 500
Felt pen on transparent paper
38.2 x 59.7 cm
Signed: 4 B, gez. A. v. Eyck

Footbridge over Landwehr Canal in place of former "Graf Spee Bridge"
Planning 1985/86

Klaus Theo Brenner
Benedict Tonon, Berlin

with Matthias Essig, Charly Pauli

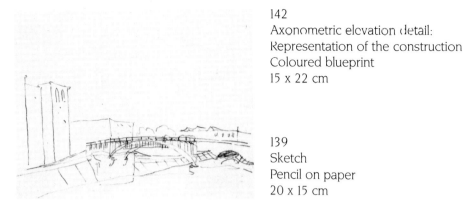

142
Axonometric elevation detail:
Representation of the construction
Coloured blueprint
15 x 22 cm

139
Sketch
Pencil on paper
20 x 15 cm

140
Sketch
Pencil on paper
20 x 15 cm

141
Perspective of the bridge, scale 1:50
Ink on transparent paper
60 x 135 cm

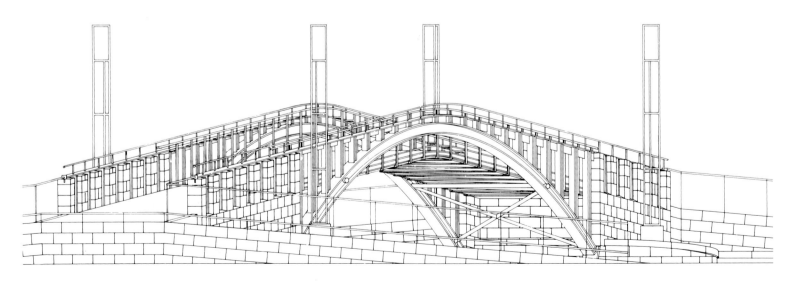

93

Survey "Am Karlsbad", 1982

Richard Meier & Partners
Richard Meier
Gunter Standke, New York

with Stanley Allen, Andrew Buchsbaum,
Bernd Echtermeyer, Hans Christoph
Goedeking, Marc Hacker, Hans Li, Jim Tice

143
Axonometric representation of
the development proposal
The Landwehr Canal in the foreground
(eastern section), scale 1:200
India ink on PE foil
105.1 x 105.1 cm

144
Axonometric representation of
the development proposal
(western section), scale 1 : 200
India ink on PE foil
104.9 x 105 cm

**Residential Project "Am Karlsbad",
Corner of Potsdamer Strasse and
Am Karlsbad (Houses 3–6)
Planning 1983/84
Completed 1985**

Jürgen Sawade, Berlin

with Axel Schulz, Knut Niederstadt,
Berndt Zachariae

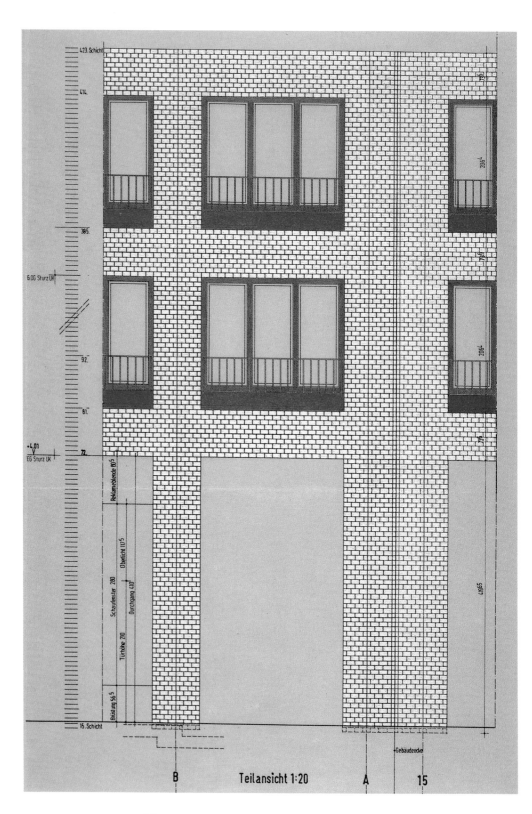

145
House No. 5, partial front elevation
Construction plan, scale 1 : 20
Crayon on transparent copy
68.5 x 61.5 cm

**Residential Project "Am Karlsbad",
Corner of Potsdamer Strasse and
Bissingzeile (Houses 7–9)
Planning 1983/84
Completed 1985**

**Georg Heinrichs and Partners, Berlin
Georg Heinrichs
Lutz Linneweber**

with Hans-Jürgen Grosse

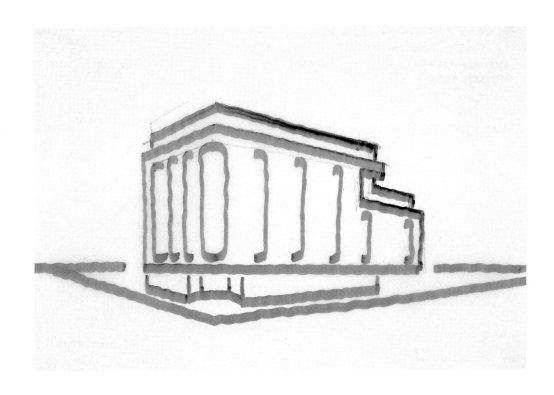

146
Sketch of structure C
Felt pen on transparent paper
21 x 29.7 cm

147
Houses Nos. 8–9, elevation from the
Bissingzeile, construction plan, scale 1 : 50
India ink and foil on transparent blueprint
61.7 x 151.6 cm
Dated: 6.12.83

**Residential Project "Am Karlsbad",
Am Karlsbad 2 (Houses 1 and 2)
Planning 1983/84
Completed 1985**

**Heinz Hilmer
Christoph Sattler, Munich**

with Dieter Pichler

148
Houses Nos. 1 and 2, elevation from
Am Karlsbad, construction plan, scale 1 : 50
India ink and foil on transparent paper
64.6 x 123.1 cm
Dated: 16. 8. 1984

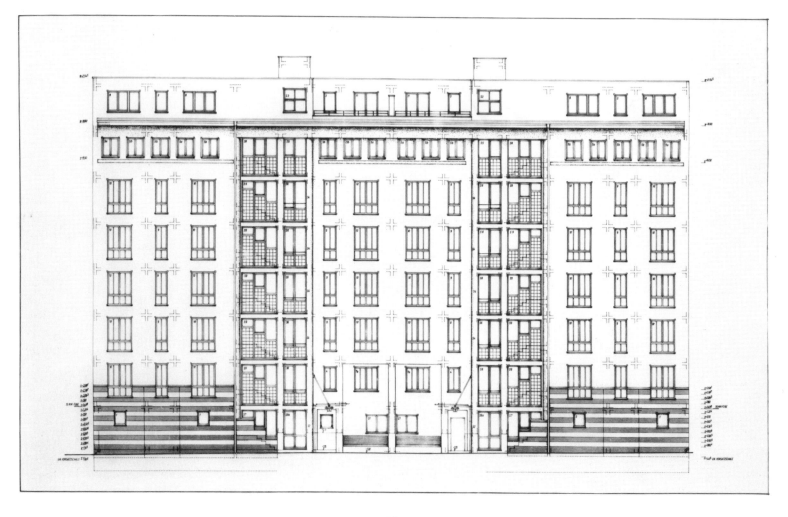

**Planning survey for Science Centre
Berlin 1979/80**

Mario Botta, Lugano

with Martin Boesch

149
Perspective from southeast,
Reichspietschufer
India ink on transparent paper
48.3 x 86 cm

150
General view with Tiergarten
India ink on transparent paper/original
lost, reduction on photocopy

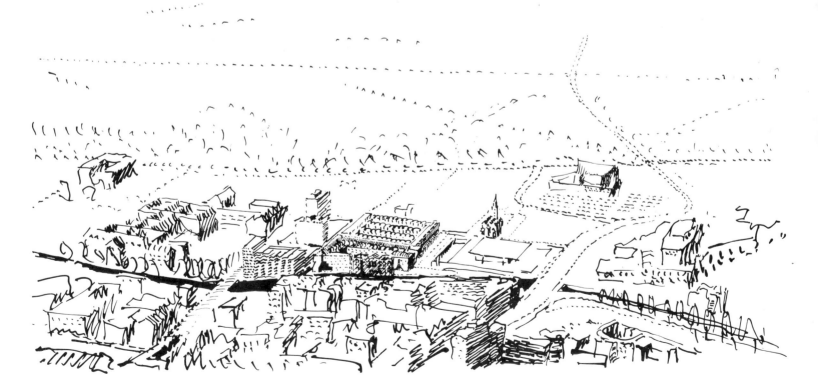

**Planning Survey for Science Centre
Berlin 1979/80**

**First Prize
James Stirling
Michael Wilford and Associates,
London**

with Walter Nägeli, Peter Schaad,
John Tuomey

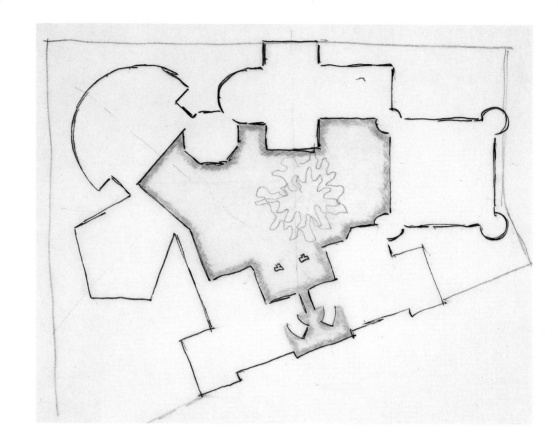

151
Sketch 1 of shapes and position
of structures
India ink, crayon and felt pen
on transparent paper
18.2 x 23.3 cm
(Passepartout detail)

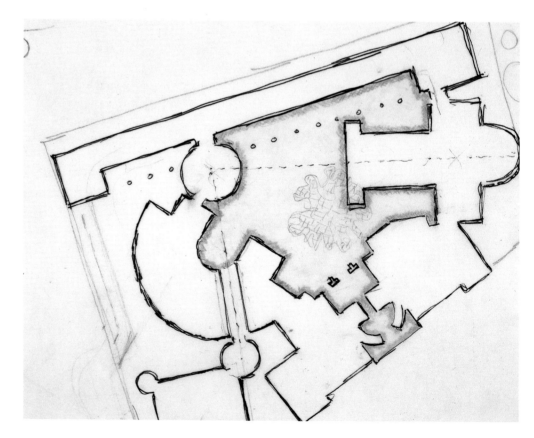

152
Sketch 2 of shapes and position
of structures
Pencil, felt pen and crayon
on transparent paper
18.2 x 23.3 cm
(Passepartout detail)

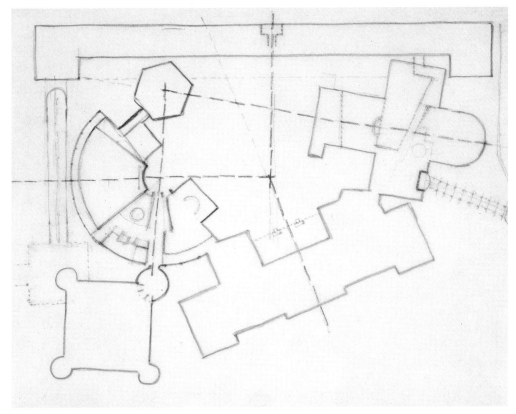

155
Sketch
Elevation and sectional detail
Ballpoint pen and crayon on paper
14.7 x 10.5 cm

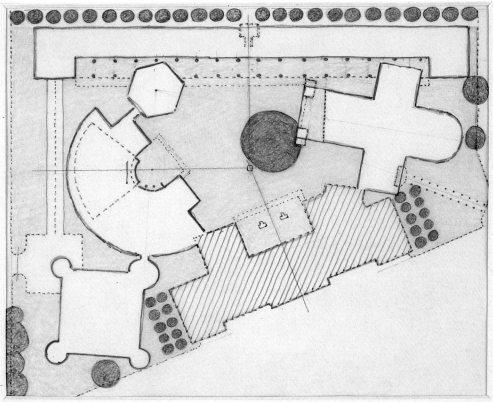

153
Sketch 3 with related axes
Pencil and felt pen on transparent paper
18.3 x 23.3 cm
(Passepartout detail)

154
Sketch 4 of site
Felt pen and crayon on transparent paper
18.2 x 23.2 cm
(Passepartout detail)

156
Sketch
Elevation and sectional detail
Ballpoint pen and crayon on paper
14.5 x 10.5 cm

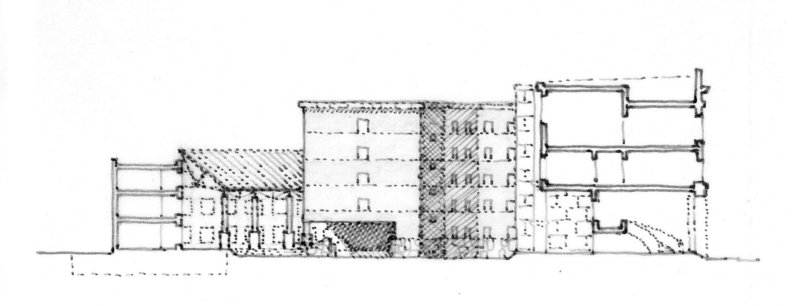

157
Sketch
West elevation
Felt pen and crayon on transparent paper
9.8 x 18.4 cm
(Passepartout detail)

158
Sketch
Courtyard elevation, section through old
building and structure E
Felt pen and crayon on transparent paper
9.8 x 18.3 cm
(Passepartout detail)

Science Centre Berlin,
Reichspietschufer 48–58
Plans and working drawings 1980–87
Under construction since 1984

James Stirling
Michael Wilford and Associates,
London/Berlin

with Walter Nägeli, Siegfried Wernik
(Peter Ray 1980)
and Alois Albert, Hannelore Deubzer,
Volker Eich, Alexander Kolbe, Hanne
Lutterbach, Robert Niess, Heike Nordmann

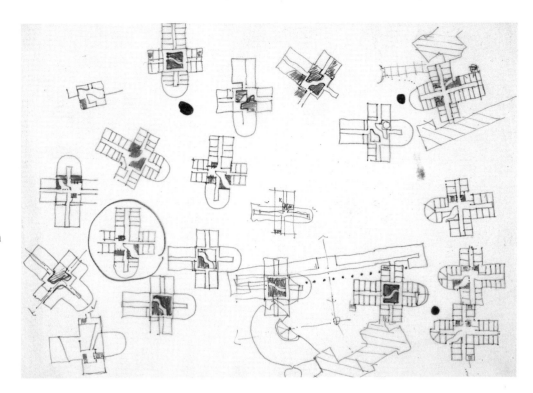

159
Sketches of plan of structure C
Felt pen on transparent paper
20.9 x 29.9 cm

160
Sketches of plan of structure D
Felt pen on transparent paper
20.9 x 29.7 cm

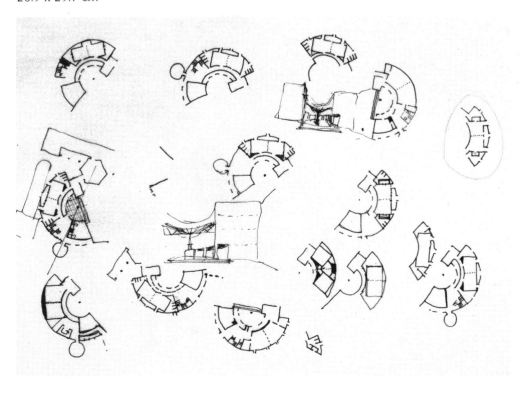

161
Office study
Pencil and crayon on transparent paper
11.6 x 7 cm

162
Office study
Pencil and crayon on transparent paper
12.5 x 8 cm

164
Axonometric study of the front of the
arcade in structure E with detail sketches
Pencil, crayon and felt pen on blueprint
59.6 x 51.7 cm

163
Office studies
Ballpoint pen and crayon on paper
20.9 x 29.7 cm

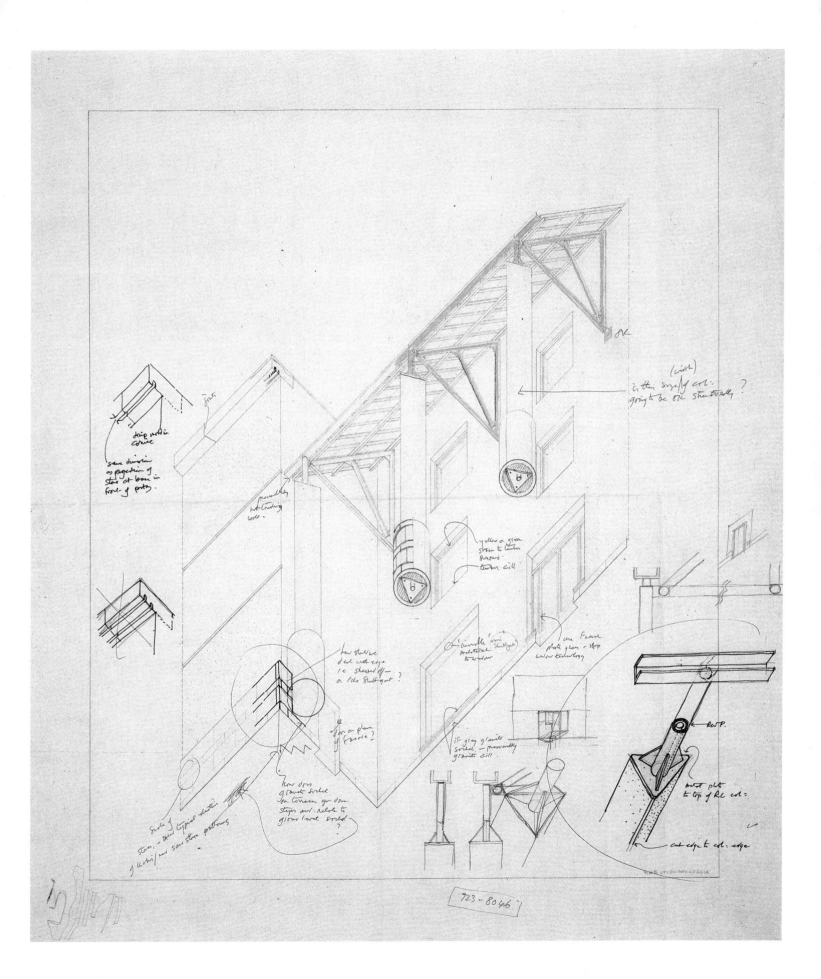

**Restricted International Competition
"Extension to National Gallery and
Residential Project in Cultural Forum",
1981**

Peter C. von Siedlein, Munich

with Horst Fischer, Egon Konrad, Hansjörg
Schrade, Peter Seeger, Albert Stoll, Ursula
Zoll

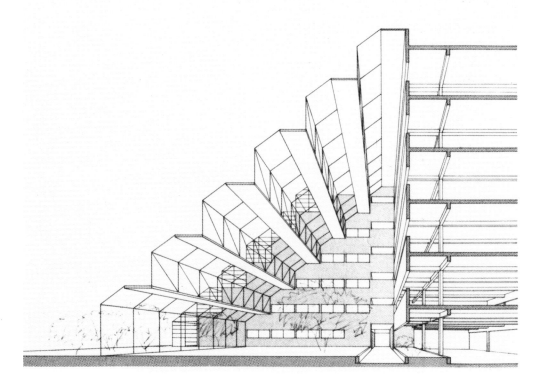

165
Sectional perspective of the Wintergarten
India ink, pencil and foil on transparent
paper (blueprint)
21.6 x 41.7 cm

166
East-west section
Scale 1 : 200
Ink on transparent paper
60.5 x 192.2 cm

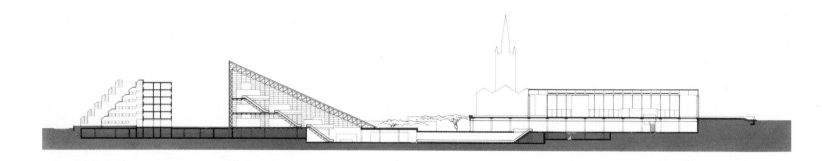

**Residential Project in Cultural Forum
Hitzigallee 17–21, Sigismundstrasse
5–9
Planning 1982–84
Completed 1985**

**Kurt Ackermann
Peter Jaeger, Munich**

with Richard Fischer, Harry Schöpke

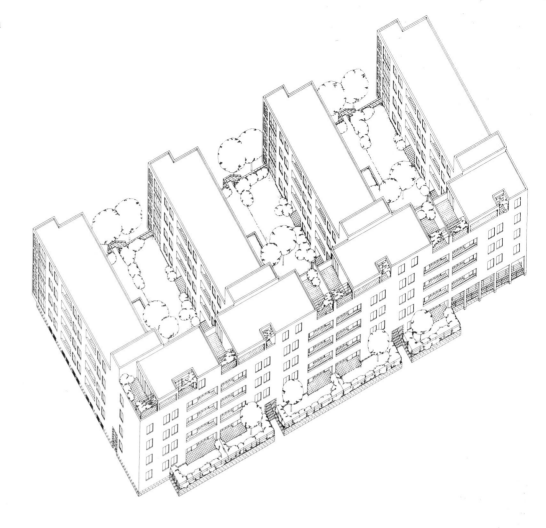

167
Axonometric
Scale reduced from 1 : 100
Photocopy on transparent paper
30 x 65 cm

168
West façade
Scale reduced from 1 : 100
Part of larger scheme
Photocopy on transparent paper
30 x 65 cm

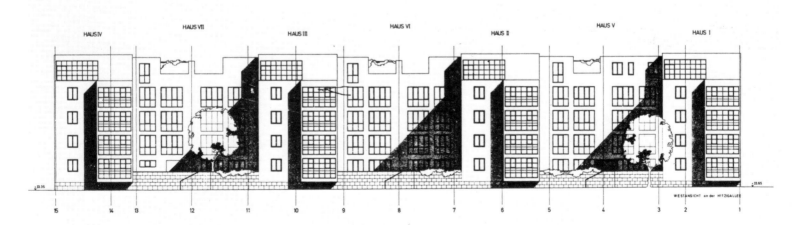

**German-Japanese Centre Berlin
in former Japanese Embassy
Tiergartenstrasse 24–27, Graf-Spee-
Strasse 2–4
Planning since 1983
Demolition and reconstruction since
1986**

**Kisho Kurokawa
Architect & Associates, Tokyo**

with Taiji Yamaguchi

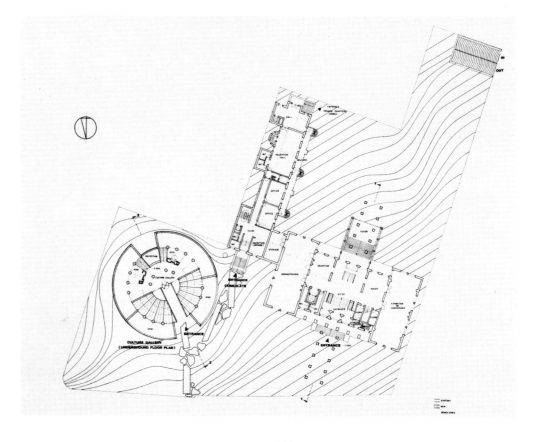

169
Ground floor plan A, scale 1 : 200
Blueprint on Capa board
73 x 83.9 cm
Dated: April 1984

170
Section 1.1 A, scale 1 : 200
Coloured blueprint on Capa board
73 x 83.9 cm

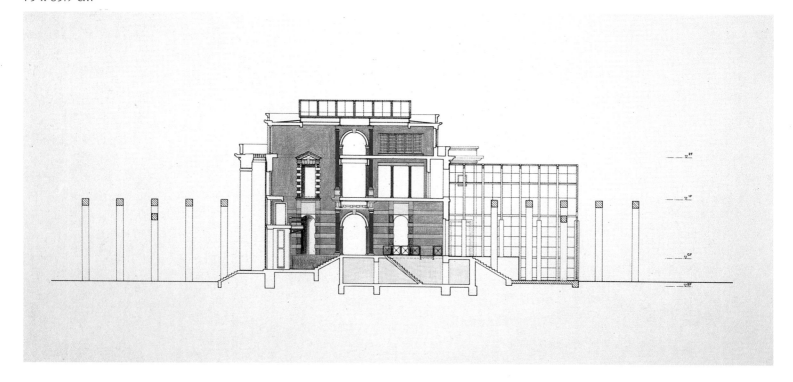

**Reconfiguration of Greek Embassy,
Apartment House Graf-Spee-Strasse 17
Planning 1983**

Stephan Braunfels, Munich

171
Corner perspective
India ink on transparent paper
62.4 x 88 cm
Signed: Sign. Stephan Braunfels 1984

Project for Restoration and Conversion of former Italian Embassy Berlin, 1982

Paolo Portoghesi, Rome

with H. Banks, M. Checchi, G. Cundari,
L. Garibaldi, E. Montrone, E. N. Schulz

172
South elevation
Coloured photo
16.5 x 18 cm

173
Façade sketches
Ink on paper
23.5 x 16.5 cm

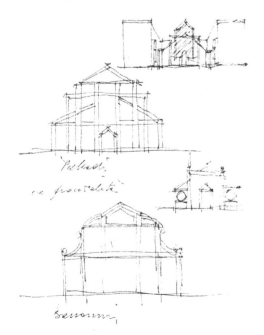

174
Preliminary façade
Sketches
Ink on paper
23.5 x 16.5 cm

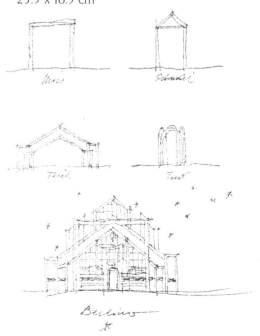

International Survey Cultural Forum Berlin, 1983

Hans Hollein, Vienna

with August Sarnitz, Othmar Hasler, Franz Madl, Klaus Matauschek, Hans Streitner, Ulrike Liebl, Erich Pedevilla, Hsia-Wei Wang, Josef Braid, Dieter Nehring, Rainer Pirker, Betty Thürlimann, Holger Nettbaum

175
Site plan, scale 1 : 1000
Coloured blueprint
123 x 121 cm

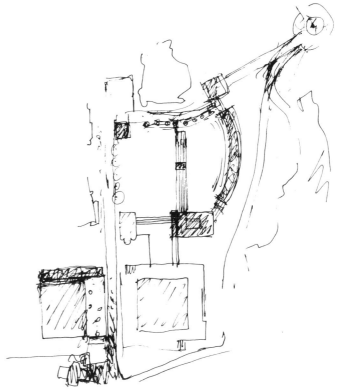

176
Sketch
Felt pen on paper
20.9 x 29.6 cm

111

**International Survey Cultural Forum
Berlin
Revision of Competition Project, 1984**

Hans Hollein, Vienna

with August Sarnitz, Josef Braid, Dieter
Nehring, Rainer Pirker, Erich Pedevilla,
Betty Thürlimann, Hsia-Wei Wang, Holger
Nettbaum

177
Aerial view
Pencil on paper
29.7 x 42 cm

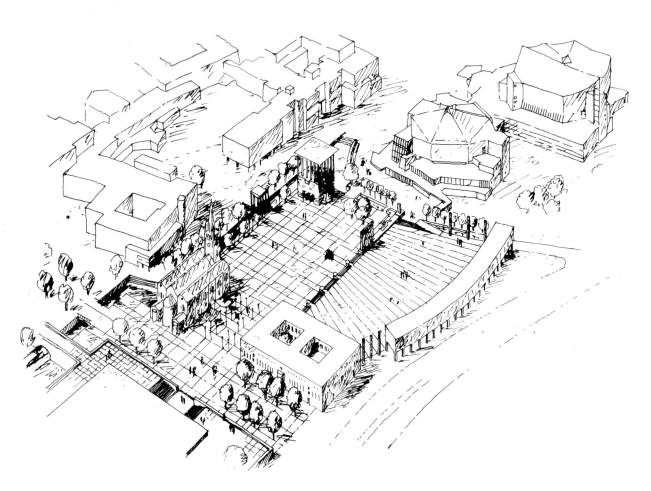

178
Sketch Bible Museum
Felt pen on white paper
19.1 x 15.5 cm

International Survey Cultural Forum
Berlin, 1983

Oswald Mathias Ungers
Max Dudler, Cologne

with Jo Franzke, Alfram von Hoessle,
Horst Jentschura, Thomas Kubisch,
Hinrich Reyelts, Holger Rübsamen, Renzo
Vallebuona, Karlheinz Wieland

179
Axonometric drawing (west, partial
section), scale 1:1000
India ink on transparent paper
124 x 62 cm

180–183
Perspectives
180 Matthäi Churchyard
181 Apartment houses, Potsdamer Station
182 Corner houses, Potsdamer Strasse
183 Extension, National Gallery

India ink on transparent paper
Shadows masked by foil
62 x 62 cm

180

182

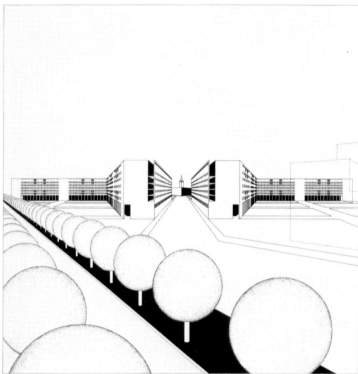

181

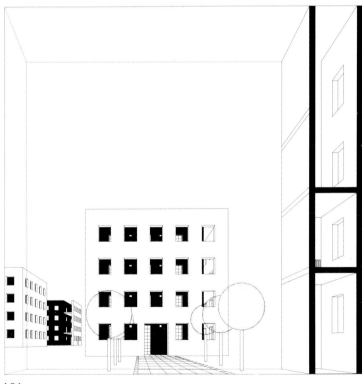

183

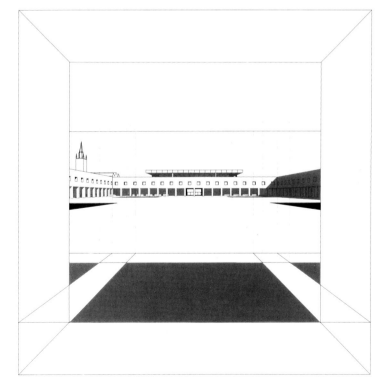

International Competition
Rauchstrasse, 1980

First Prize
Rob Krier, Echternach/Luxemburg

184
Site plan, scale 1 : 500
India ink on transparent paper
47.5 x 63.7 cm
Signed: Stadthäuser am Tiergarten in
Berlin, August 80, sign. Krier

185
Perspective of garden court, west view
India ink on transparent paper
45.5 x 47.5 cm
Signed: Rauchstr. Berlin 29. 8. 80, sign. Krier

**International Competition
Rauchstrasse, 1980**

**Highly Commended
Klaus Theo Brenner
Benedict Tonon, Berlin**

186
Site plan, scale 1:1000 (detail)
Crayon on blueprint
59.9 x 59.9 cm

187
Axonometric drawing, scale 1:500
Spray technique, collage
57.8 x 59.8 cm

Urban Villa on Rauchstrasse,
Houses 5/6
Planning 1982–84
Completed 1984

Rob Krier, Luxemburg/Vienna

188
Façade drawing with Italian and German
towers and sketch of ground plan
Colour crayon on transparent paper
15 x 15 cm

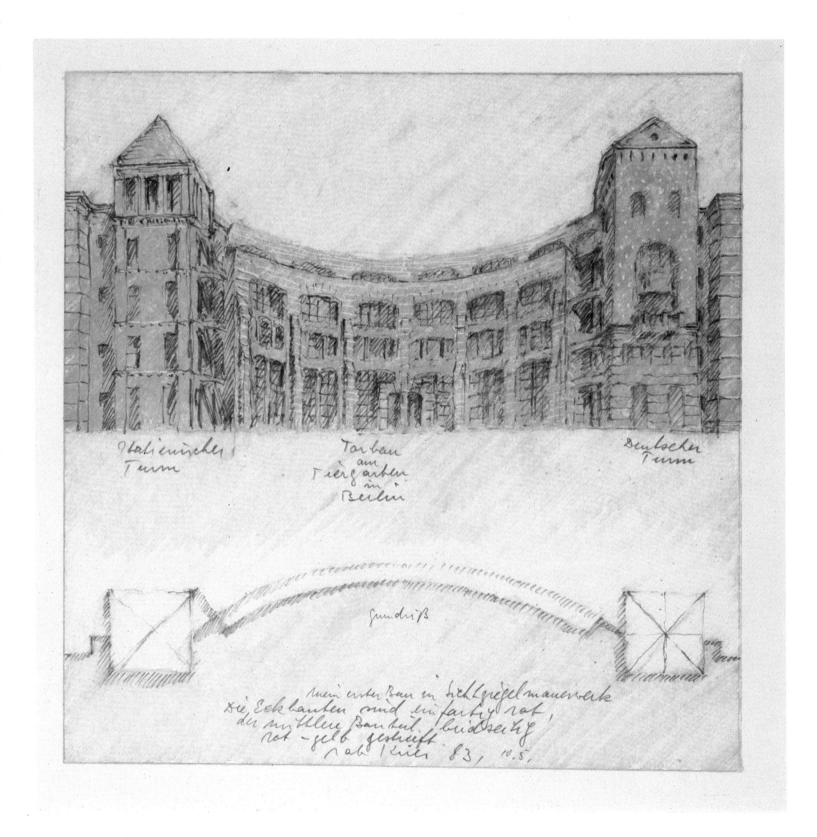

Urban Villas on Rauchstrasse, House 4
Planning 1982–84
Completed 1985

Klaus Theo Brenner
Benedict Tonon, Berlin

with Joshimi Yamaguchi-Essig, Christian
Behrla

189
Preliminary sketch
Volume and façade study, scale 1 : 500
Pencil and crayon on yellow tracing paper
30.4 x 56.6 cm

190
Four axonometric drawings, scale 1 : 500
Pencil and crayon on yellow tracing paper
30.7 x 57.7 cm

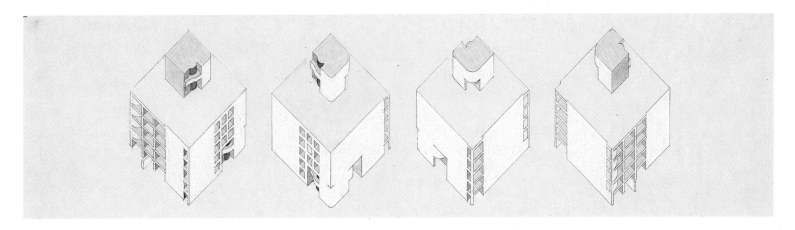

Urban Villas on Rauchstrasse, House 8
Planning 1983/84
Completed 1985

Hans Hollein, Vienna

with Hans Streitner, Willi Fritsch, Ulrike
Liebl, Klaus Matauschek, Franz Madl, Dieter
Nehring, Erich Pedevilla, Hsia-Wei Wang,
Betty Thürlimann

191
Axonometric drawing of
the southeast corner
Coloured blueprint

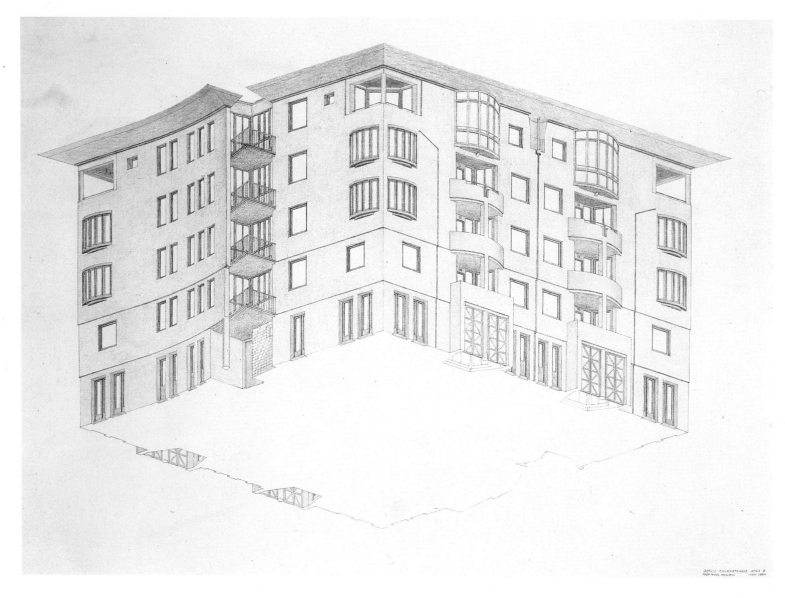

192
Axonometric drawing of
the northwest corner
Coloured blueprint

Urban Villas on Rauchstrasse, House 1
Planning 1982–84
Completed 1984

Aldo Rossi
Gianni Braghieri, Milan

with Christopher Stead, Gabriele Geronzi

193
Ground plan, elevation and perspective
(sketch)
Felt pen on paper, coloured in

194
Sketch: plan, elevations, axonometric
drawing, scale 1 : 200
Pencil on brown transparent paper
74.7 x 50 cm

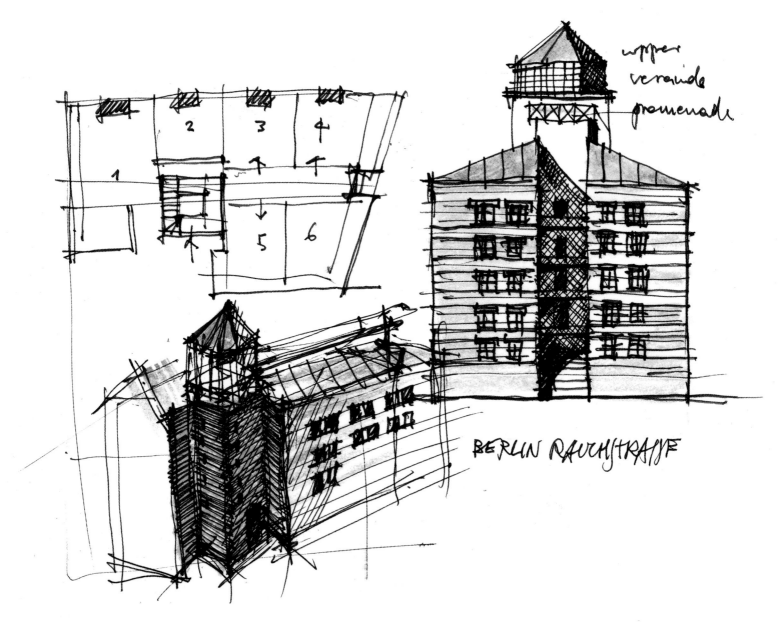

upper
verande
promenade

BERLIN RAUCHSTRASSE

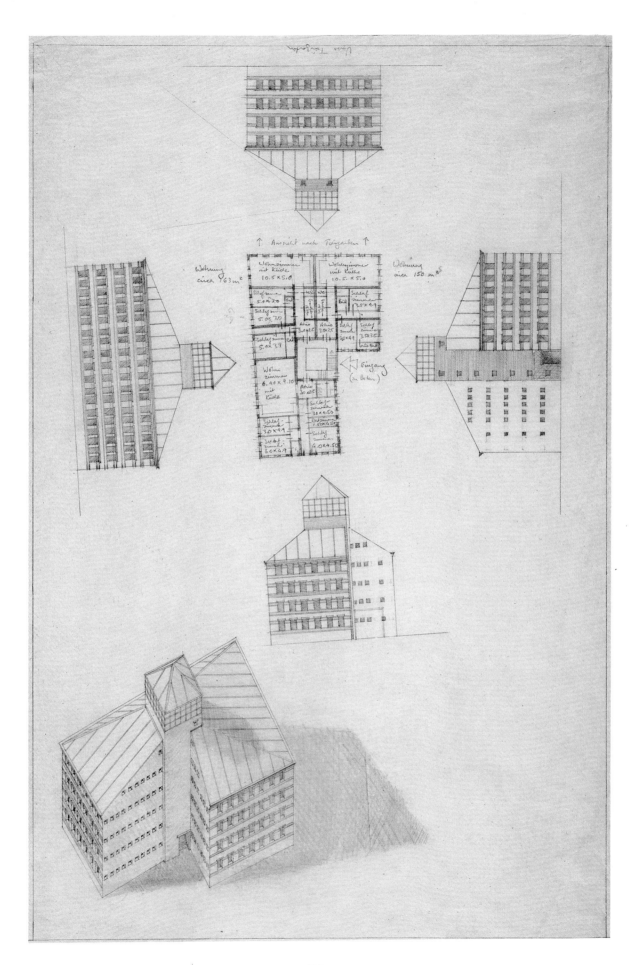

Urban Villas on Rauchstrasse, House 3
Planning 1982–84
Completed 1984

Giorgio Grassi
Edoardo Guazzoni, Milan

with Guido Zanella, Nicola Di Battista

195
Preliminary study
Elevations, sections, top views, scale 1:200
Pencil and felt pen on reverse side of
a blueprint
43.5 x 53.2 cm
Signed: G. Grassi '83

196
Façade studies, scale 1:100
Pencil and felt pen on reverse side of
a blueprint
81.6 x 67 cm
Signed: per Josef Kleihues con amicizia
1983. Berlino-casa Rauch-/Dehlerstr.
sign. Giorgio Grassi
Date stamp

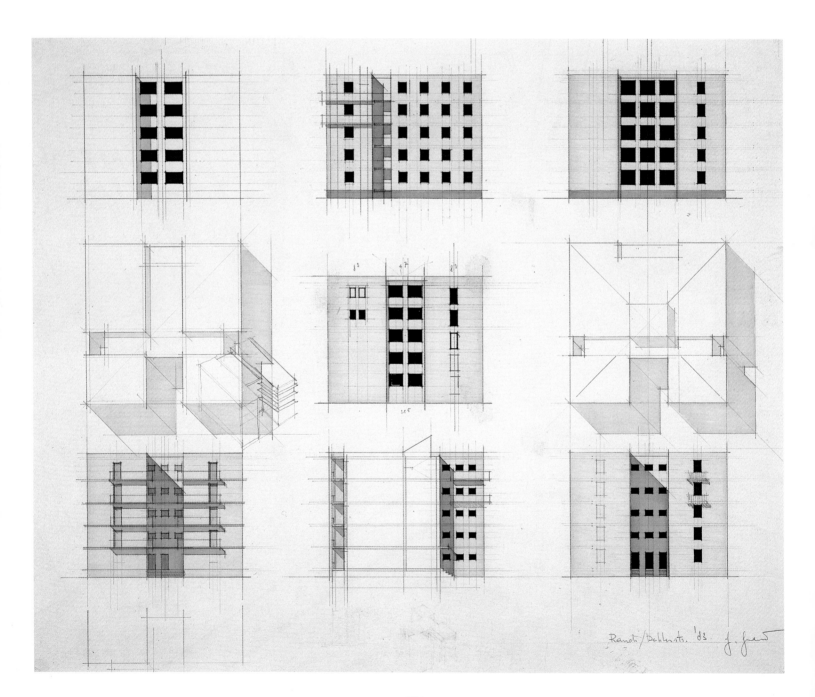

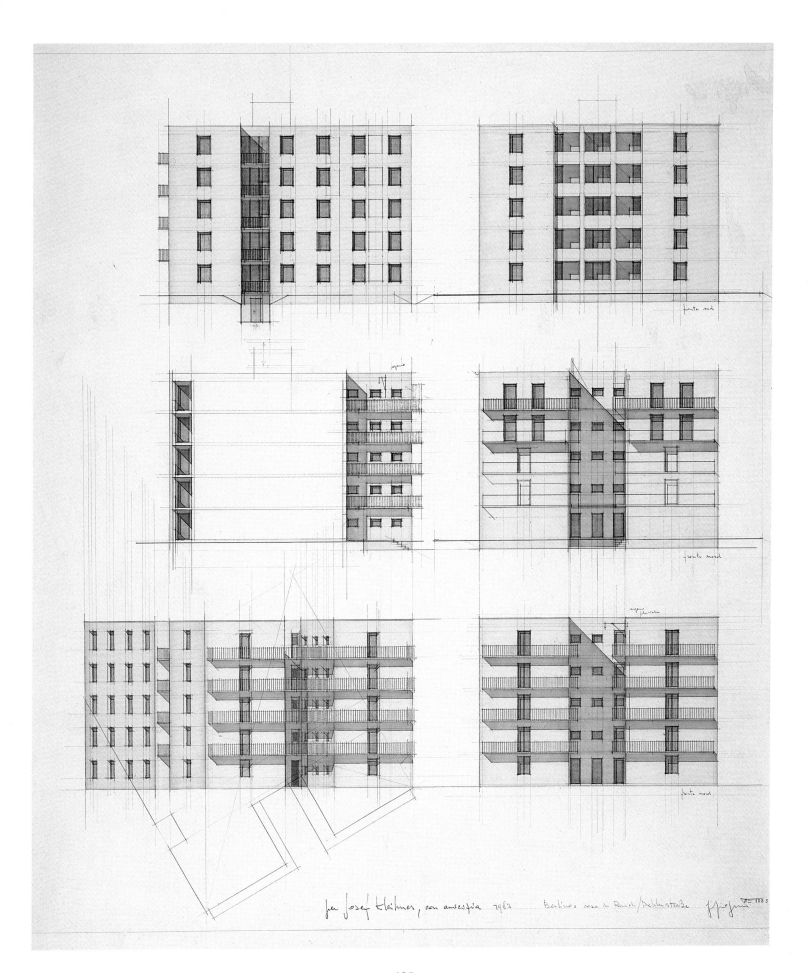

**Preliminary Design for Rauchstrasse,
House 9
Planning 1982/83**

Mario Botta, Lugano

with Urs Külling

Hans Hollein later took over the planning.

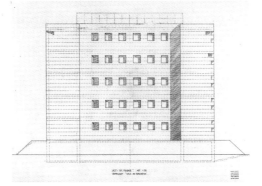

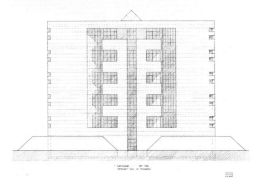

197
West and east façades, scale 1 : 50
Pencil on PE foil
55.5 x 64.6 cm

198
Elevation Rauchstrasse (southern façade),
scale 1 : 50
Pencil on PE foil
55 x 64.5 cm

199
Sketches
Plan, scale 1 : 100, perspective
Pencil on transparent paper
29.8 x 48.2 cm

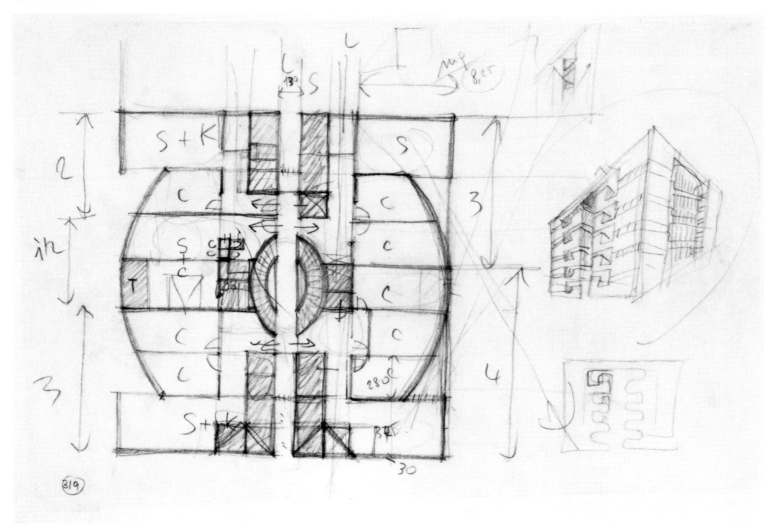

New Urban Building

Demonstration Area
Southern Friedrichstadt

Southern Friedrichstadt

**Rudiments of history
Place of contradictions
Critical reconstruction**

"In Maurilia the traveller is invited to inspect the town and also to look at certain picture post-cards which show what it used to be like: the very same square with a chicken in place of the bus station, the music pavilion instead of the flyover, two young ladies with white parasols instead of the ammunition plant. To avoid dis-appointing the locals, the traveller must praise the town on the postcard and say how he prefers it to the present-day town, being careful though to keep his expressions of regret within the well-defined limits laid down by convention."

Italo Calvino

"Indeed, if we are prepared to accept that the methods of science and of bricolage are approaches that exist side-by-side simultaneously, if we are willing to grant that both are ways of tackling problems, ... it might even be possible to suppose that the way could be paved for a really practical future dialectic."

Colin Rowe

Southern Friedrichstadt came practically undamaged through the Second World War until shortly before its end. It was only the air-raids of February 1945 and the final battle for the erstwhile capital of the Reich that raged soon afterward that spelt total destruction for this centrally situated Kreuzberg district. In the first two postwar decades, the little that remained fell victim to a mania of destruction that is absolutely incomprehensible to us today. Absurd motorway projects, widening and rerouting of streets, and new edifices springing up like mushrooms devastated this urban area so that one would hardly recognize it. Cleared sites and stark fireproof walls, relics of the architecture of two centuries and isolated new buildings, Angel of Peace and Checkpoint Charlie: a bizarre "collage d'histoire".

Despite brutal acts of destruction it is the urban ground-plan that offers the most clues to its baroque origins, if we look closely. The topographic layout of the his-torical city, however, no longer exists, the visual axes have lost their "points de vue". Only in the view from Markgrafenstrasse to the south does the present-day Berlin

Museum stand as evidence of the history of the eighteenth century. To the north, the wall stifles the town.

More than any other demonstration ground of the IBA, this area of contradic-tions presented a challenge for the experi-ment of a critical reconstruction.

When I speak of the rediscovery of the architecture and the critical reconstruction of the city, my premise is that conventions developed in the course of Europe's his-tory that helped to shape her architectural and urbanistic culture. This in no way con-tradicts the other statement, that each city possesses its own peculiar quality which results from its own history and, procee-ding therefrom, a specific way of relating to architecture and urbanism.

In his passionate utterances on the city, Italo Calvino once said that there was no point in trying to determine "whether Zenobia is to be numbered among the happy or the unhappy cities. The rational way is to allocate cities not to these two categories, but to two others: those which always give man's wishes a form, their form, though the years may pass and changes take place, and those where the wishes either are capable of blotting out the city or are blotted out by it".

Zenobia, though, is for each of us the city in which we live. It is the same everywhere and yet the unique city, when it is able to "give man's wishes a form", its form, "though the years may pass and changes take place". This by no means rules out caesuras and new directions – without which continuity would not be possible. But at various points in Berlin, and espe-cially in southern Friedrichstadt we have been obliged to watch town-planning pro-jects being pursued to that razor's edge point "where the wishes ... are capable of blotting out the city".

Over the centuries, conventions have evolved for architecture and urban deve-lopment: these conventions have universal character. Nevertheless, each city has its own particular character, its own history, and conventions of its own. Ignorance of this truth can only lead to the decay of urbanistic culture and of the city as a place to live in. Thanks to the modern industrial society, dizzy rates of growth and the devastations of war, many of these con-ventions have been set aside or simply for-gotten. This has led to great insecurity in

our relationship with nature, in planning our cities, and even in housing pro-grammes.

Thus it is obvious and inevitable that we had to rediscover the principles underlying the historical urban entity. The idea of reconstruction, though, is liable to dege-nerate rapidly into nostalgia. We must therefore strive to promulgate a new, broader understanding of reconstruction. That is why, lest misconceptions arise, I speak of a critical reconstruction of the city, which can only be achieved on the basis of a rational examination of the constituent elements of the city. Along with the *ground-plan*, the permanent "gene struc-ture" of the city, the other main elements are the *organization of buildings* and the *image* of the city. The word "city" implies these constituent parts as well as the whole.

It is the *ground-plan* in particular that testi-fies to the spiritual and cultural idea behind the founding of a city. The urban ground-plan presets the programme for the inter-play of factors governing the economy, social and intercourse traffic, and defines the fundamental character of the place for years to come. It is after all the founda-tions of a city that continue to provide, after it has passed away, reliable evidence of its one-time development.

But only the *organization of buildings* on the urban ground-plan defines the relationship of the corporeal to the spatial. The city is a *three-dimensional model*, and this conception is inescapably bound up with the ground-plan. And yet, however much the urban ground-plan predetermines the idea of the three-dimensional city, its role is a passive one in regard to the changing types and styles of buildings that are erected upon it. This we can observe in the long history of Rome, or in the dynamic evolution of Manhattan. And southern Friedrichstadt? We can only get an idea of eighteenth cen-tury architectural practices from old prints or, as a concrete example, the former Col-legium building, now the Berlin Museum. Whatever programme the ground-plan lays down, it will not take definite shape until a superstructure has been erected: streets, squares and parks, the grey, green or blue arteries provided or suggested to planners by the city's layout only come to life in conjunction with an urban building pro-gramme.

Kochstrasse, corner of Charlottenstrasse (Ullstein Publishers building), as it was in 1930.

Alte Jakobstrasse, headquarters of the German Metalworkers' Union. Built in 1929/1930 to plans by Erich Mendelsohn and Rudolf W. Reichel.

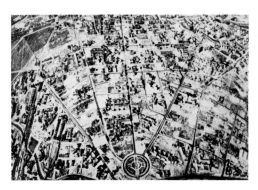

Southern Friedrichstadt, c. 1955, with Mehringplatz in foreground.

It is the *image* of a city especially, the physiognomy of its houses, that – transcending the geometry of the city – reveals the spiritual and cultural values of changing epochs.

Only by looking at the visible image of architecture can we appreciate its substance. In literature, the cheap romance competes with the quality novel; in music, the pop song competes with the symphony; similarly, architecture is a battleground between two poles. Architecture's equivalents to the cheap romance or the pop song, its sensationalist spectacles, are acclaimed by many. Truth, love, and aesthetic values, however, do not always triumph. This has been brought home to us in the debate on the "right" decision in terms of urban development and on the quality of architecture.

At the beginning of the IBA, in the year that marked the hundredth anniversary of the birth of Bruno Taut, I recalled in the preamble to the international competition Koch – Friedrichstrasse that he called for "clarity" in architecture. "To strive for clarity", Taut said, "means, in the field of housing: to simplify, to seek rational solutions to technical and design problems, to express the ground-plan in the architecture – in short, to exercise restraint."

Many projects will comply with this standard, but certainly not all. Then, again, there are other criteria which also claim moral and artistic legitimacy – criteria associated with terms like synthesis, communication, complexity, or historicality, attempts to adapt the classic idea of dialectic to the vocabulary and circumstances of modern times.

It remains to be seen whether the process by which the uncompromisingly reductive vocabulary of the "classical modern" school has given way to a multiplicity of new interpretations of the wishes expressed by architectural theory and aesthetics, whether this process can be called a new "dialectic", whether it will pass the practical test. The passage of time will separate the wheat from the chaff – this also applies to the projects of the International Building Exhibition.

Still, some of the architects and projects represented in the IBA, pointers in a new direction, and the experiment of the "critical reconstruction" of the city pave the way for a modern, dialectically organized grammar of architecture. We shall elaborate this theme in the documentation on Southern Friedrichstadt (Vol. III of the series "Documents and Projects, the New Building Areas of the IBA"). The architectural drawings presented in the exhibition in the German Museum of Architecture form a part of this series.

Josef Paul Kleihues

Survey for Block I, 1982

Oswald Mathias Ungers
Hans C. Müller
Bernd G. Faskel

with Uwe Becker

200
Ground floor plan, scale 1 : 500
Coloured blueprint
64 x 64.1 cm

201
General floor plan, scale 1 : 500
Coloured blueprint
64.1 x 63.9 cm

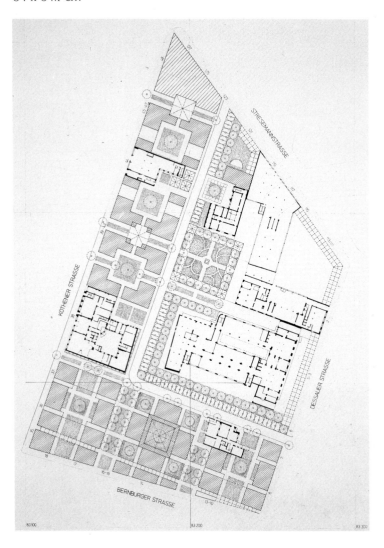

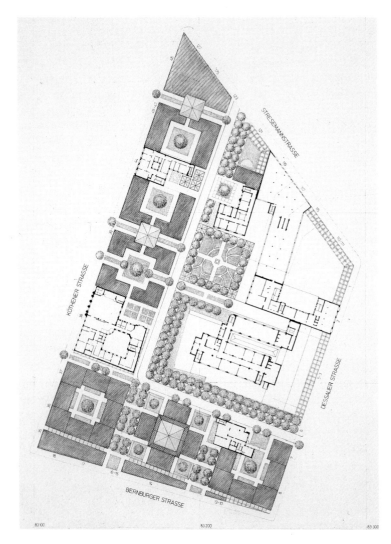

**Residential Development Köthener
Strasse 39–43, Block I
Planning 1984
Completed 1985**

Hans Christian Müller, Berlin

with Moritz Müller

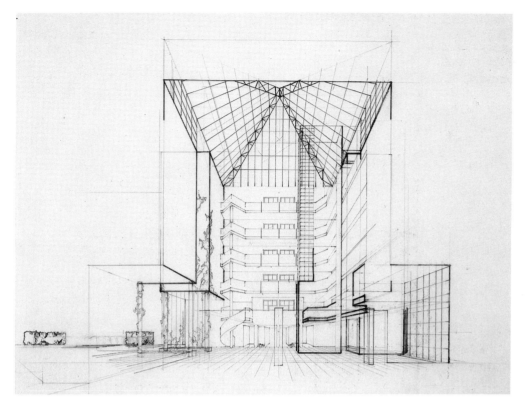

202
Interior perspective
Spatial study of the central stairwell
between the garden courts
Pencil and felt pen on transparent paper
41.8 x 78.4 cm

203
Municipal development
Ist perspective representation of a possible
square structure with glass hall
Felt pen on transparent paper
31.8 x 43.5 cm

**Residential Development Köthener
Strasse 35–37
Corner of Bernburger Strasse 16–18,
Block I
Planning 1984–86**

Oswald Mathias Ungers, Cologne

with Emanuela von Branca, Jürgen von
Brandt, Karl Lothar Dietzsch

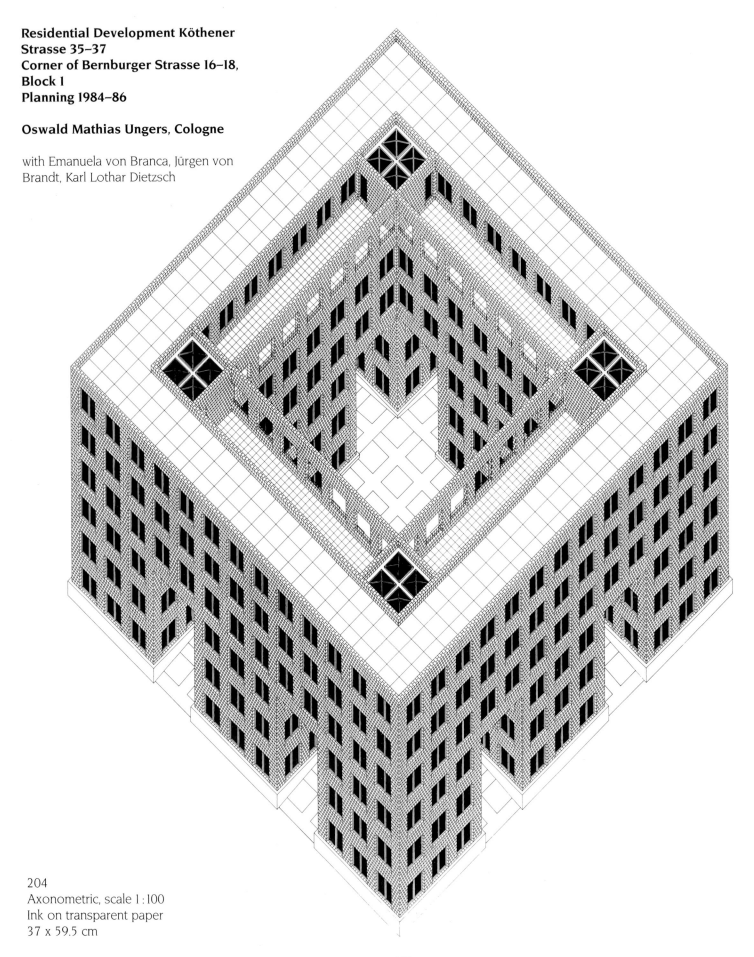

204
Axonometric, scale 1 : 100
Ink on transparent paper
37 x 59.5 cm

Extension to Federal Railway Administration Building on Halle Embankment, on top of an air-raid shelter, Block 14 Design study 1986

Christoph Mäckler, Frankfurt

with Regine Beckmann,
Thomas Baumgarten

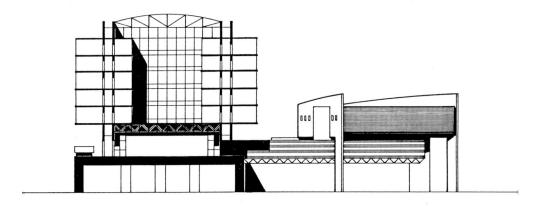

205
Section, scale 1:500
Ink on transparent paper
42 x 80 cm

206
Perspective
Ink on transparent paper
42 x 80 cm

Open Competition to articulate site of former Prince Albrecht Palace, 1984, Block 3

Highly Commended
Architektursalon Elvira
Elisabeth Lux
Martin Wiedemann, Berlin

207
Surface analysis of the shaped parts
Coloured foils on photocopy, mounted on cardboard
32.4 x 32.4 cm

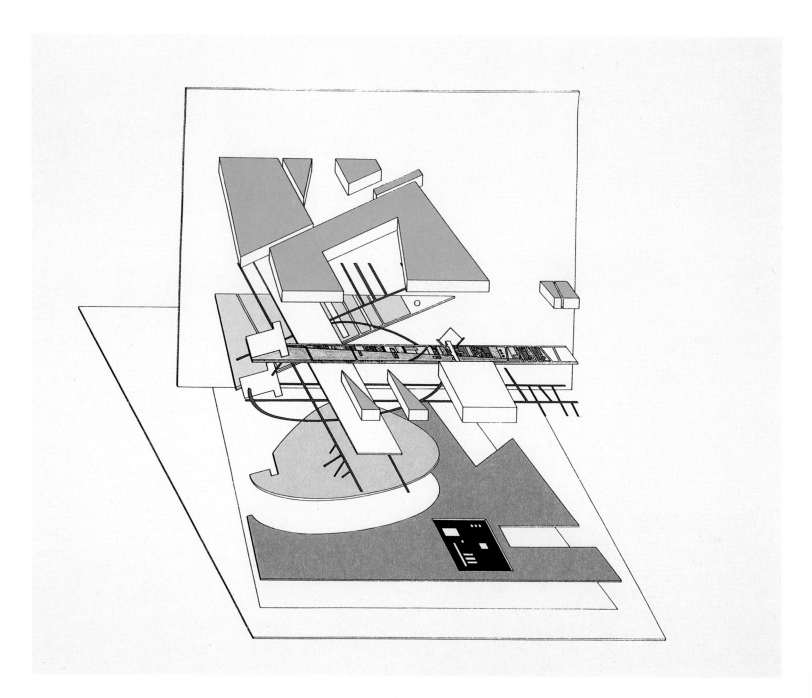

208
Aerial view
Coloured foil on photocopy, mounted
on cardboard
32.4 x 32.4 cm

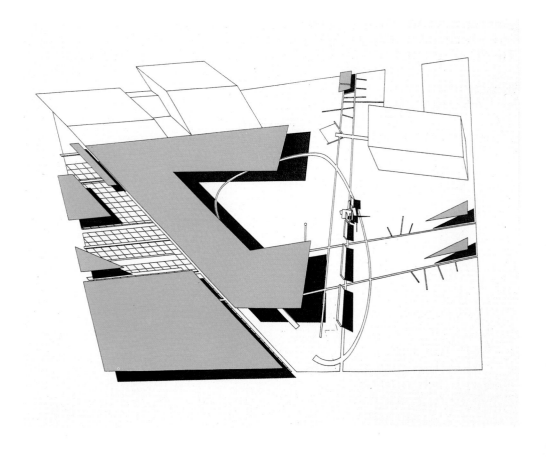

209
Road network with design elements
Coloured foil on photocopy, mounted
on cardboard
32.4 x 32.4 cm

A Rudimentary area – historical relic (ruins) of
  devastated city
B Place of reflection. Recreation for city dwellers
C Urban square – different surface structures of
  paved areas, typical look of urban square
D Strip of emptiness – area of non-design
E Federal strip – compression of significance,
  place of challenge and debate

 1 Abstract monument of what happened – clay
 2 Active museum – dramatization of the archive wall
 3 Traces of the PPA – space for public remembrance
   ceremonies
 4 Artistic activities plaza
 5 Gropius building as multifunctional exhibition hall,
   temple of the imagination
 6 Wooded areas as optically and acoustically
   transparent element, incorporating existing trees
 7 Groups of trees to mark off sectors of urban
   square
 8 Groups of trees accenting presence of "The Wall"
 9 Groups of trees to mark approach situations
10 Random paths as starting points for beaten tracks
11 Access paths for open-air art
12 Parking

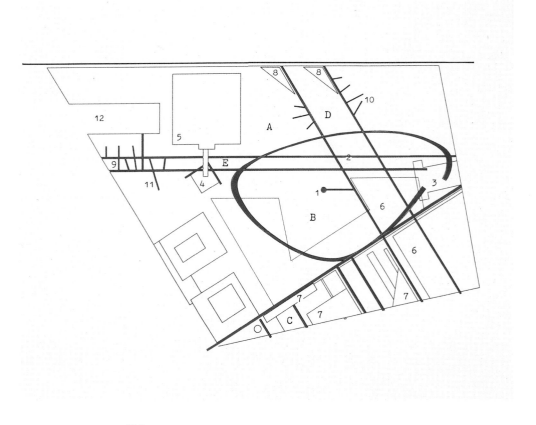

Open Competition to articulate site of former Prince Albrecht Palace, 1984, Block 3

Second Prize
Giorgio Grassi, Milan

with Agostino Renna, Nicola Di Battista, Francesco Collotti, Guido Zanella and Enzo Collotti (historian), Claudio Crespi (model)

210
Modification of the Prince Albrecht Palace and annexes
Upper floor plan and elevations, scale 1 : 200
Coloured blueprint
75.2 x 102.1 cm

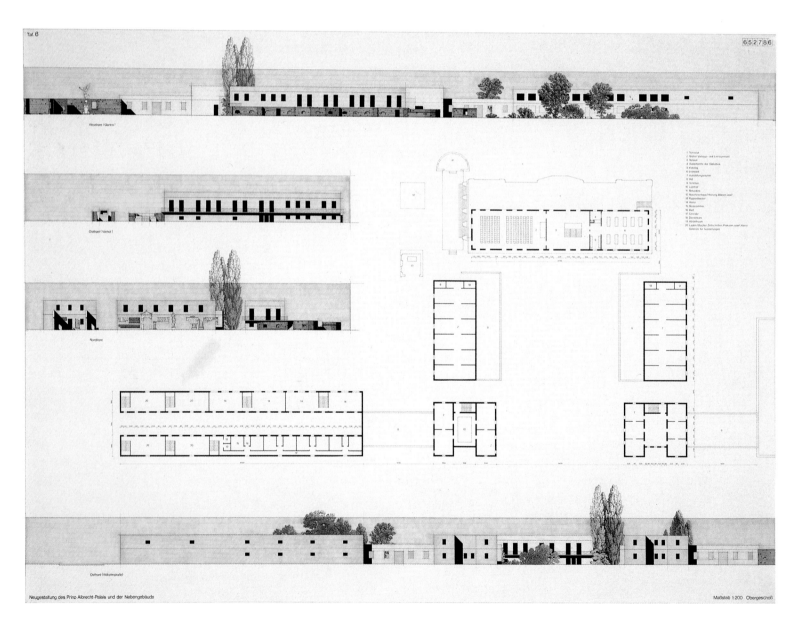

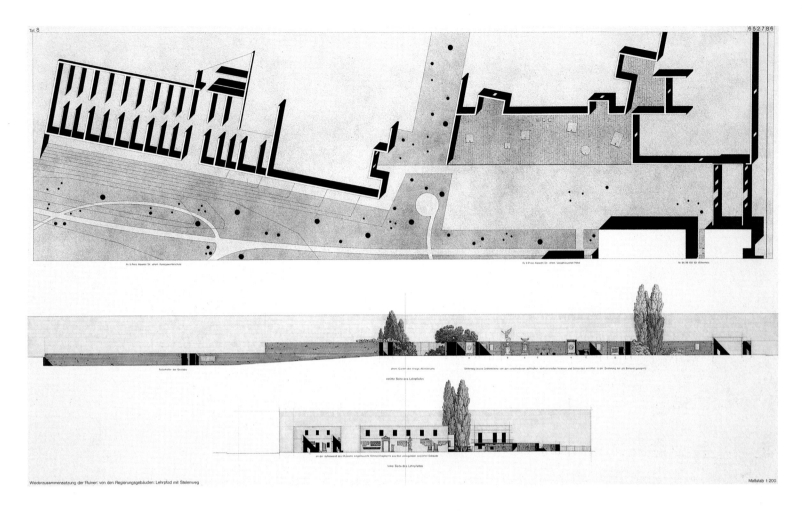

211
Recomposition of the "ruins" of the
government buildings
Aerial view and elevations, scale 1:200
Coloured blueprint
68.1 x 114.3 cm

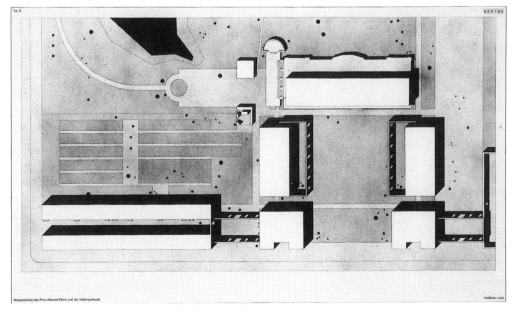

212
Modification of the Prince Albrecht Palace
and annexes
Aerial view, scale 1:200
India ink and spray technique
on transparent blueprint
56.5 x 97.1 cm

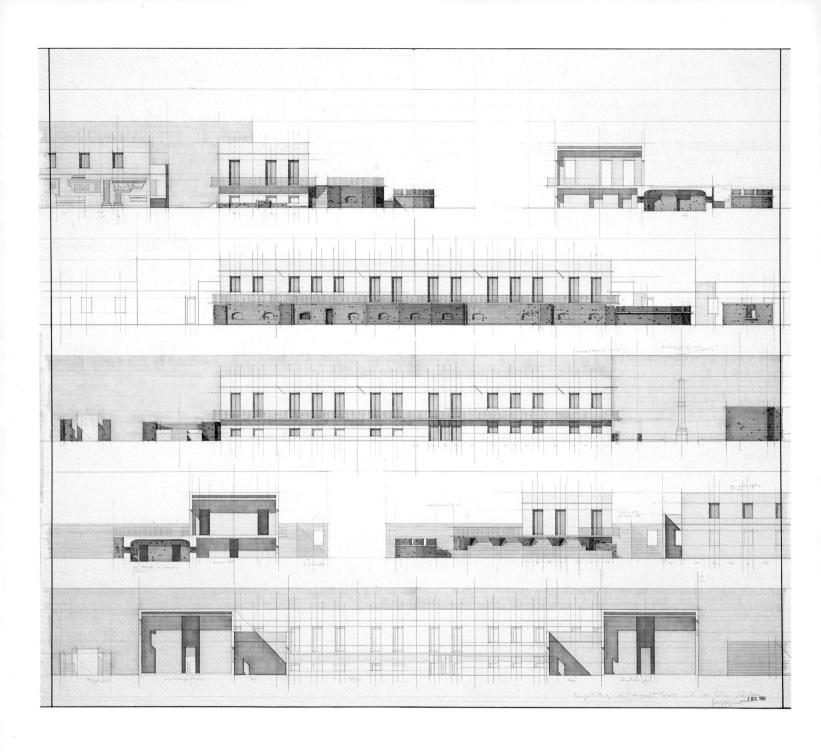

213
Modification of the Prince Albrecht Palace
Elevations and sections, scale 1:100
Pencil and felt pen on the reverse side
of a blueprint
81.2 x 94.5 cm
Signed: Dic. 1983 Giorgio Grassi

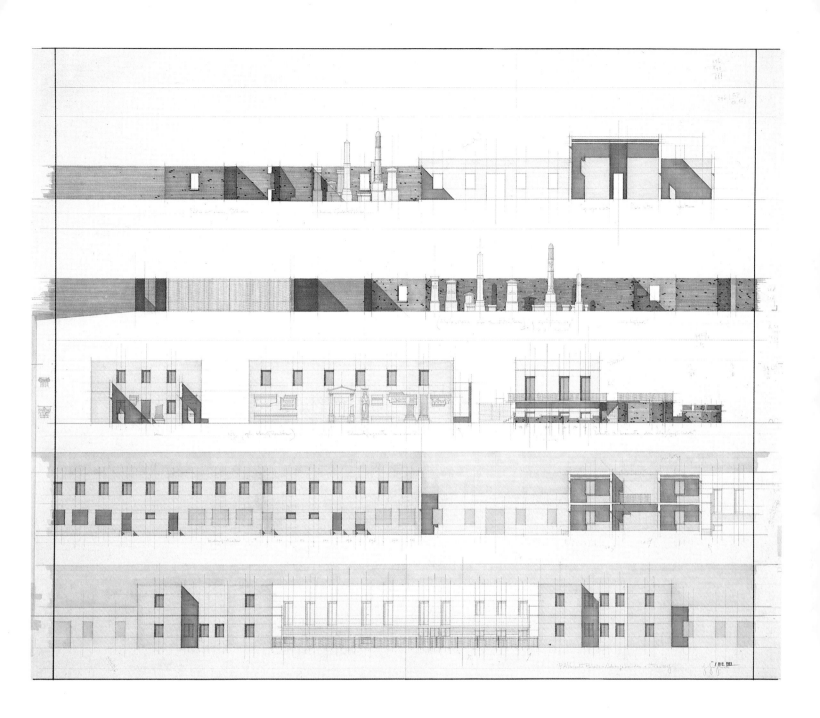

214
Stelenweg and modification of the
Prince Albrecht Palace and annexes
Elevations, scale 1:100
Pencil and felt pen on the reverse side
of a blueprint
82.4 x 97.3 cm
Signed: Dic. 1983 Giorgio Grassi

**Open Competition to articulate site of
former Prince Albrecht Palace, 1984,
Block 3**

José Rafael Moneo, Madrid

215
Sketch of the stone building
India ink on paper
26.7 x 20.6 cm
(Passepartout detail)

216
Sketch of the municipal development
context
India ink on paper
21 x 29 cm

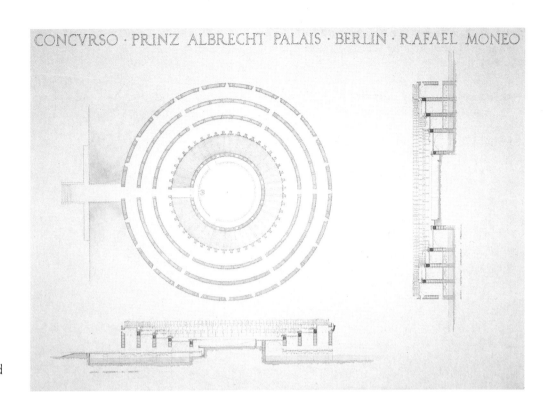

217
The stone building in the lake
Plan and section, scale 1 : 250
Pencil and watercolour on drawing board
73 x 102 cm

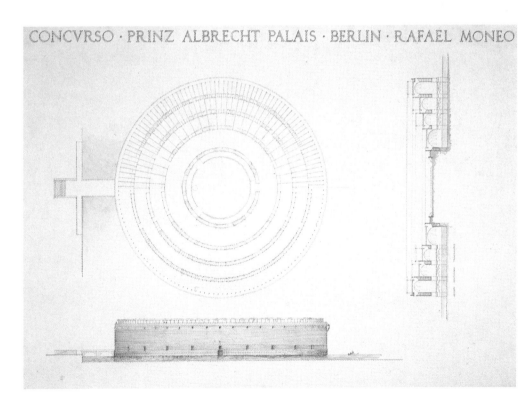

218
The stone building in the lake
Elevation, aerial view, cross section,
scale 1 : 250
Pencil and watercolour on drawing board
73 x 102 cm

Open Competition to articulate site of former Prince Albrecht Palace, 1984, Block 3

Highly Commended
Raimund Abraham, New York

with Brad Liperts, Warren Ser, Adi Shamir

219
Sections, model photos, scale 1 : 250
Coloured blueprint
106 x 121 cm

220
Model photograph on transparent sepia
paper, coloured in pencil

221
The central block
Horizontal section
Superimposed on vertical section
Pencil on handmade paper

Open Competition to articulate site of former Prince Albrecht Palace, 1984, Block 3

Highly Commended
John Hejduk, New York

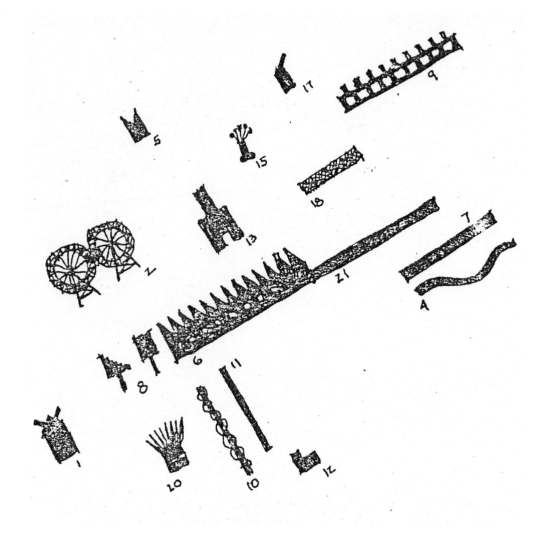

222
Sketches
Photocopy on Japanese rice paper
42 x 29.7 cm

223
Site plan, scale 1:250
Eastern and western section
Black and white photograph
152 x 212 cm

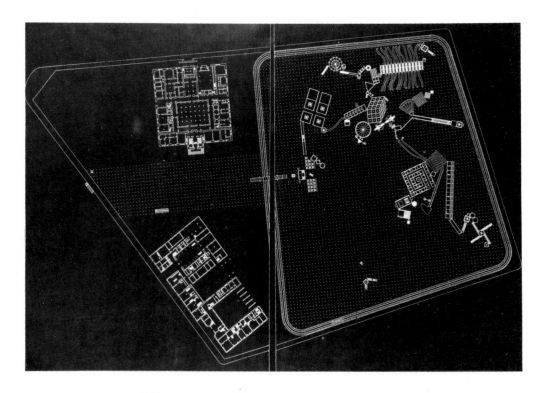

224
Sketch
Photocopy on Japanese rice paper
21 x 29.7 cm (detail)

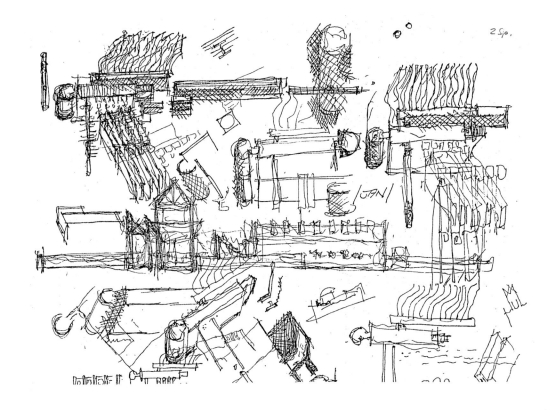

225
Structural drawing, scale 1 : 100
Colour pencil on transparent paper
90.6 x 156.1 cm

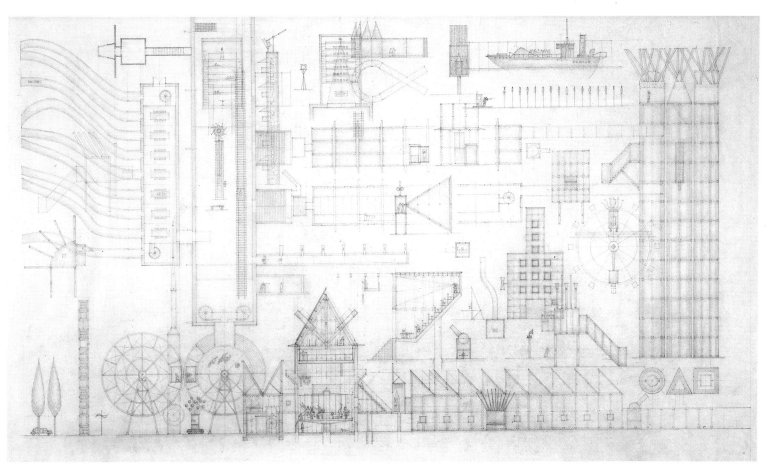

BERLIN

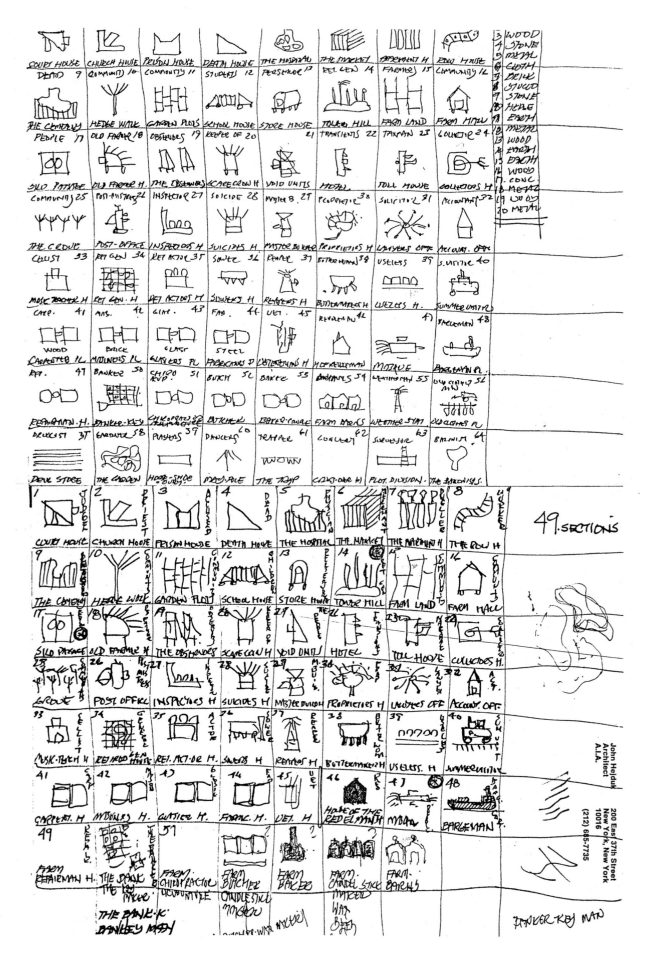

49. SECTIONS

John Hejduk
Architect
A.I.A.

200 East 37th Street
New York, New York
10016

(212) 685-7735

**Restricted International Competition
Living and Working in Southern Fried-
richstadt
Kochstrasse/Friedrichstrasse, 1981
Block 4**

**One of the Prizes
Oriol Bohigas
David Mackay
Josep Martorell, Barcelona**

229
Perspective
West view of Kochstrasse
Pencil on transparent paper

**Residential and Commercial Premises
Kochstrasse 65, Zimmerstrasse 19
Block 4
Planning since 1985**

**Josep Martorell
Oriol Bohigas
David Mackay, Barcelona**

232
Axonometric façade detail, scale 1 : 50
India ink and crayon on Ingres paper
70 x 52 cm

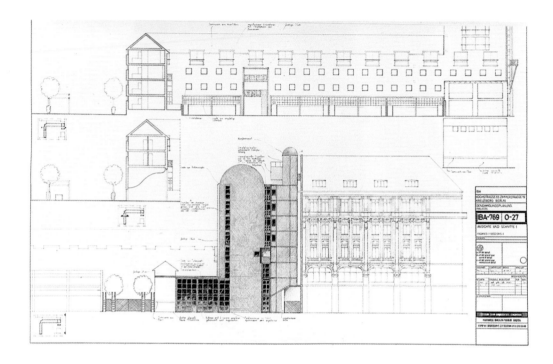

230
Section elevation, perpendicular
to Kochstrasse
Kochstrasse elevation, scale 1 : 100
Crayon on Ingres paper
60 x 95 cm

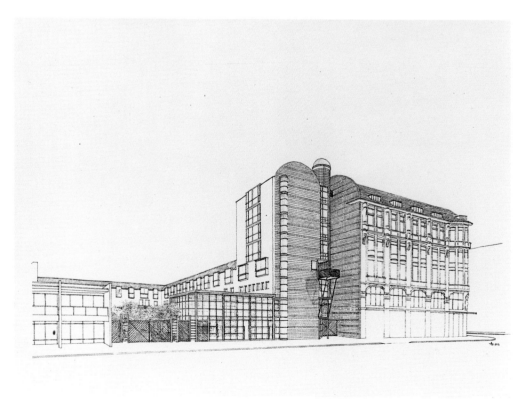

231
Northeast perspective of Kochstrasse
Crayon on Ingres paper
35 x 59 cm

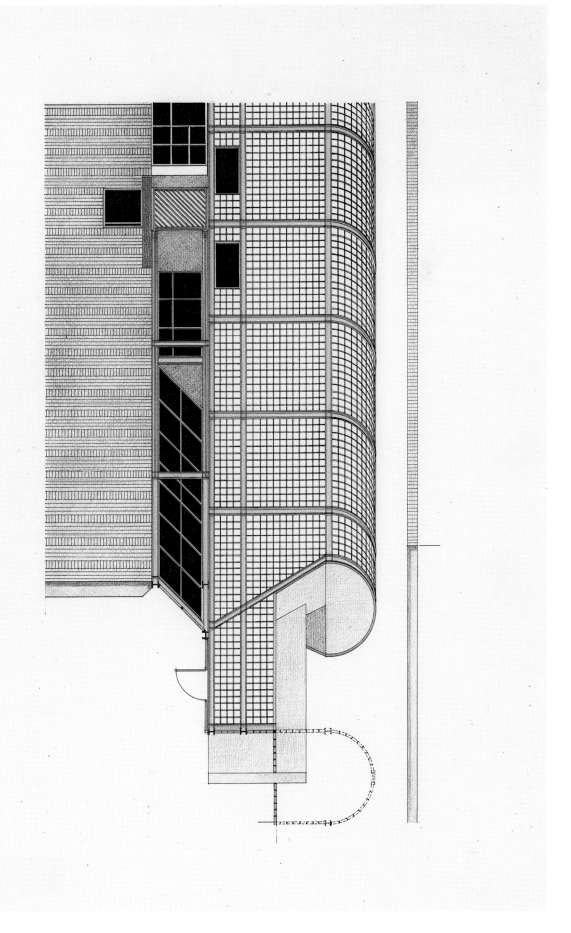

151

**Residential and Commercial Premises
Kochstrasse 67–72, Block 4
Planning since 1985**

**Josep Martorell
Oriol Bohigas
David Mackay, Barcelona**

236
Partial view of the Kochstrasse façade,
scale 1:50
India ink and crayon on Ingres paper
70 x 52 cm

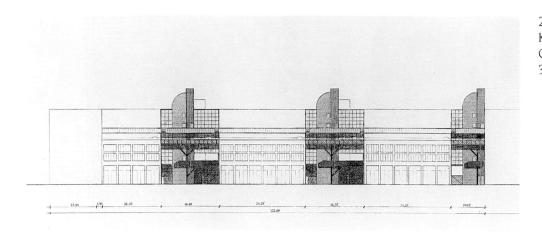

233
Kochstrasse elevation, scale 1:200
Crayon on Ingres paper
30 x 76 cm

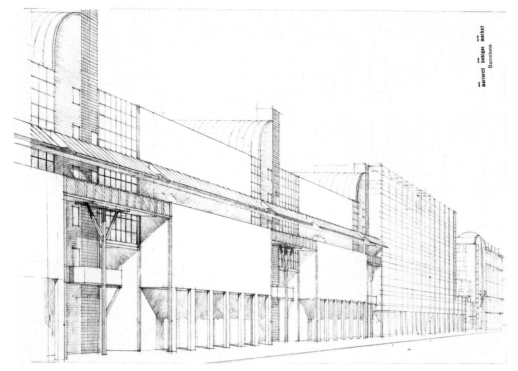

234
East perspective
Background: Kochstrasse project 65

235
Façade study of Kochstrasse elevation,
scale 1:100
Crayon on paper
70 x 50 cm

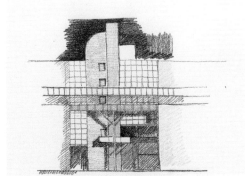

**International Competition
Living and Working in Southern Fried-
richstadt
Kochstrasse/Friedrichstrasse, 1981**

**Highly Commended
Office for Metropolitan Architecture,
OMA, London
Rem Koolhaas
Stefano de Martino, London**

with Herman de Kovel, Richard Perlmutter,
Batsheva Rouen, Ricardo Simonini, Ron
Steiner, Alex Wall

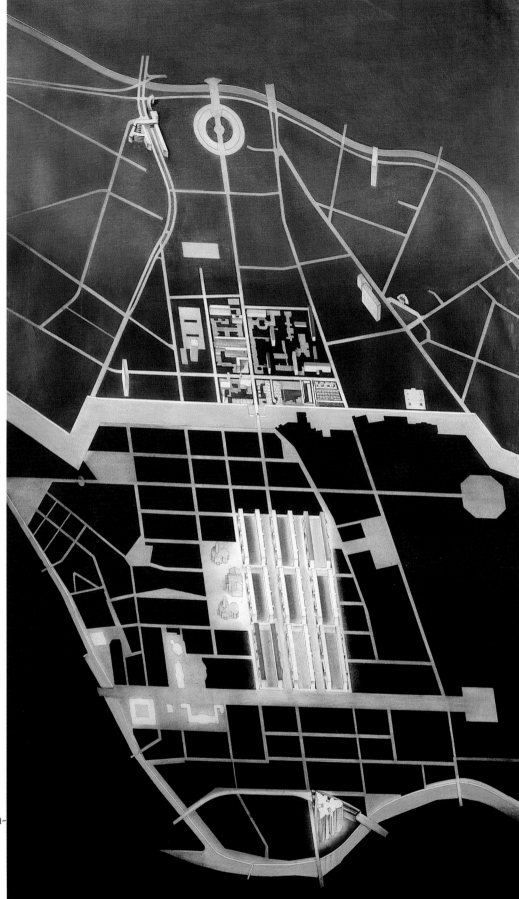

237
Site plan, Friedrichstrasse, station
to Mehringplatz
Axonometric representation of historic
projects (Mies van der Rohe's glass
building, Karl Friedrich Schinkel's
Gendarme market, Hilbersheimer's residential blocks, Mendelson's Trades Union
House) and proposed development
India ink, crayon and spray technique
on cardboard
160.5 x 95.3 cm

238
Axonometric overall plan of the complete
municipal concept
Blocks 4, 5, 10 and 11, scale 1 : 500
India ink, watercolour and gouache
on cardboard
97.8 x 123 cm

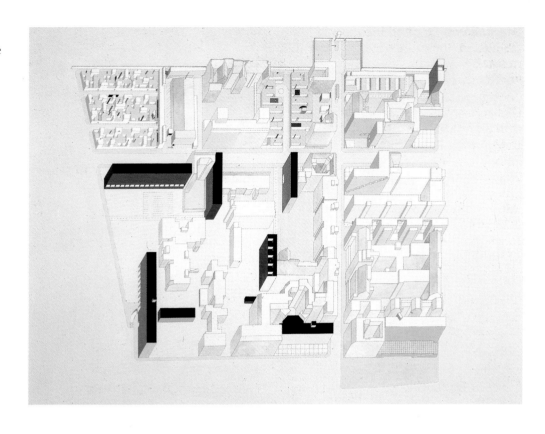

239
Axonometric general view of residential
housing
Block 4, western section
a) Stairwell core
b) Stairwell and wall elements
c) Volumetrics
India ink, chalk and crayon on cardboard
101.5 x 230 cm

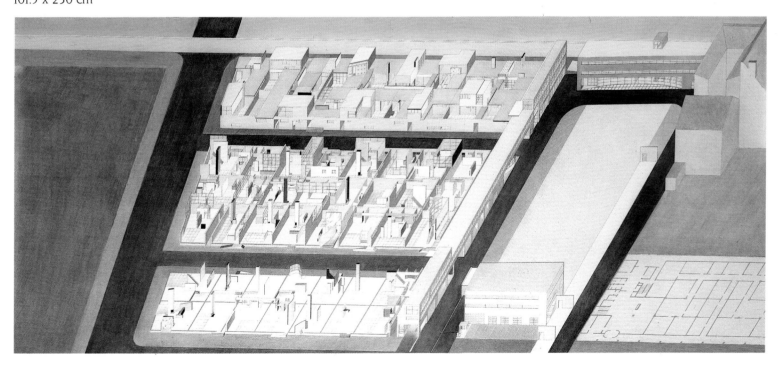

**Apartment House Friedrichstrasse
207/208**

**Office for Metropolitan Architecture,
OMA, London
Elia Zenghelis
Rem Koolhaas
Matthias Sauerbruch**

with Alex Wall, Eleni Dean, John McMinn

240
Axonometric drawing of the elements:
Roof, structure, ground floor, scale 1 : 500
India ink and foil on transparent paper
29.7 x 42 cm

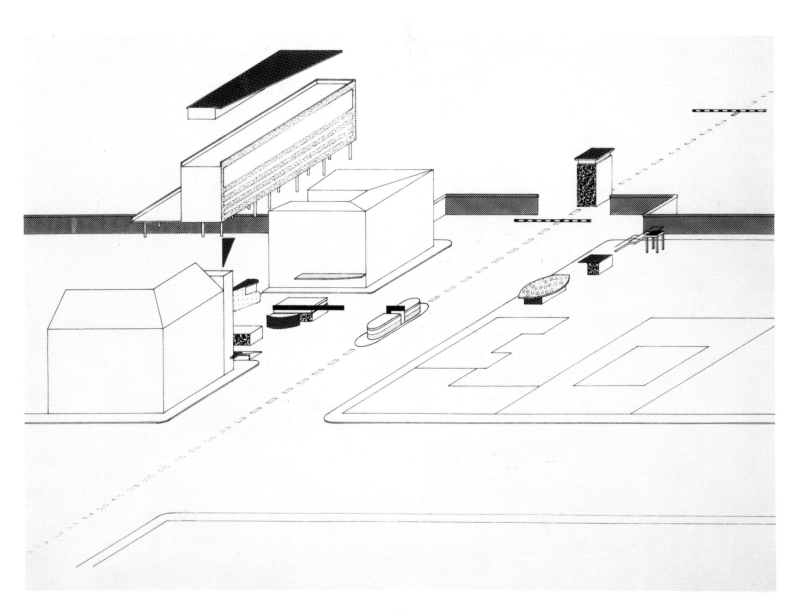

241
Axonometric drawing, from below,
scale 1:200
India ink and foil on transparent paper
29.7 x 42 cm

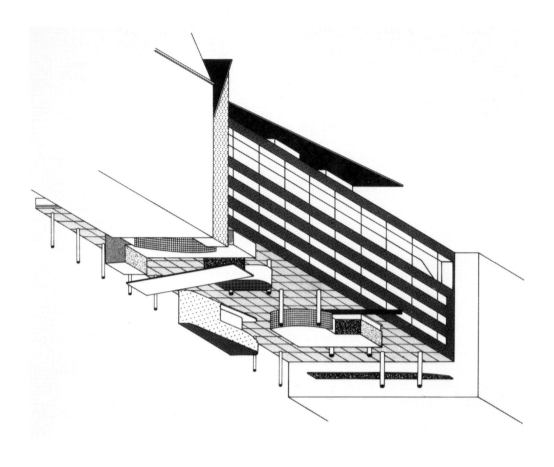

242
Section II-II, scale 1:100
India ink on transparent paper
39 x 59 cm, heading excluded
Dated: 1.9.85

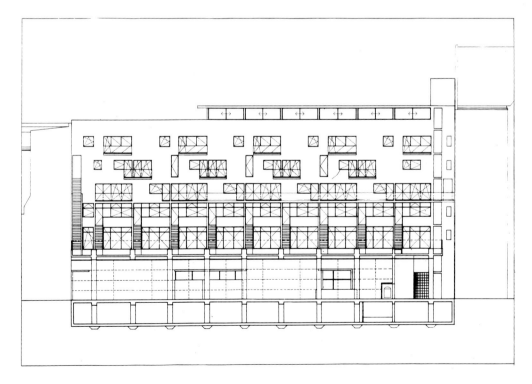

**Gatehouse Wilhelmstrasse 41/42,
Block 4
Planning since 1985**

**Herbert Pfeifer,
Lüdinghausen/Westfalen**

with Bernhard Leusder, Manfred Heinrich

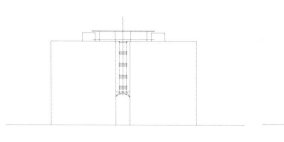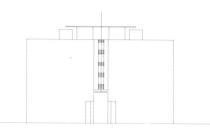

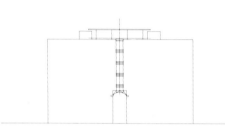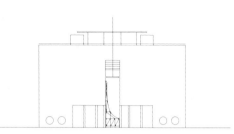

243–247
Schematic drawings
Variations on the gateway situation
View of Wilhelmstrasse, scale 1 : 200
India ink on transparent paper
5 sheets 29.7 x 21 cm

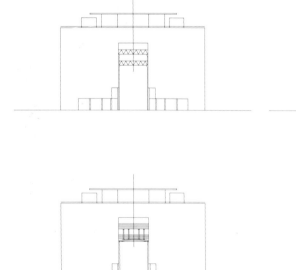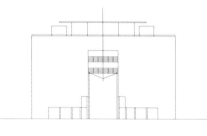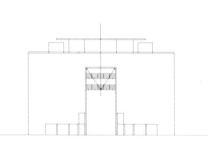

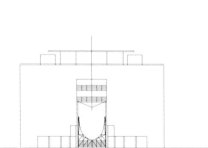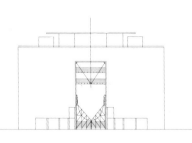

**Residential Development House B,
Zimmerstrasse 1/2, Corner of
Wilhelmstrasse 42/42 A, Block 4
Planning since 1985**

**Joachim Schürmann
Margot Schürmann, Cologne**

with Wolf Dittmann, Martin Orawiec, Jens
Bothe, Wilfried Euskirchen, Margaretha
Lange, Georg Rattay, Ruth Raasch-Nowak,
Wolfgang Raderschall, Herbert Süselbeck,
Hadi Teherani, Tilmann Weber

248
Façade model towards Wilhelmstrasse
Plastic, coloured cardboard
60.5 x 60.5 cm (frame size)

249
Façade model towards Zimmerstrasse
Plastic, coloured cardboard
60.5 x 60.5 cm

**Residential and Commercial Premises,
Corner of Wilhelmstrasse and
Kochstrasse
Planning since 1985**

**Jean Flammang
Burkhard Grashorn
Aldo Licker, Dortmund**

250
Wilhelmstrasse elevation
Jean Flammang
Gouache on blue paper
65 x 50 cm
Signed: Jean Flammang 1986

251
Elevation sketch
Burkhard Grashorn
Pencil on transparent paper
63.3 x 45.7 cm
Dated: 19.11.85

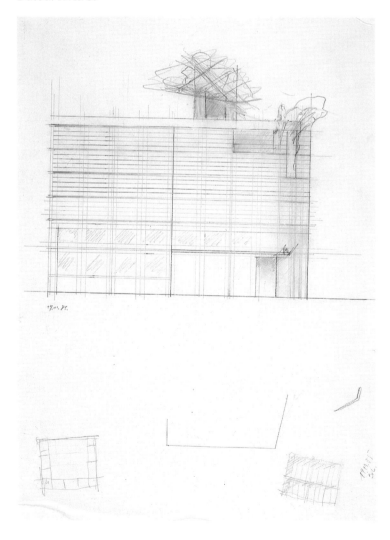

Former Baroque House near Check-point Charlie
Corner of Friedrichstrasse and
Zimmerstrasse
Research and Planning 1984/85

Christian Koch, Berlin

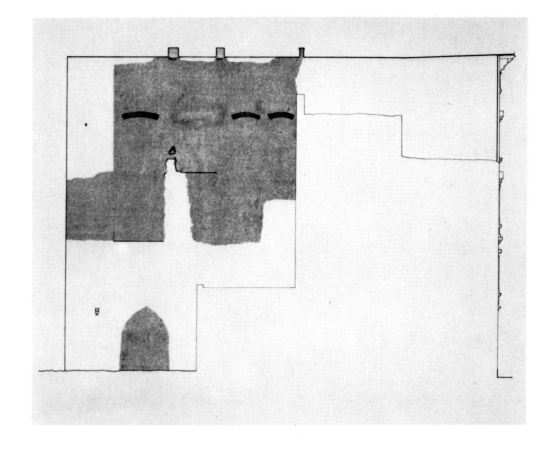

252
Ground floor plan, scale 1:50
Blueprint
59.2 x 84 cm

253
Brandwand elevation (west), scale 1:50
Blueprint
59.2 x 84.1 cm

254
Ground floor plan showing arrangement
of beams, scale 1:50
Photocopy
59.3 x 84.2 cm

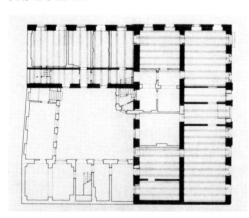

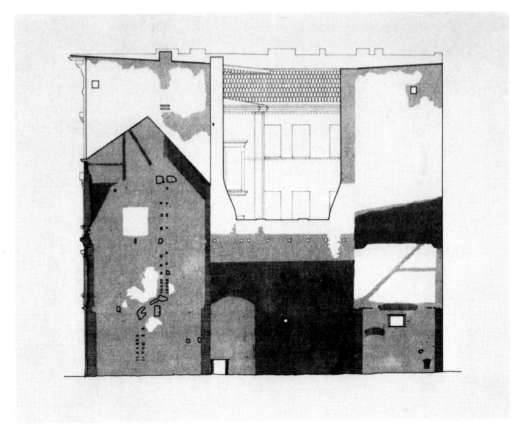

**Apartment House, Corner of Koch-
strasse and Charlottenstrasse, Block 5
Planning 1982–84
Completed 1985**

**Hans Kammerer
Walter Belz
Klaus Kucher and Partner, Stuttgart**

with Marie-José Acra, Tilman Stroheker,
Michael Wagner

255
Kochstrasse elevation with plan of access
ramp, scale 1 : 50
Pencil on transparent paper
91.5 x 129.1 cm
Signed: 9. 8. 89 gez. MA

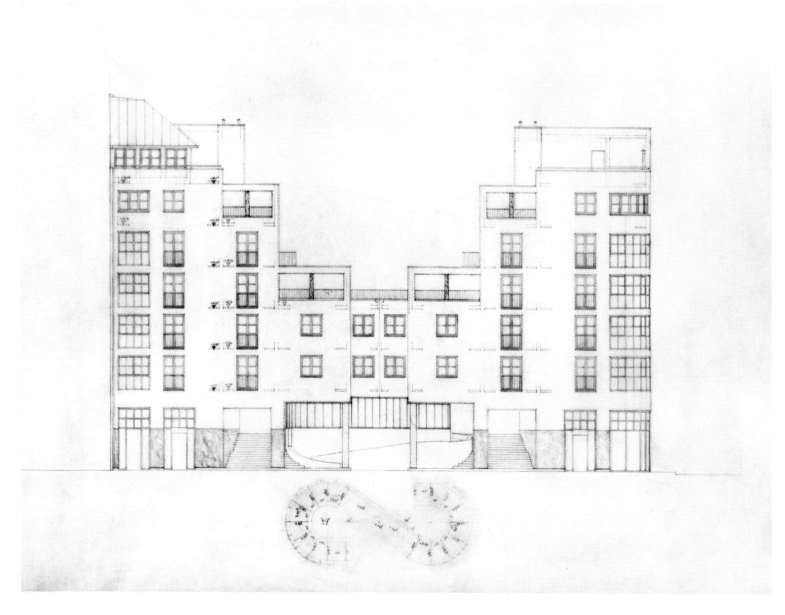

256
Approach to the inner courtyard, access
stairs and ramp, elevation of the project
plans, scale 1 : 20
Pencil on transparent paper
49.5 x 155.2 cm
Signed: 13.8.84 gez. ZI

257
Approach to inner courtyard, access stairs
and ramp, working drawing of floor plan,
scale 1 : 20
Pencil on transparent paper
49.7 x 166 cm
Signed: 13.6.85 gez. ZI/MIA

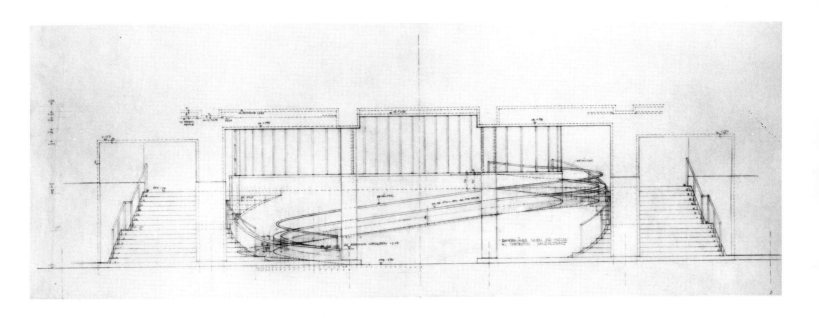

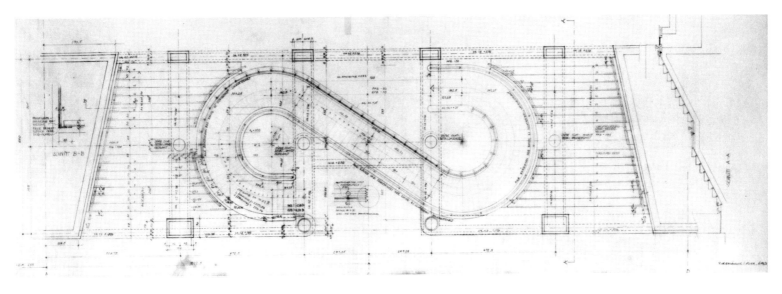

**Restricted International Competition
Living and Working in Southern Friedrichstadt
Kochstrasse/Friedrichstrasse, Block 5,
1981**

**Special Prize
Peter Eisenman
Jaquelin Robertson, New York**

with Christopher Glaister, Tom Hut, Thomas
Leeser, Michelle Andrew (drawing), John
Leeper (model)

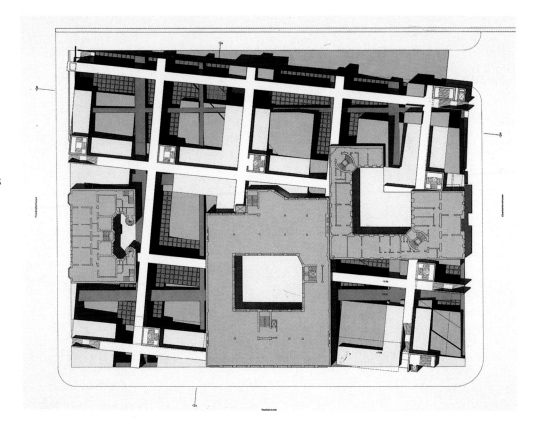

258
Aerial view, scale 1:200
Foil on black and white photographic
reproduction, mounted on Capa board
91.5 x 91.5 cm

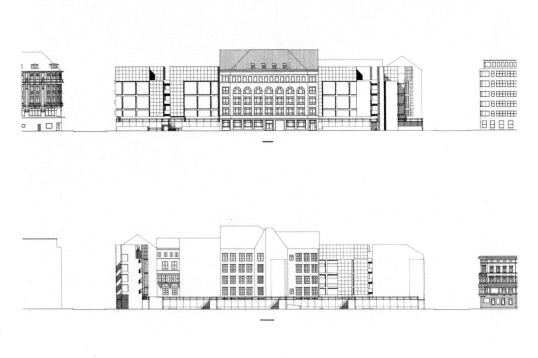

259
Elevations, scale 1:200
above: Kochstrasse; below: Zimmerstrasse
Photo reproduction on Capa board
91.5 x 91.5 cm

260
Perspective, southwest view over the
"Museum of the artificially excavated city"
Pencil and crayon on paper, mounted
on Capa board
91.5 x 91.5 cm

261
Perspective, southeast view
Pencil and crayon on paper, mounted
on Capa board
91.5 x 91.5 cm

**Residential and Commercial Premises,
Corner of Kochstrasse and Friedrich-
strasse, Block 5
Planning 1982–84
Completed 1986**

**Eisenman/Robertson, New York
Peter Eisenman**

with Thomas Leeser

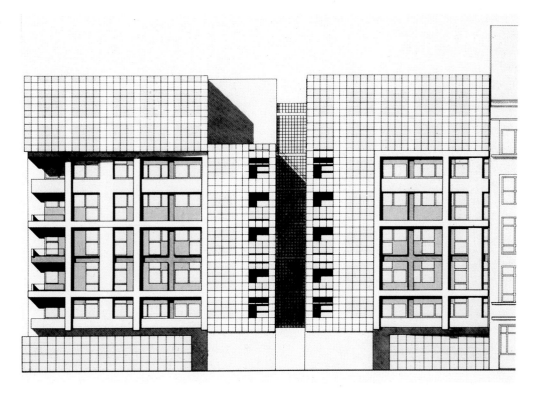

262
South façade towards Kochstrasse,
scale 1:200
Foil on photoreproduction or blueprint
(original lost)

263
North façade (courtyard), scale 1:200
Foil on photoreproduction or blueprint
(original lost)

264
West façade towards Friedrichstrasse,
scale 1:200
Foil on photoreproduction or photocopy
(original lost)

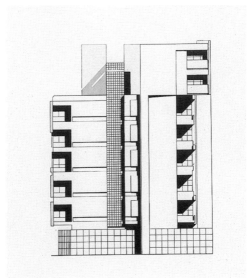

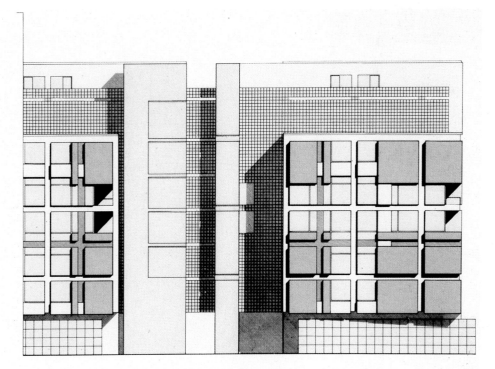

167

**Park Layout near Checkpoint Charlie,
Block 5
Planning 1985**

**Eisenman/Robertson, New York
Peter Eisenman**

with Thomas Leeser

266
Axonometric drawing, scale 1:200
Foil on photographic reproduction
on Capa board
60.9 x 91.6 cm
Signed: 1. Mai 1985 TL

265
Plan, scale 1:200
Foil on photographic reproduction
on Capa board
61 x 91.5 cm
Signed: 1. Mai 1985 TL

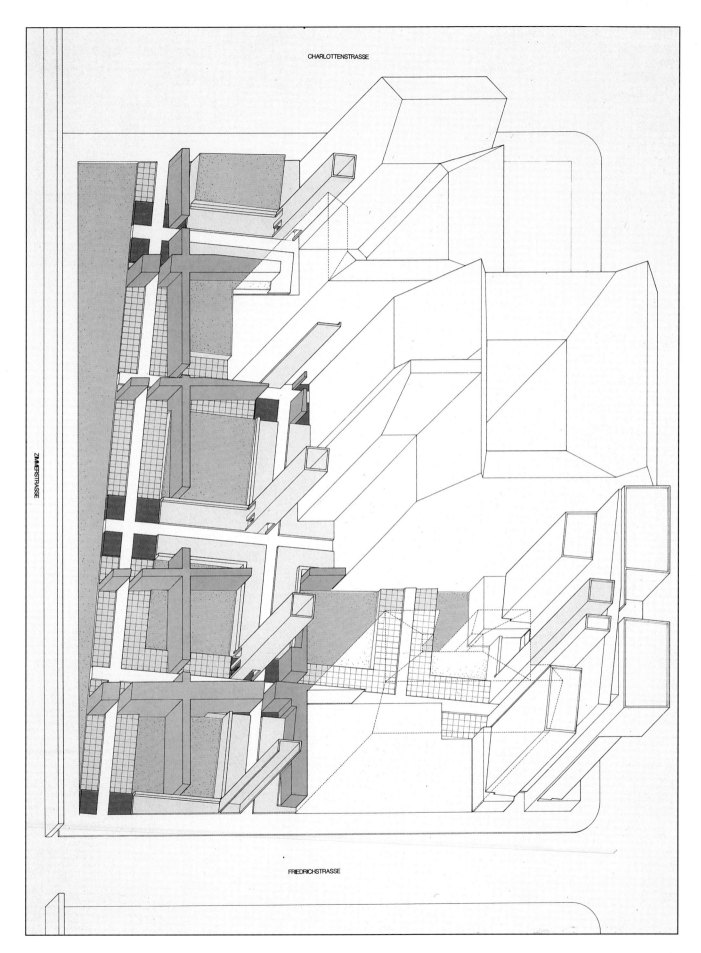

CHARLOTTENSTRASSE

ZIMMERSTRASSE

FRIEDRICHSTRASSE

169

**Restricted International Competition
Living and Working in Southern Fried-
richstadt
Kochstrasse/Friedrichstrasse, 1981
Block 10**

**A Special Prize
Aldo Rossi
Gianni Braghieri, Milan**

with Christopher Stead, Jay Johnson

269
Perspective, sketch of building corner
Pencil and crayon on paper
29.7 x 21 cm
Signed: Berlin AR 10 Ott 80

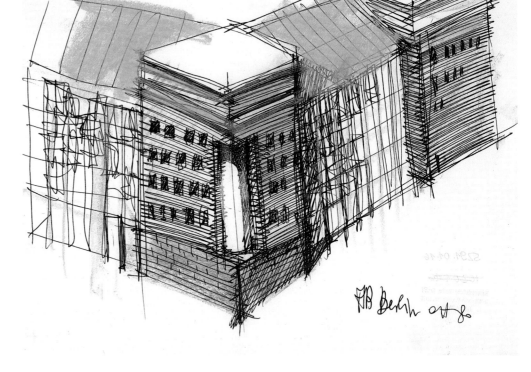

267
Preliminary sketch of building corner
Felt pen and chalk on paper
21 x 29.7 cm
Signed: AR Berlin Ott 80

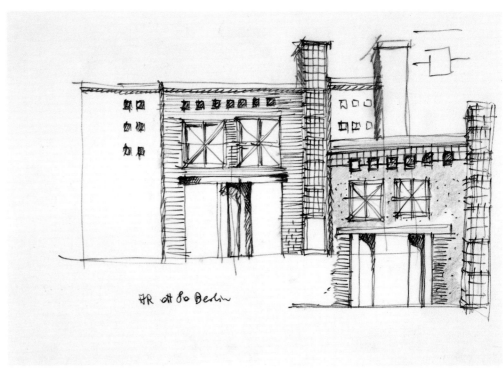

268
Study façade sketch
Pencil, felt pen and crayon
on transparent paper
21 x 29.7 cm
Signed: AR Ott 80 Berlin

Berlin AR 10 ott. 80.

270
Street and courtyard elevations, scale 1 : 100
Felt pen and oil crayon on blueprint
54.7 x 109.4 cm

271
Wilhelmstrasse, elevation and standard
floor plan, scale 1 : 200
Sheet 3
Felt pen and oil crayon on blueprint
54.5 x 165.8 cm

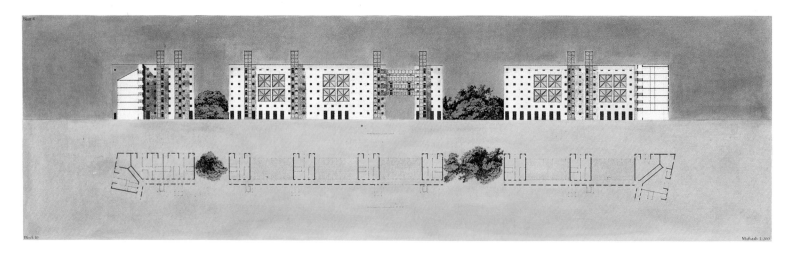

272
Perspective with superimposed plan and
façade sketches
Pencil and India ink on transparent paper
71.8 x 109.5 cm

273
Wilhelmstrasse, street view and typical
floor plan, scale 1 : 200
Felt pen and crayon on photocopy
54.8 x 165.5 cm

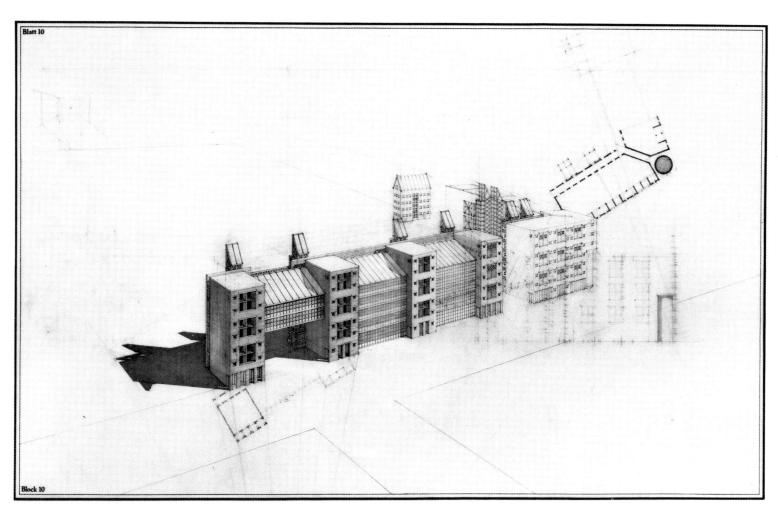

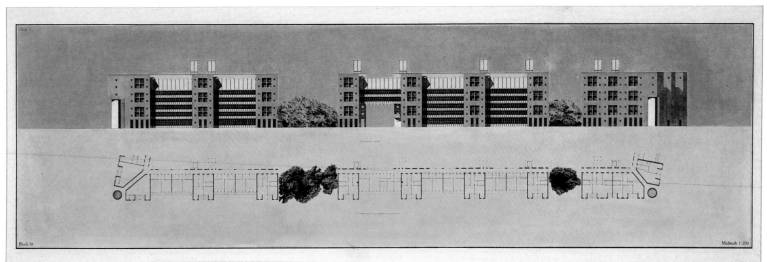

**Residential Development
Koch-/Wilhelm-/Puttkamerstrasse,
Block 10
Planning 1983/84
Under construction since 1986**

**Aldo Rossi
Gianni Braghieri, Milan**

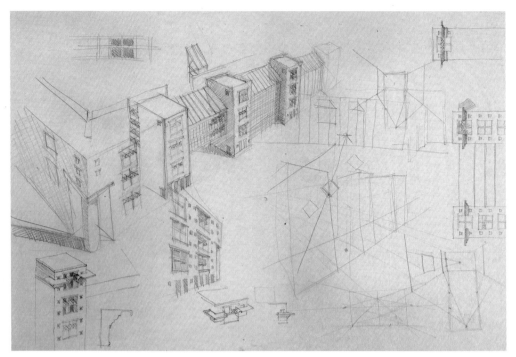

274
Modification of the preliminary drawing
Perspective sketches
Pencil on brown transparent paper
50 x 74.5 cm

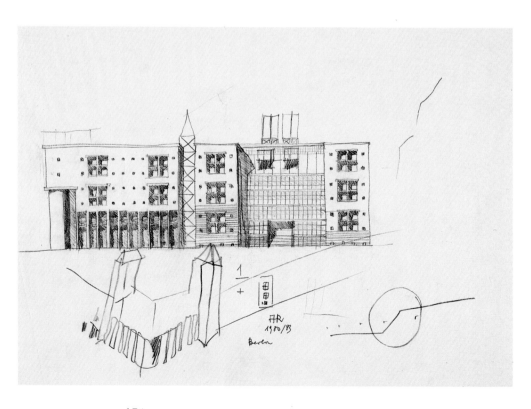

275
Study of façade, elevation and
corner drawing
Pencil on yellow tracing paper
37 x 53 cm
Signed: AR 1980/83 Berlin

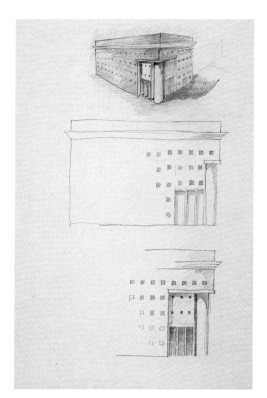

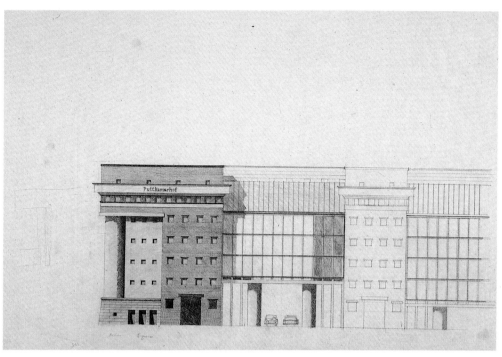

276
Sketch of building corner
Perspective, elevations
Pencil and crayon on brown
transparent paper
74.6 x 49.9 cm

277
Study of Puttkamerhof façade, scale 1:100
Pencil and crayon on brown
transparent paper
49.8 x 74.5 cm

278
Study of Wilhelmstrasse façade, gateway
to the inner courtyard, scale 1:100
Pencil and crayon on brown
transparent paper
50 x 74.5 cm

175

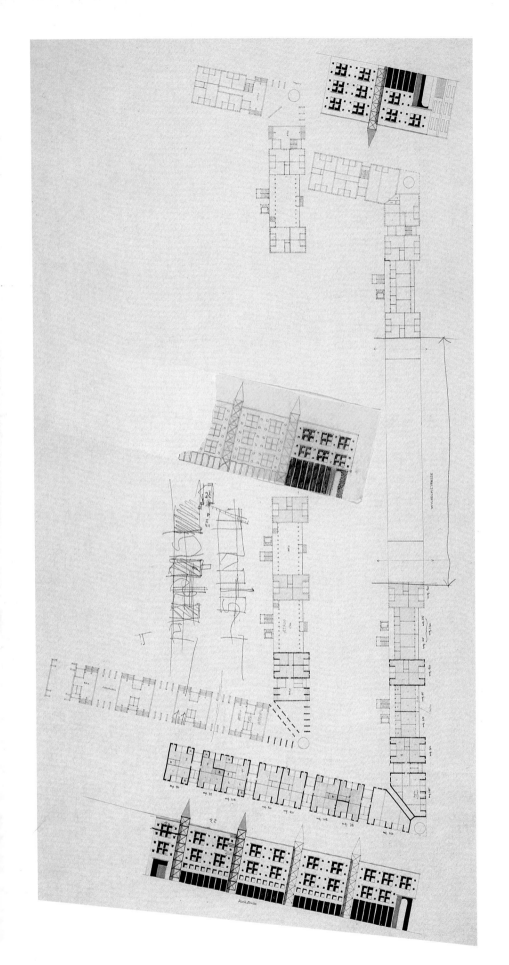

279
Modification of the preliminary drawing
Plans, elevations, sketches, scale 1:200
Coloured blueprint, sketch on yellow
transparent paper glued on
86 x 160.5 cm
Signed: (Stamp) Aldo Rossi

280
Elevation scale 1 : 50
Coloured blueprint
59.6 x 62.5 cm
Dated: Agosto '84

**Restricted International Competition
Living and Working in Southern Fried-
richstadt
Kochstrasse/Friedrichstrasse, 1981
Block 10**

**One of the Prizes
Raimund Abraham, New York**

with Kevin Bone, Robert James, Joseph
Levine

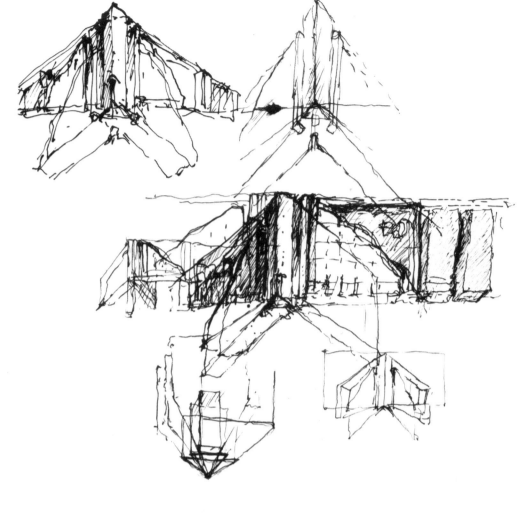

281
Axonometric studies of building corner
Felt pen on paper
31 x 24 cm

282
Axonometric sketch of the block
Felt pen on paper
31 x 24 cm

178

283–285
Elevations, scale 1 : 200
India ink, pencil and crayon
on transparent paper

286
Site plan study of Kochstrasse/Wilhelm-
strasse/Puttkamerstrasse block
Pencil and crayon on transparent paper
51 x 40 cm

Kochstrasse elevation 46 x 165 cm

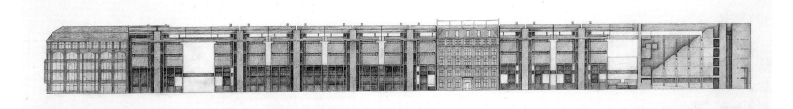

Wilhelmstrasse elevation 46 x 164.5 cm

Puttkamerstrasse elevation 39.5 x 180 cm

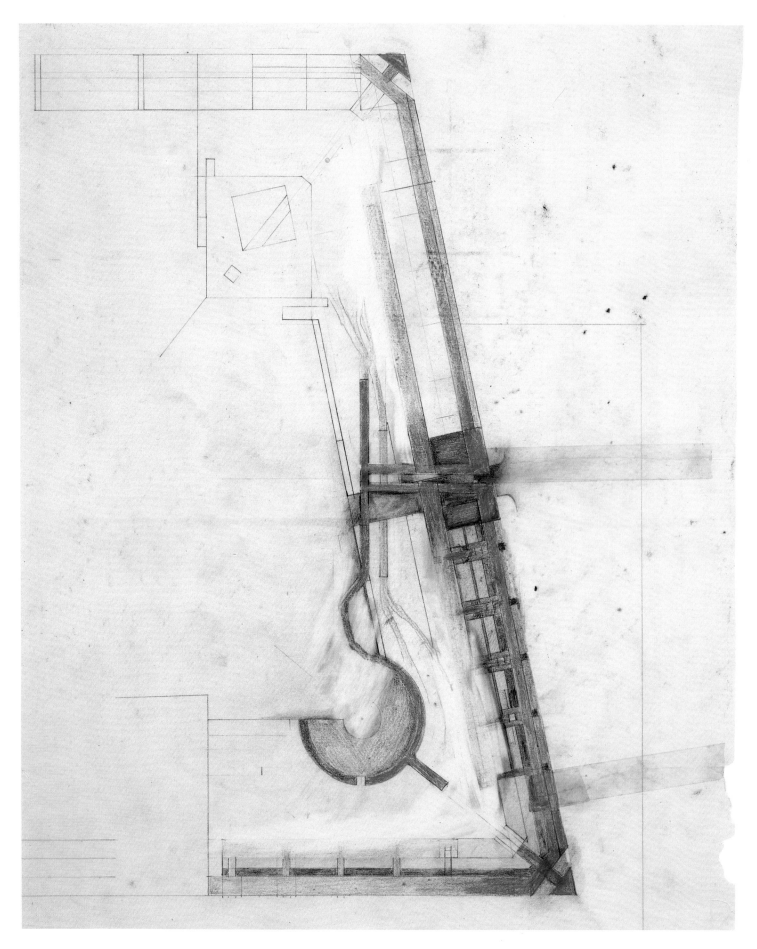

Restricted International Competition
Living and Working in Southern Fried-
richstadt
Kochstrasse/Friedrichstrasse, 1981
Block 10
Revised Version of Competition Entry

Dietmar Grötzebach
Günter Plessow
Reinhold Ehlers, Berlin

with Peter Krop, Kay Marlow, Martin Wuttig

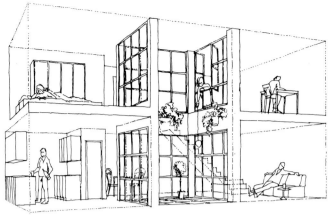

287
Axonometric section of drawing of
a maisonette with double-storey
winter garden
Felt pen on transparent paper
21 x 29.7 cm

288
Perspective elevation Kochstrasse
Coloured photocopy
50 x 70.2 cm
Signed: Grö 23.9.82

Südliche Friedrichstadt, Kochstr. 8–14, Straßenansicht Grö 23/9 82

**Restricted International Competition
Living and Working in Southern Fried-
richstadt
Kochstrasse/Friedrichstrasse, 1981
Block 11**

**One of the Prizes
Marie-Claude Bétrix
Eraldo Consolascio
Bruno Reichlin
Fabio Reinhard, Zürich**

with Patrik Huber
Engineers: Santiago Calatrave, Zürich,
Schuler/Künzle/Sägesser, Zürich

290
Kochstrasse façade, scale 1:50
Pencil, felt pen, ballpoint pen, crayon and
spray technique on drawing board
101.8 x 72.9 cm

289
Friedrichstrasse, Kochstrasse and
Charlottenstrasse elevations, scale 1:200
Silkscreen and spray technique
82.8 x 132.1 cm

183

**Residential and Commercial Premises,
Corner of Kochstrasse and Friedrich-
strasse, Block 11
Planning since 1982**

**Bruno Reichlin
Fabio Reinhard, Zürich**

with Eddi Imhoff

291
Elevations and section, scale 1:200
Coloured blueprint
116.2 x 98.5 cm

292
Ground floor plan, scale 1:200
Coloured blueprint
119.4 x 99.1 cm

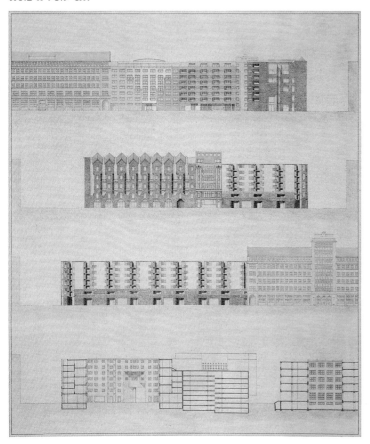

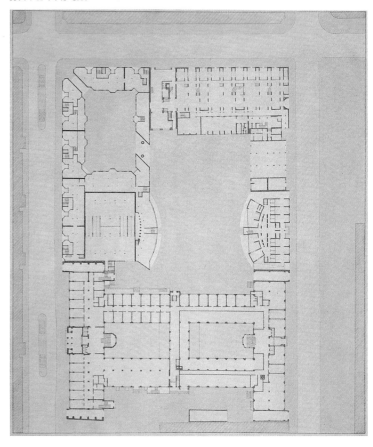

293
Perspective of Kochstrasse/
Friedrichstrasse corner
Chalk and crayon on blueprint
62.4 x 62.4 cm

**Residential and Commercial Premises
Friedrichstrasse 32/33, Block 11
Planning since 1983
Under construction since 1986**

Raimund Abraham, New York

with Heike Büttner, Claus Neumann

294
Sketches
Elevations and axonometric drawings
Felt pen on paper
21 x 24 cm

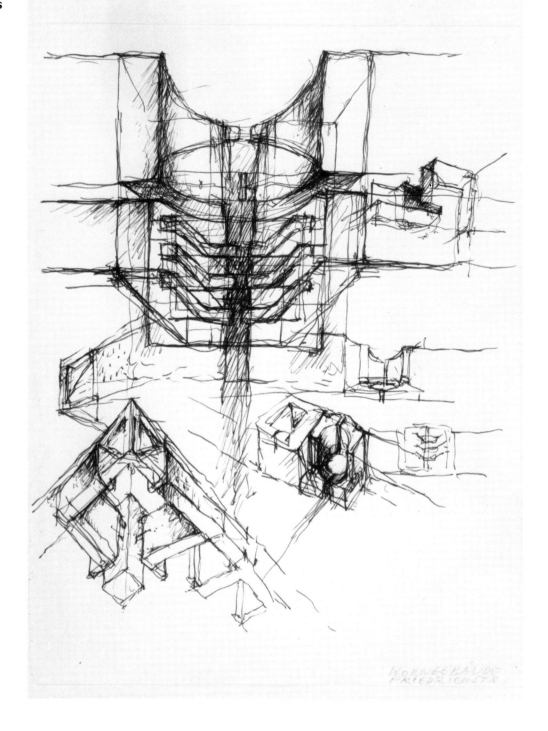

295
Courtyard elevation, scale 1:100
Pencil and crayon on paper
45 x 60 cm

296
Sectional view, scale 1:100
Pencil and crayon on paper
45 x 60 cm

297
Friedrichstrasse elevation, scale 1:100
Pencil and crayon on paper
45 x 60 cm

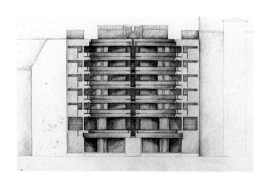
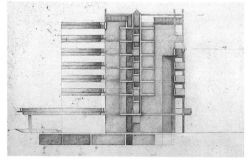
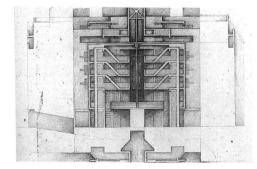

**Residential Development, Studio
Tower, Musician and Painter
Block 11
Planning since 1982**

John Hejduk, New York

From the sketchbook

298 + 299
Design sketches for residential
development and studio tower
Photocopies, drawings and postcard

300
Sketch for Musician
Photocopy

301 + 302
Sketches for Painter
Photocopies

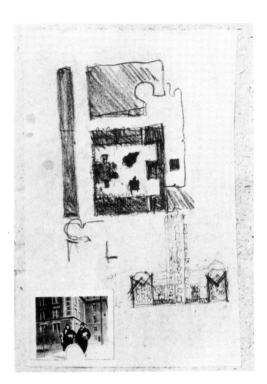

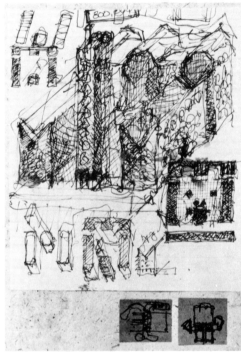

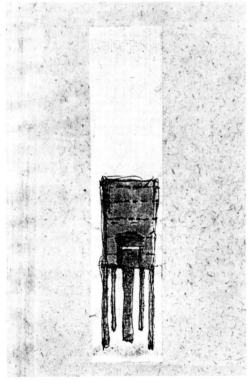

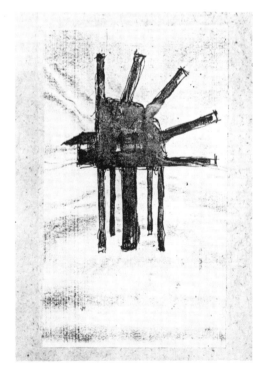

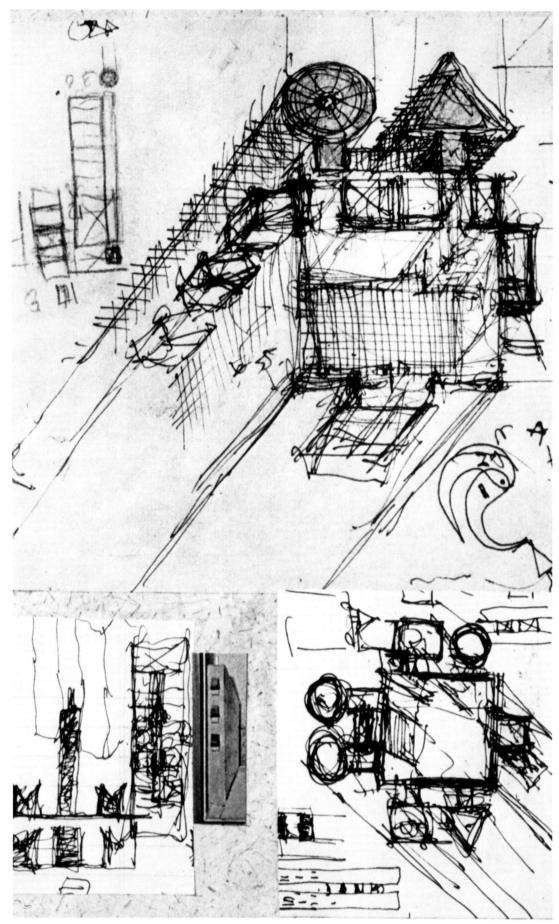

303
Sketches of three projects
Ground plans and elevations, superimposed in parts, sepia print
123.8 x 92.9 cm

From the sketchbook

304
Sketches for studio tower
Photocopies and drawing

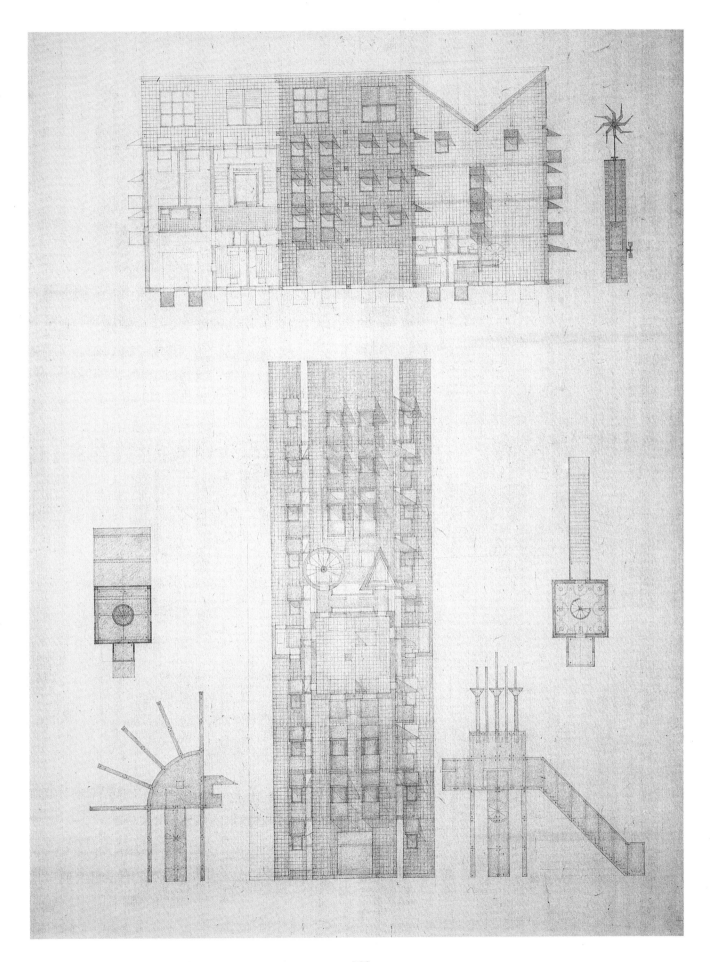

189

**Competitive Planning Survey,
Friedrichstrasse 38/39, Charlotten-
strasse 87–89, 1986
Block 11**

**Klaus Theo Brenner
Benedict Tonon, Berlin**

with Norbert Hemprich, Ulrich Pantzke

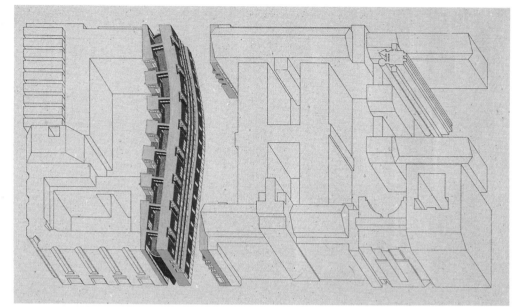

305a
Axonometric drawing, scale 1:500
Chalk on Xerox copy on brown paper
92 x 40 cm

305b
Perspective
Chalk on Xerox copy on brown paper
10.7 x 16.2 cm (detail)

**Competitive Planning Survey,
Friedrichstrasse 38/39, Charlotten-
strasse 87–89, 1986
Block 11**

**Ante Josip von Kostelac,
Seeheim-Malchen**

with Hans Bezzenberger, Kay Wilisch

307
Site plan, scale 1 : 500
Perspectives
Xerox copy and colour crayon
80 x 80 cm

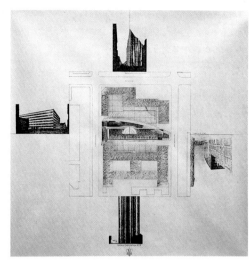

308
Friedrichstrasse elevation, courtyard elevation, scale 1 : 200
Xerox copy and colour crayon
80 x 80 cm

306
Axonometric representation of the
structural elements, scale 1 : 500
Xerox copy and colour crayon
80 x 80 cm

309
Parking house elevation,
Charlottenstrasse elevation, scale 1 : 200
Xerox copy and colour crayon
80 x 80 cm

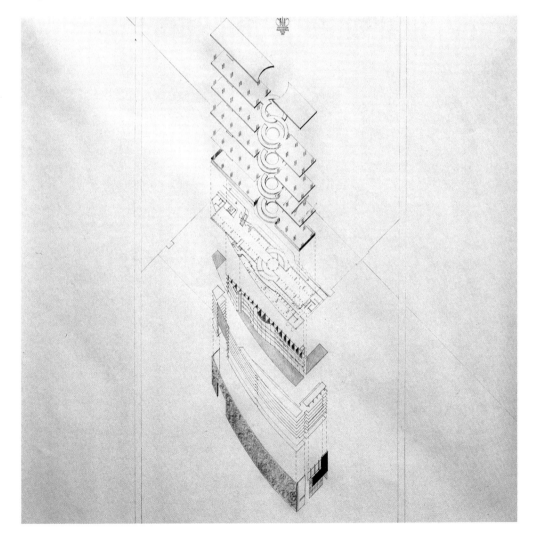

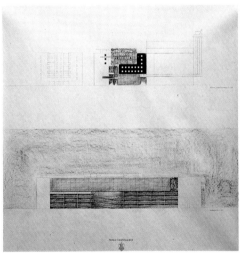

Residential Development by
Felix Mendelssohn-Bartholdy Park,
Block 7
Preliminary Design 1985

Georg Kohlmaier
Barna von Sartory, Berlin

310
Perspective
Pencil, India ink and crayon on cardboard
45 x 62.6 cm
Inscribed on reverse: 1985
Façade towards Felix-Mendelsohn-
Bartholdi-Park

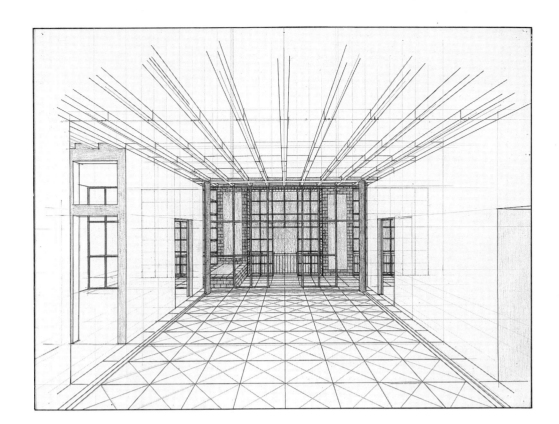

311
Interior perspective
Pencil, ink and crayon on cardboard
30 x 40 cm
Inscribed on reverse: 1985
View towards winter-garden
Living in factory building

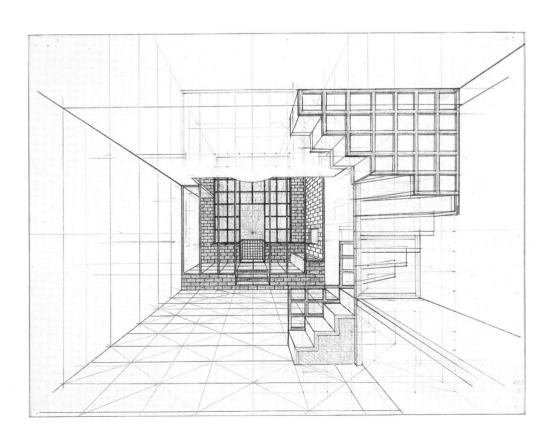

312
Interior perspective
Pencil, India ink and crayon
on cardboard
29.8 x 39.9 cm
Inscribed on reverse: 1985
View of the winter-garden
(maisonette, 3 room flat)
Wohnen im Fabrikbau

**Apartment House Schöneberger
Strasse 8
Apartment House Dessauer Strasse 22**

**Apartment House Dessauer Strasse 26
Block 7
Planning 1984–86**

**Johanne Nalbach
Gernot Nalbach, Berlin**

313
Dessauer Strasse elevation
Coloured photocopy
21 x 29.7 cm

314
Plan sketch, scale 1:200
Pencil and crayon on transparent paper
33 x 53 cm

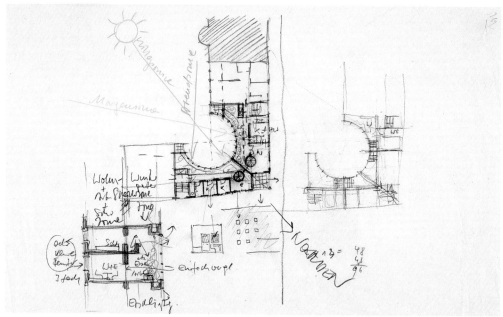

315
Schönberger Strasse elevation
Coloured photocopy
21 x 29.7 cm

316
Plan study, scale 1:100
Pencil and crayon on transparent paper
33.2 x 46.4 cm

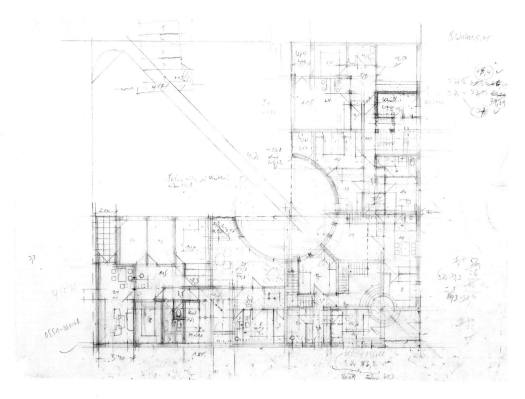

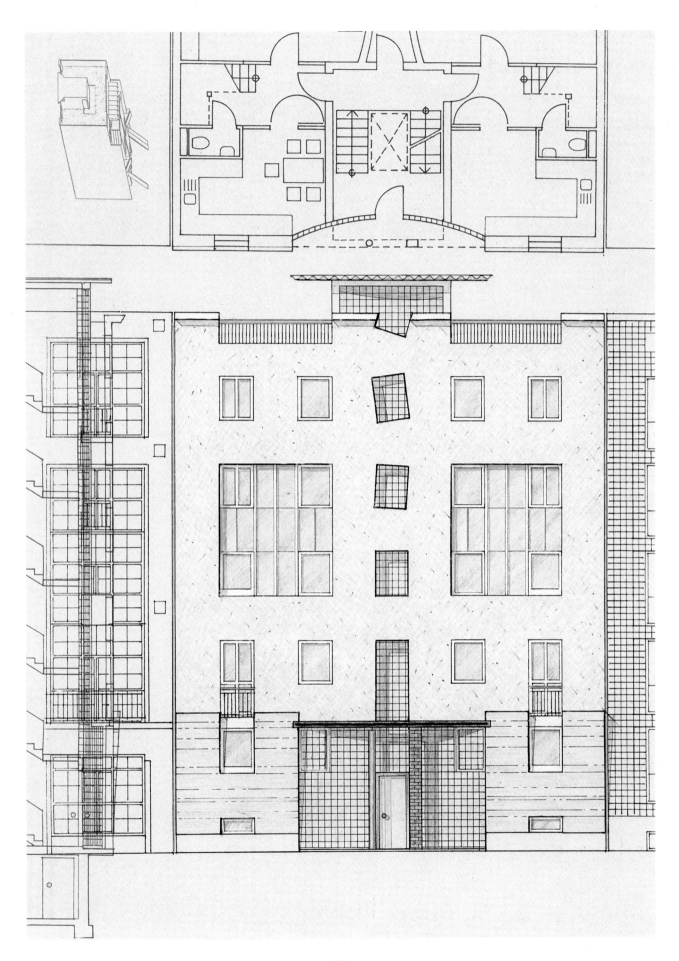

195

**Residential Development
Schöneberger Strasse 10–12
Apartment House Dessauer Strasse 23
Block 7
Planning since 1985**

**Haus-Rucker-Co., Düsseldorf
Günter Zamp Kelp
Laurids Ortner
Manfred Ortner**

with Grzegorz Rybacki

318
Perspective
Schöneberger Strasse elevation
Photocopy on paper, coloured
72.7 x 101.6 cm

PERSPEKTIVE   HAUS - RUCKER - CO   IBA BERLIN 1987

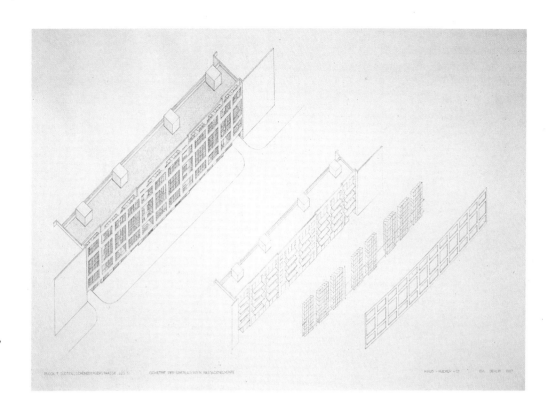

319
Axonometric drawing of façade elements,
scale 1 : 200
Pencil and crayon on drawing board
73 x 102 cm

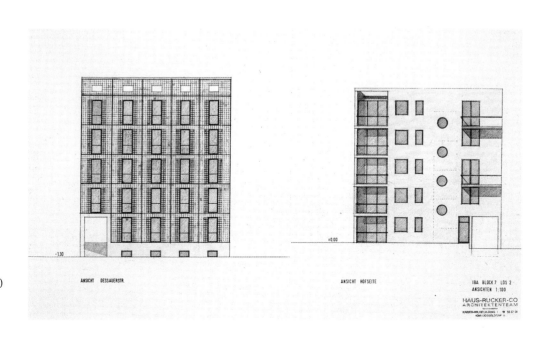

320
Left: Dessauer Strasse elevation
Right: courtyard side elevation, scale 1 : 100
Coloured Photocopy
30 x 50.8 cm

**House by the Fire Wall
Schöneberger Strasse 5
Block 7, House 7
Planning 1985/86**

Josef Paul Kleihues, Berlin

with Stephan Gallant, Sabine Häcker,
Thomas Müller, Ulrike Schröder

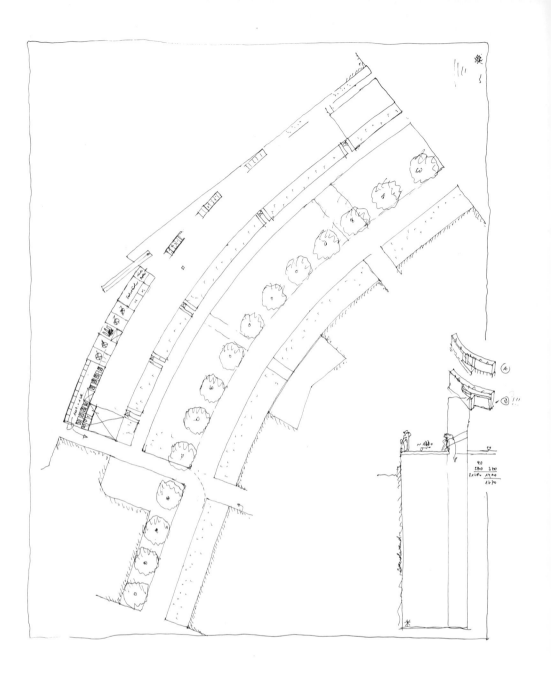

321
Sketch, ground floor plan
with open spaces
Felt pen on yellow tracing paper
81.5 x 65.7 cm

322
Site plan, scale 1 : 2000
Taken from official site plan
Black and red ink on paper
20.5 x 20.5 cm

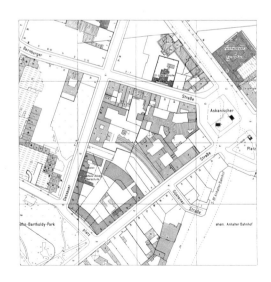

323
Elevation (part), scale 1 : 50
Pencil, ink and crayon
on brown paper
80 x 69.7 cm

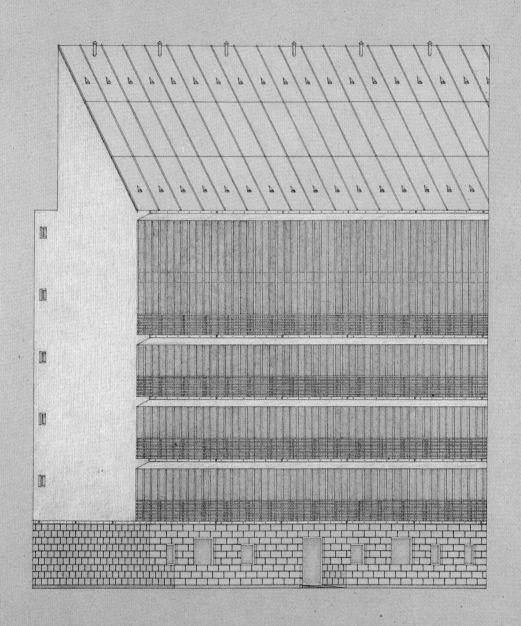

**International Competition for Ideas
in Urbanism "Living in Friedrichstadt",
1980, Block 33**

**One of the First Prizes
Gerald Brunner
Franz Rendl
Reinhard Hörl
Walter Kirchmayr
Georg Driendl, Vienna**

324
Axonometric drawing with shadows,
scale 1 : 500
Coloured blueprint
66.4 x 66.6 cm

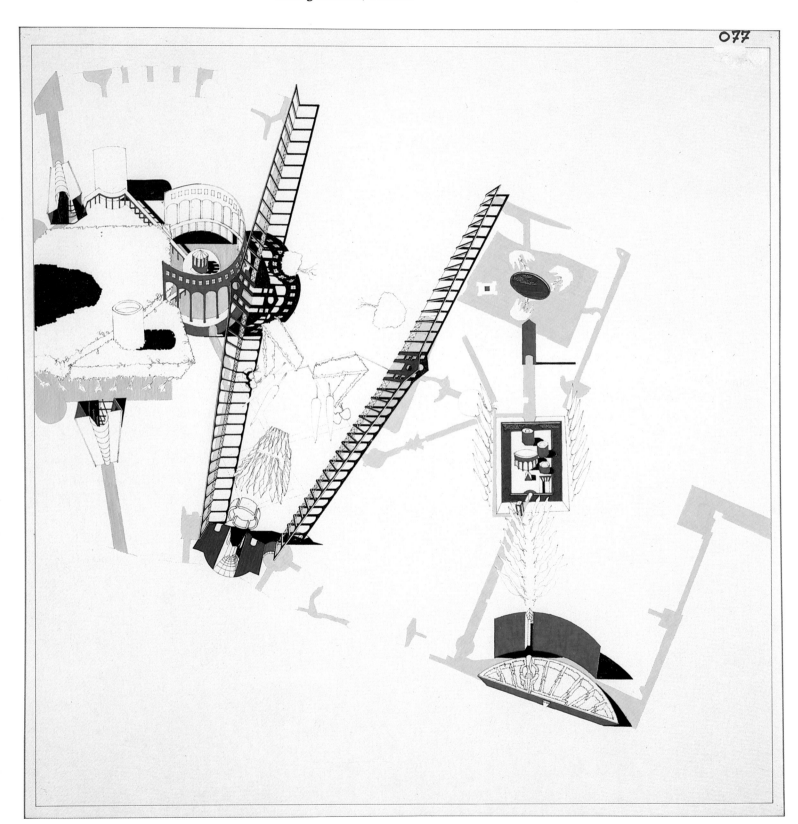

**International Competition for Ideas
in Urbanism "Living in Friedrichstadt",
1980, Block 33**

**One of the First Prizes
Hans Kollhoff, Berlin**

with Matthias Karch

325
Axonometric section drawing with plan,
scale 1 : 200
Pencil and crayon on transparent paper
34.5 x 33.8 cm

326
Axonometric drawing of the overall area
Photocopy, coloured (crayon)
66.6 x 66.8 cm

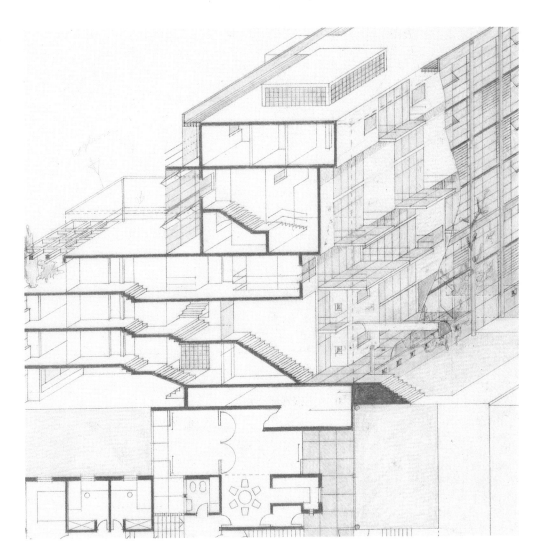

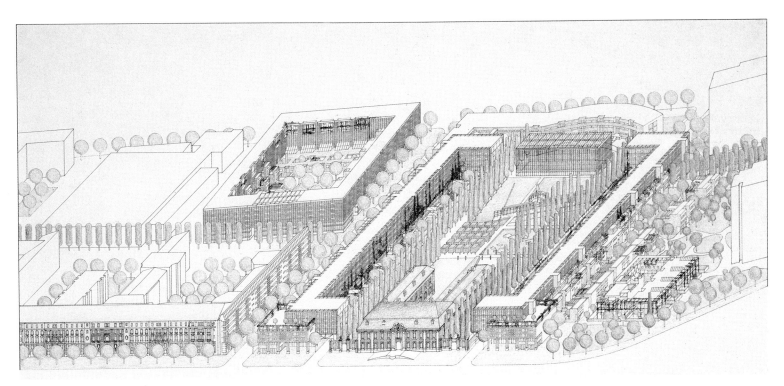

**"Living near the Berlin Museum",
House F, Block 33
Planning 1982–84
Completed 1986**

**Hans Kollhoff
Arthur Ovaska, Berlin**

with Almut Geier

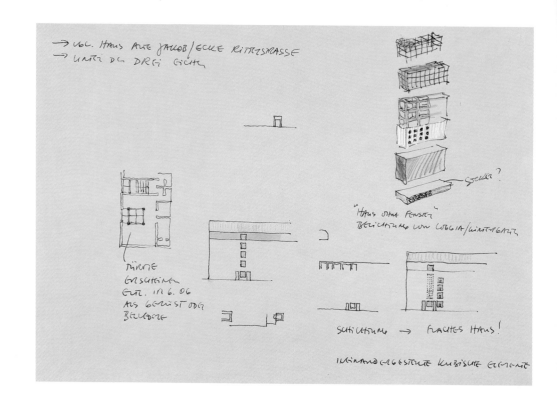

327
Sketch of the horizontal structure
India ink and crayon on yellow
tracing paper
32 x 45.4 cm

328
Plan and façade study
Pencil and crayon on yellow
tracing paper
45.5 x 95.6 cm

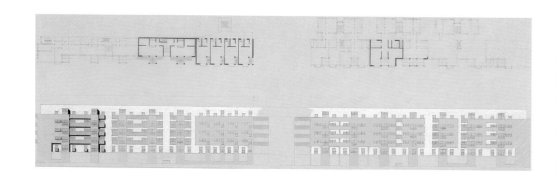

329
Façade sketch, scale 1 : 200
India ink and crayon on paper
40.5 x 97.8 cm

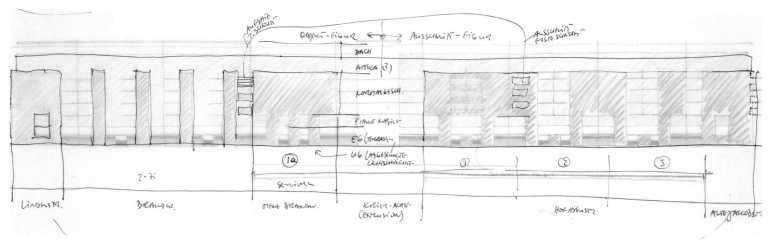

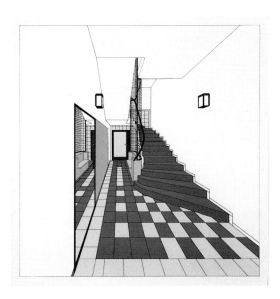

330
Interior perspective
House F 1 entrance
Foil on contrast
copy
36 x 35.8 cm

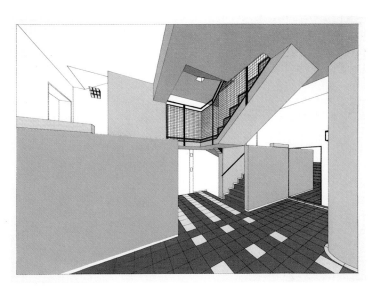

331
Interior perspective
Houses F 2, 3
entrance
Foil on contrast
paper
36 x 48.3 cm

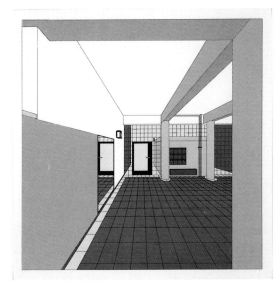

332
Interior perspective
Houses F 6, 7, 8
entrance
View toward
private road
Foil on contrast
copy
36 x 36.1 cm

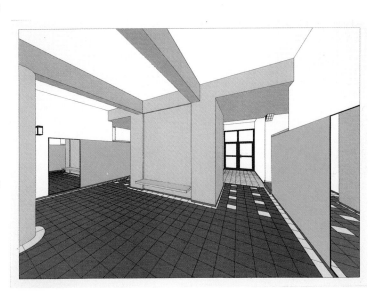

333
Interior perspective
Houses F 6, 7, 8
entrance
View of courtyard
Foil on contrast
paper
36 x 48.2 cm

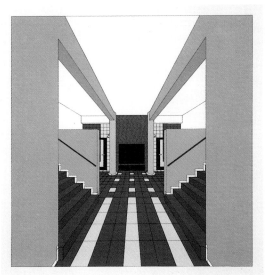

334
Interior perspective
House F 4 entrance
View toward
private road
Foil on contrast
paper
37.8 x 37.9 cm

335
Interior perspective
House F 4 entrance
View of courtyard
Foil on contrast
copy
36 x 48.5 cm

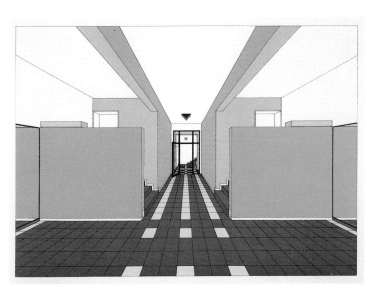

336
Entrance lighting fixture with house number
Detail plan, scale 1:5 and 1:2
Pencil on transparent paper
38 x 98.1 cm
Signed: 24.6.85 gez. AL

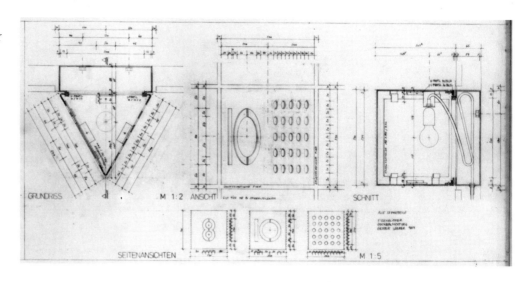

337
Passage from the private road to
the interior courtyard
Detail plan, column axes 22, scale 1:10
Pencil on transparent paper
87.7 x 158.8 cm
Signed: 8.11.84 AR/GE/MN

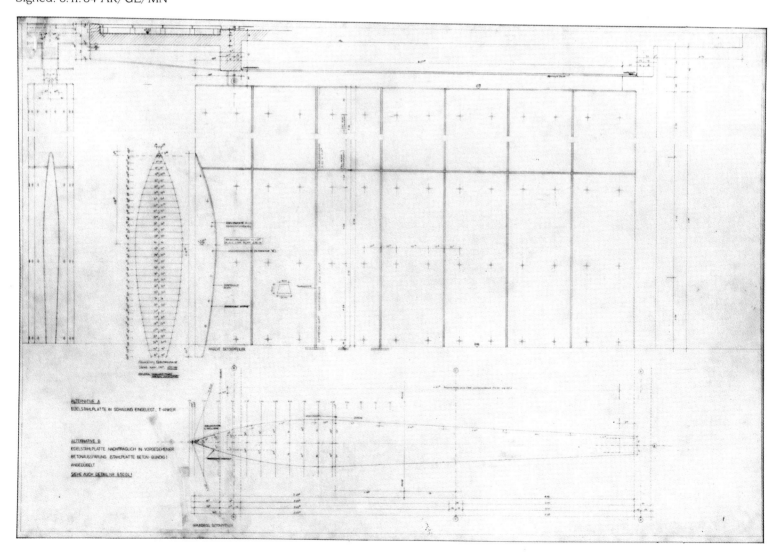

**Garden by the Berlin Museum,
Block 33
Planning since 1981**

**Hans Kollhoff
Arthur Ovaska, Berlin**

with Almut Geier

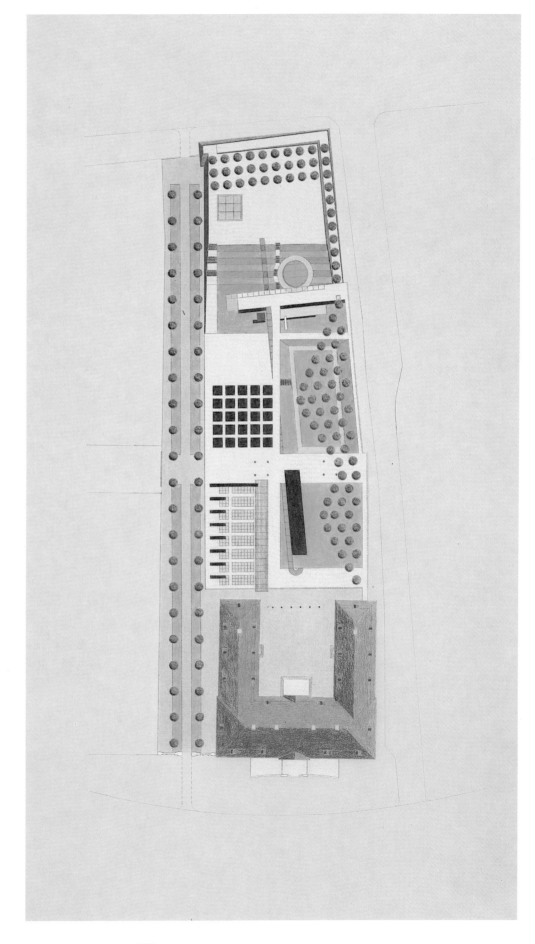

338
Site plan, scale 1 : 500
Pencil and crayon on yellow
tracing paper
40 x 64.8 cm

**"Living near the Berlin Museum",
House J, Block 33
Planning 1982–84
Completed 1986**

**Dieter Frowein
Gerhard Spangenberg, Berlin**

with Brigitte Steinkilberg, Bodo von Essen

339
Houses 4 and 5
Alte Jacobstrasse elevation
Project plan, scale 1 : 50
India ink on transparent paper
65.3 x 127.2 cm
Dated: 20.1.85

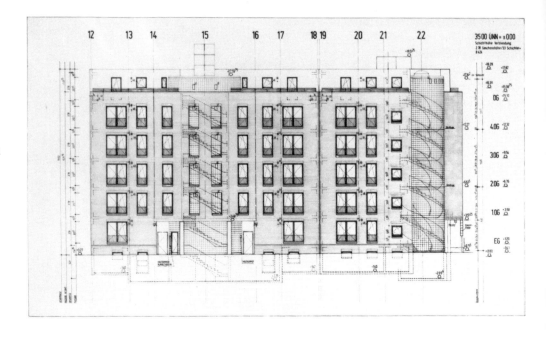

340
House 5
Detail plan of the stairwell,
ground floor plan, scale 1 : 10
India ink on transparent paper
90.7 x 123.8 cm
Dated: 19.11.84

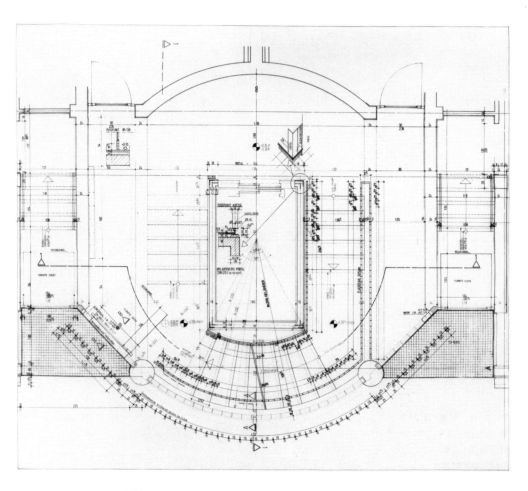

**"Living near the Berlin Museum",
House A, Block 33
Planning 1982–84
Completed 1985**

**Werner Kreis
Ulrich Schaad
Peter Schaad, London/Zürich**

with Mike Gallagher

341
Capriccio
Crayon on transparent paper
24.6 x 22.5 cm

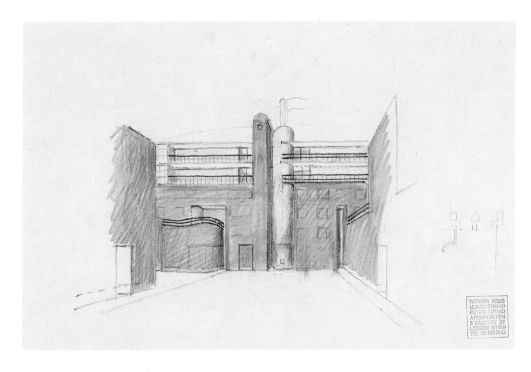

342
Study of courtyard
Pencil and crayon on yellow
tracing paper
23.2 x 35.6 cm

343
Façade study
Lindenstrasse elevation, scale 1 : 100
Pencil, felt pen and crayon
on transparent paper
32.9 x 63.8 cm

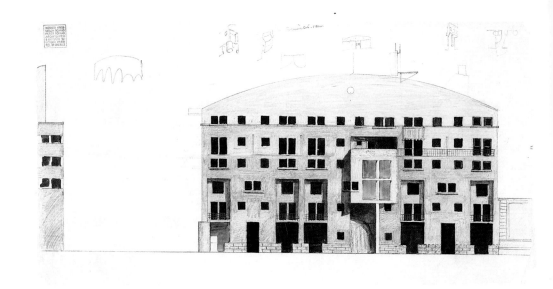

344
Lindenstrasse elevation, scale 1 : 100
Coloured blueprint
31.8 x 43.9 cm

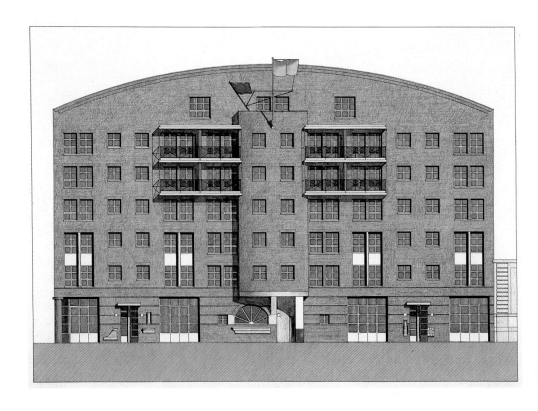

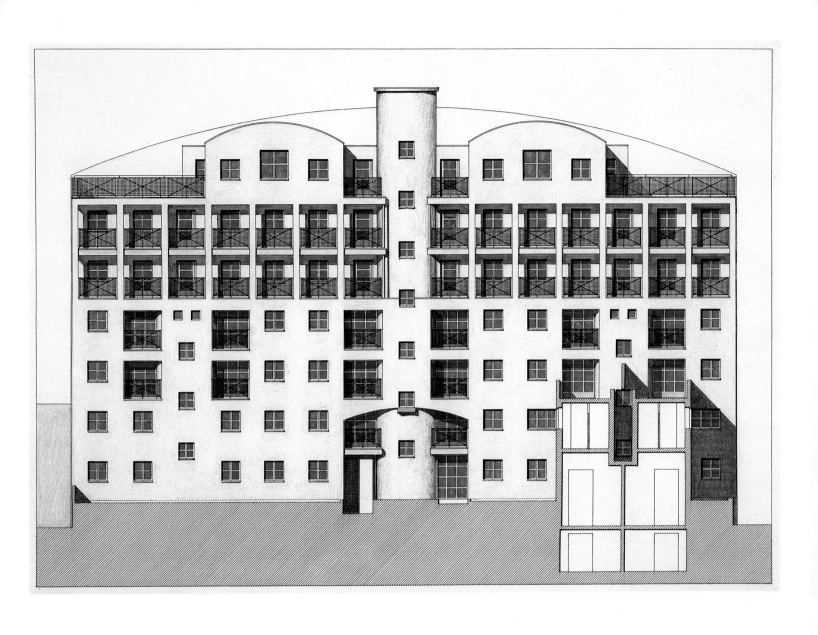

345
Courtyard façade with section of
connecting building to house B1
Coloured blueprint
31.7 x 44.1 cm

**"Living near the Berlin Museum",
House G, Block 33
Planning 1982–84
Completed 1986**

**Arata Isozaki & Associates, Tokyo
Arata Isozaki
Eisaku Ushida
Hans Karil**

347
Axonometric elevation of the Schmuckhof
of the former Victoria Insurance building,
scale 1:100
India ink and crayon on transparent paper
84.4 x 68.2 cm

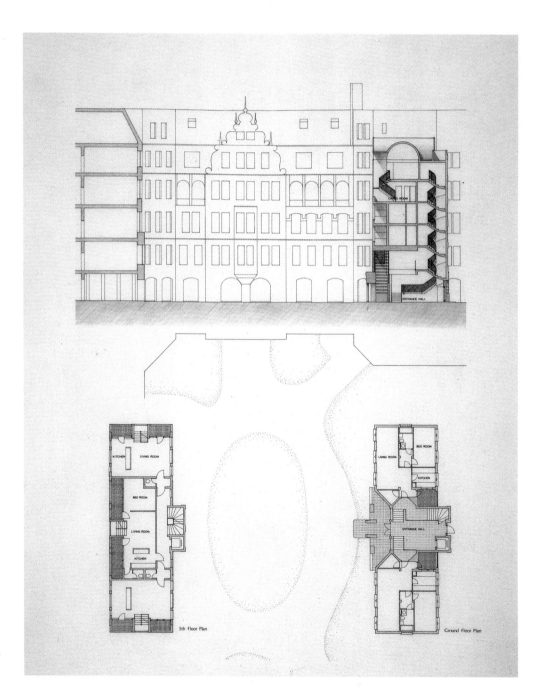

346
Cross section with elevation of the former
Victoria Insurance building
Plan of ground and fifth floors,
scale 1:100
India ink and crayon on transparent paper
84.2 x 68.2 cm

HAUS 2 im BLOCK 4

211

**"Living near the Berlin Museum",
House E, Block 33
Planning 1982–84
Completed 1985**

**Stavoprojekt Liberec, ČSSR
John Eisler
Emil Přikryl
Jiri Suchomel**

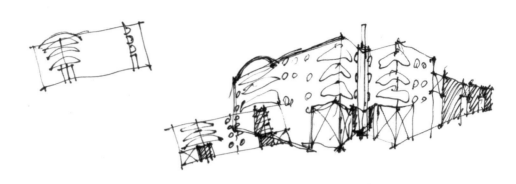

348
Sketch of the corner Alte Jacobstrasse/
private road
Felt pen on transparent paper
13.7 x 28 cm
Signed: Suchomel

349
East elevation, scale 1:100
India ink and foil on transparent paper
33.3 x 83.5 cm
Signed: Prelim. drawing 1.2.1983

350
South elevation, scale 1:100
India ink and foil on transparent paper
33.2 x 83.5 cm
Dated: 1.2.1983

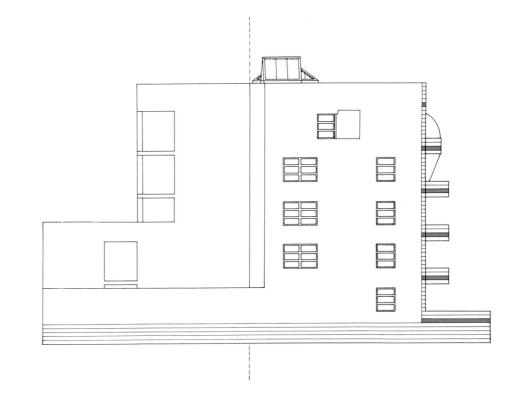

351
North elevation, scale 1:100
India ink and foil on transparent paper
33.4 x 83.4 cm
Signed: Prelim. drawing 1.2.1983

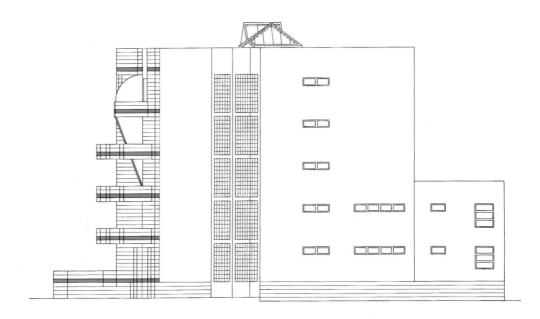

**Residential Court by Jerusalem and
New Church, Corner of Lindenstrasse
and Markgrafenstrasse, Block 30
Planning 1982–84
Completed 1986**

Herman Hertzberger, Amsterdam

with Henk de Weijer

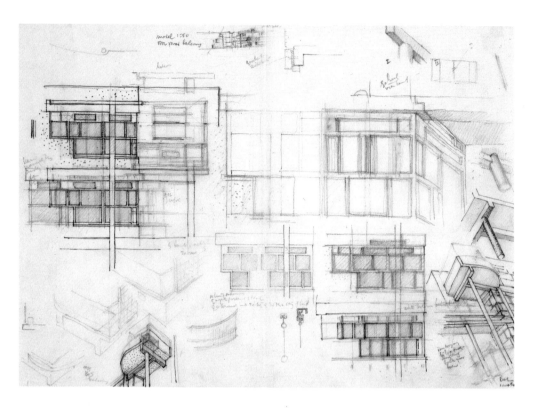

352
Sketches
Pencil, pen and crayon
on transparent paper
29.7 x 41.8 cm
Signed: Bel . . (?) 84

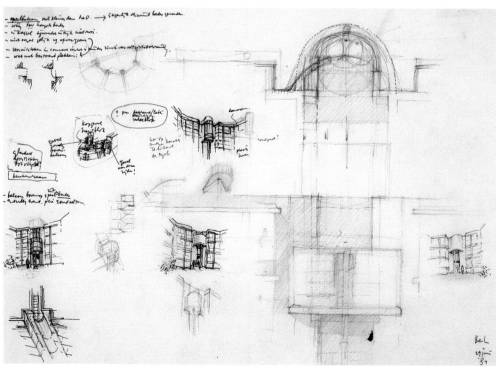

353
Sketches
Pencil, felt pen and crayon
on transparent paper
29.7 x 41.8 cm
Signed: Bel 29. Juni 84

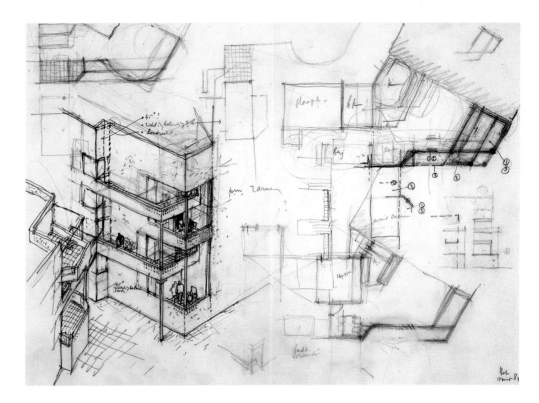

354
Sketches
Felt pen and pencil on transparent paper
29.7 x 41.8 cm
Signed: Bel 17. März 84

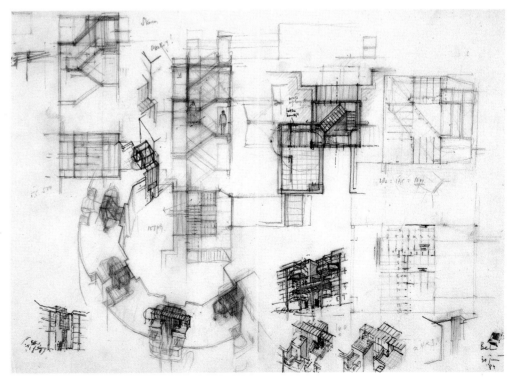

355
Sketches
Pencil, crayon, felt pen
on transparent paper
29.7 x 47.8 cm
Signed: Bel 30. Juni 86

Restricted International Competition
Wilhelmstrasse, 1981
Block 9

First Prize
Grupo 2 C:
Salvador Tarragó Cid
Juan Carlos Theilacker-Pons
Antonio Armesto Aira
Yago Bonet Correa
Juan Francisco Chico Contijoch
Antonio Ferrer Vega
Carlos Marti Aris
Santiago Padrès Creixell
Santiago Vela Parès, Barcelona

356
Perspective
View over Wilhelmstrasse
Photographic reproduction
45.6 x 51.3 cm

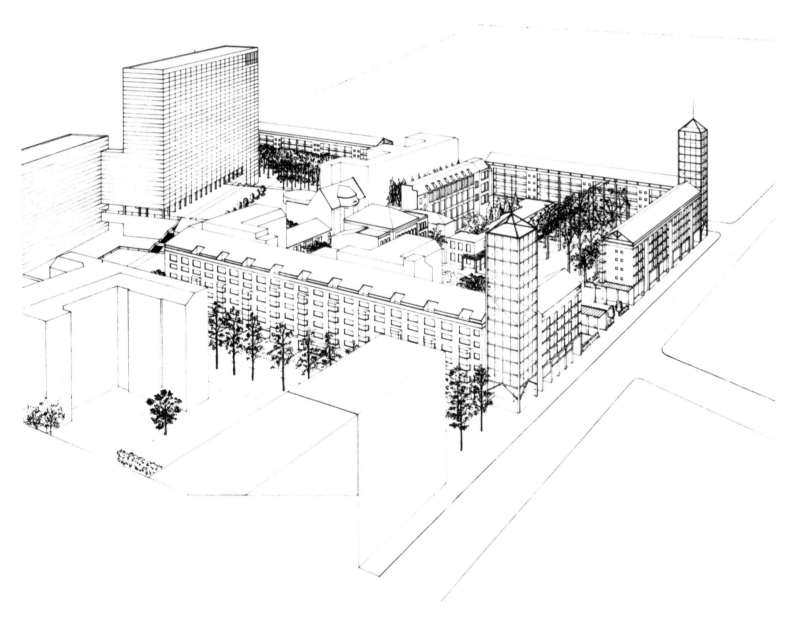

Apartment House, Corner of Wilhelm-strasse and Anhalter Strasse, Block 9
Planning since 1982
Under construction since 1986

Salvador Tarragó Cid
Juan Carlos Theilacker-Pons,
Barcelona
Helga Ruoff
Rainer Döring, Berlin

357
Axonometric drawing, scale 1:50
India ink and red ink on transparent paper
135.8 x 86.8 cm

**Highrise Apartments,
Wilhelmstrasse 119, Block 9
Planning 1986**

Pietro Derossi, Turin

with Silvanas Caffaro Rore, Franco Lattes,
Francesco di Suni, Antonio Besso
Marcheis

359
Elevations, scale 1 : 200 (reduction,
original scale 1 : 100)
Coloured crayon on transparent copy
35.8 x 26.8 cm
Dated: 17. 3. 85

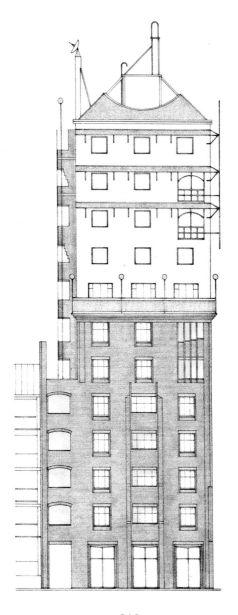

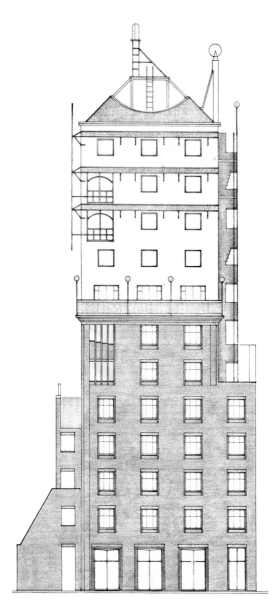

358
Elevations, scale 1 : 200 (reduced from
scale 1 : 100)
Coloured crayon on transparent copy
35.7 x 26.9 cm
Dated: 17. 3. 85

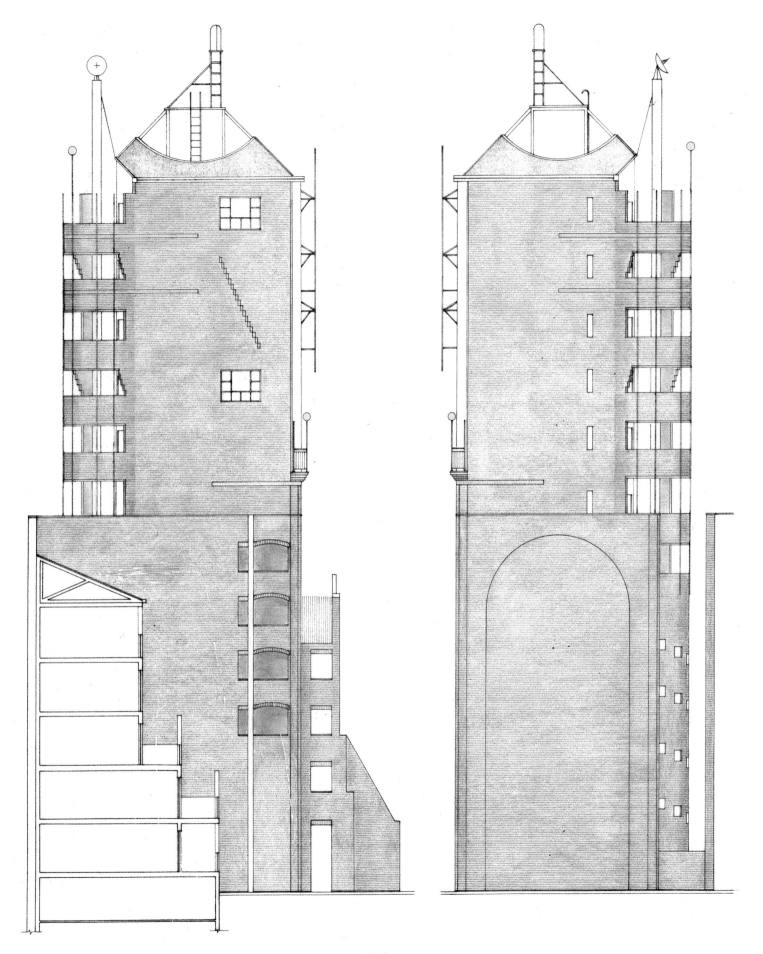

**Restricted International Competition
Wilhelmstrasse, 1981
Blocks 19, 20**

**Special Prize
John Hejduk**, New York

with Gregory Palestri

362
Site plan with Berlin Masque added
Sepia print, coloured in with crayon
117.5 x 108 cm

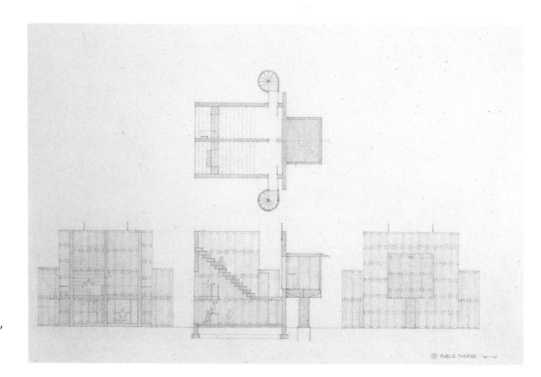

360
No. 10 Public Theater, scale 3/16″ = 1′–0″
Pencil and crayon on transparent paper
92 x 96 cm

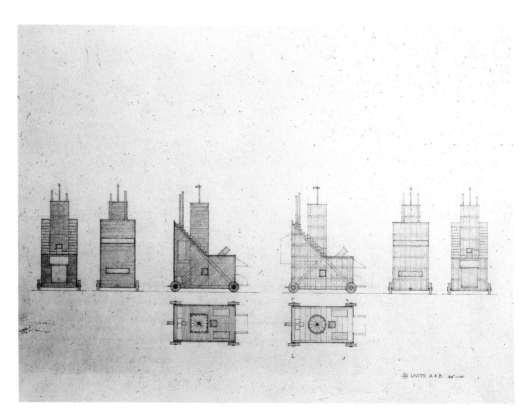

361
No. 26 Units A + B, 3/16″ = 1′–0″
Pencil and crayon on transparent paper
92 x 94 cm

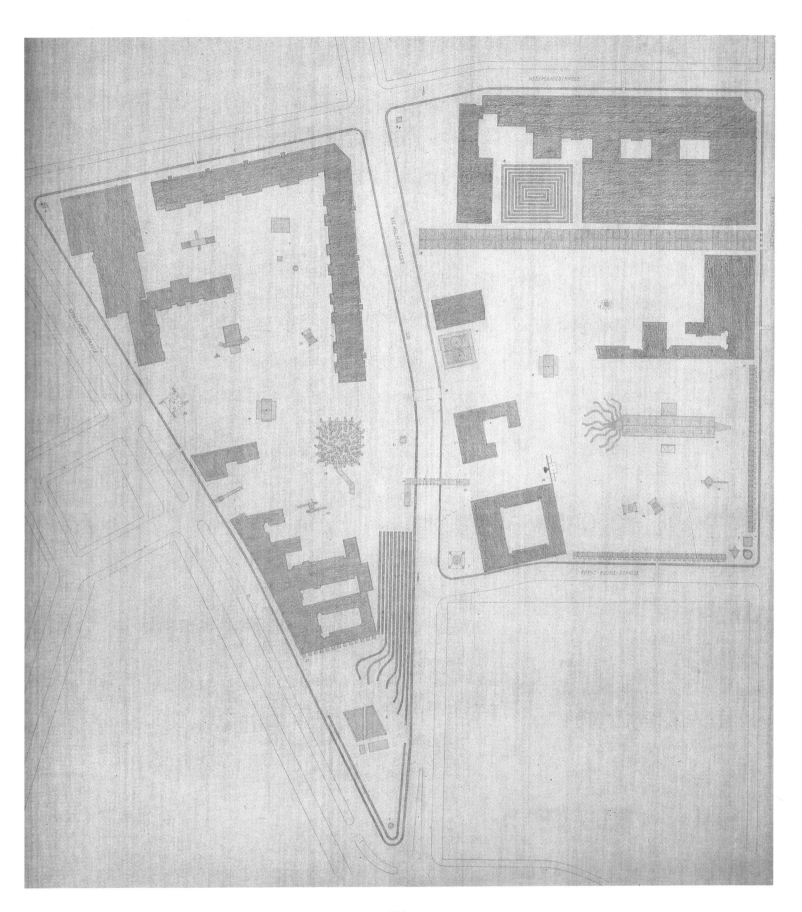

363
No. 15. Masque, cross section 3/16" =
1'–0"
Pencil and crayon on transparent paper
77 x 179 cm

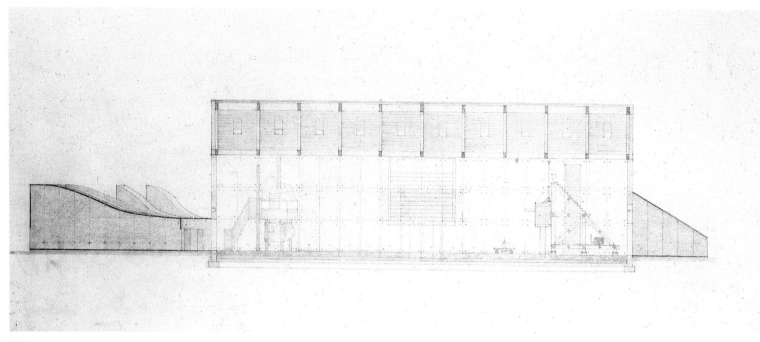

364
No. 15 Masque plan, 3/16" = 1'–0"
Pencil and crayon on transparent paper
77 x 179 cm

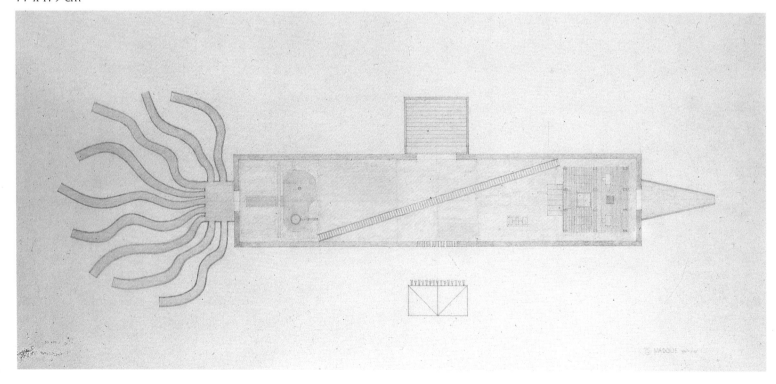

(T) GUEST TOWERS
(TT) SHOPPING BOOTHS

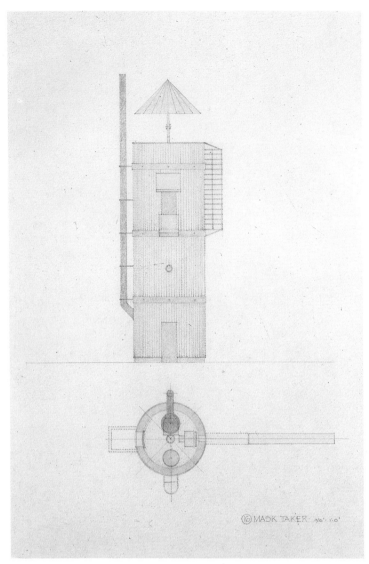

366
No. 16 Mask Taker, 3/16″ = 1′–0″
Pencil and crayon on transparent paper 90 x 77 cm

367
No. 5 Water Tower, 3/16″ = 1′–0″
Pencil and crayon on transparent paper, 104 x 93 cm

368
No. 22 House for the eldest, 3/16″ = 1′–0″
Pencil and crayon on transparent paper, 92 x 92 cm

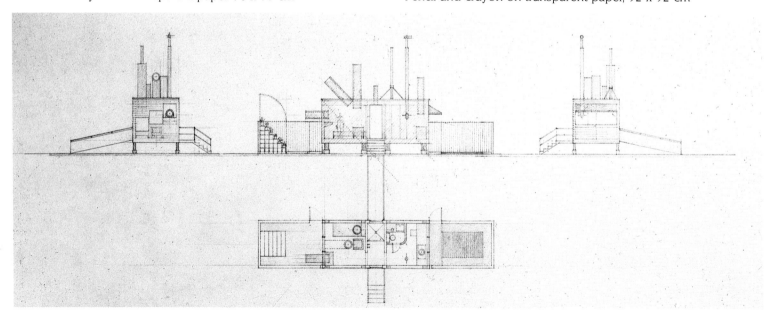

Clock House (Gatehouse)
Friedrichstrasse 234, Block 20
Planning since 1982

John Hejduk, New York

From the sketchbook

369
Façade sketches
Photocopy

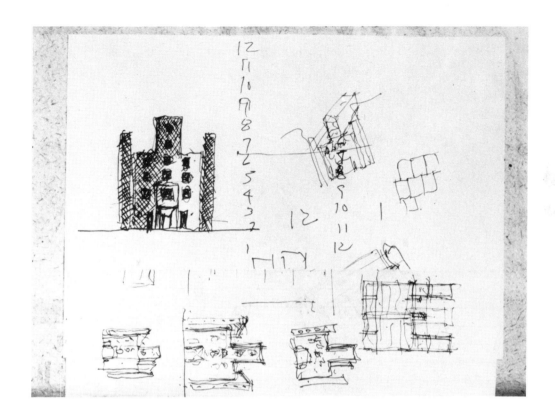

370
Friedrichstrasse elevation
Photocopy
77.2 x 62.4 cm

**Restricted International Competition
Wilhelmstrasse, 1981
Block 20**

**Second Prize
Hansjürg Zeitler
Helmut Bier
Hans Korn, Munich**

with Ute Dolle, Christoph Gatz, Sabine Pfaff,
Hossein Ghasseminejad-Raini, Michaela
Steiner, Pavel Zverina

371
Perspective of block 20
View from interior courtyard towards
the fringe development, plan superimposed
105 x 120 cm

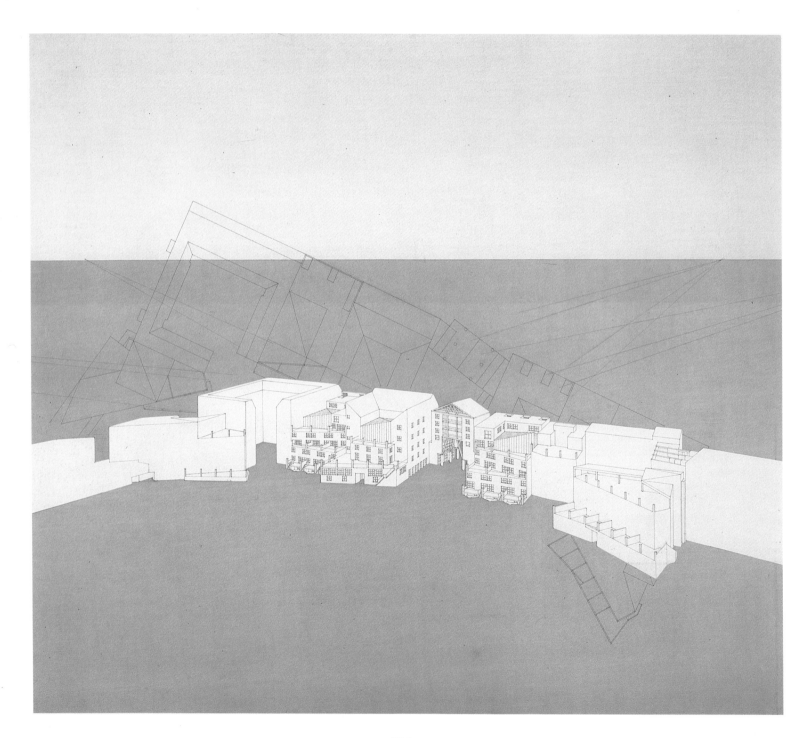

**Gatehouse Court, Wilhelmstrasse 13–14,
Block 20
Planning since 1985**

**Hansjürg Zeitler
Helmut Bier
Hans Korn**, Munich

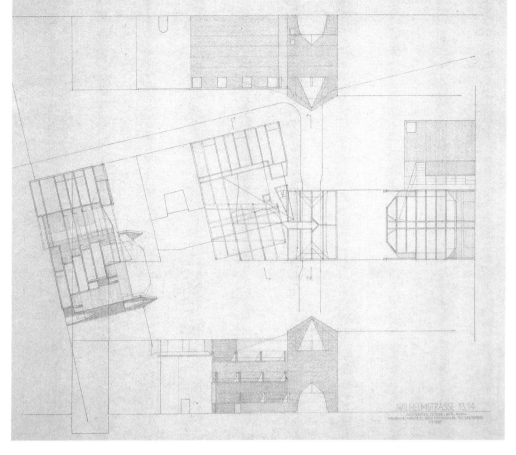

372
Ground floor plan, elevations and sections
from the courtyard and gateway houses,
schematic and superimposed, scale 1:200
Crayon on photocopy
66.7 x 76.1 cm
Dated: 1.9.85

373
Schematic axonometric drawing of the
courtyard buildings with gateway house in
the context of the neighbouring houses
Elevation from the interior courtyard,
scale 1:200
Coloured blueprint
66.6 x 75.9 cm
Dated: 1.9.85

374
South view through the glass-roofed hall of
the courtyard house
Pencil on transparent paper
90 x 89 cm

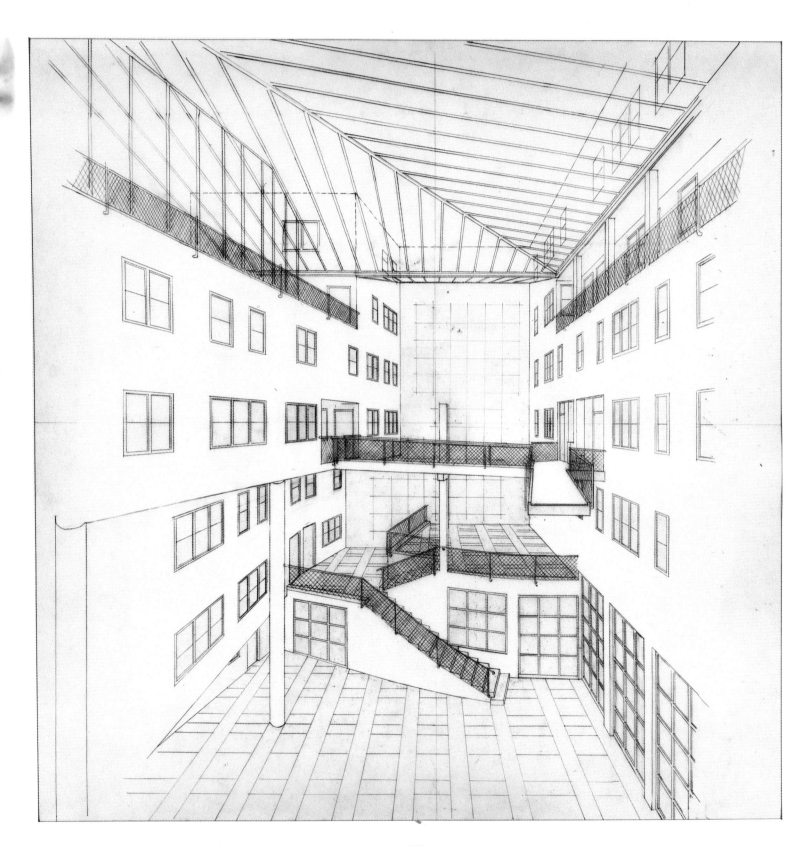

375
Perspective
North view through the glass-roofed hall
of the courtyard house
Pencil on transparent paper
90 x 89 cm

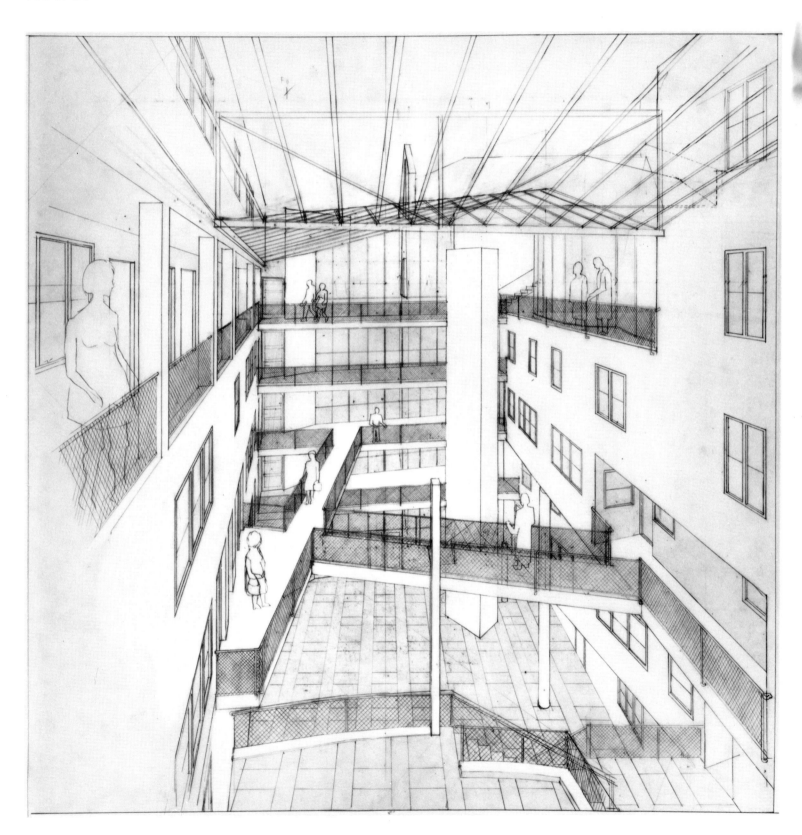

Restricted International Competition Design for an Elementary and Special School in urbanistic context with wholesale flower market and planned Bessel Park, 1983
Block 606

Gino Valle
Mario Broggi
Michael Burckhardt, Milan/Udine

with Marcella Rossin, Andrea Nulli,
Vincenzo Di Dato
(recommended for further consideration)

376
Site plan, scale 1:500
Coloured blueprint
146.3 x 98 cm

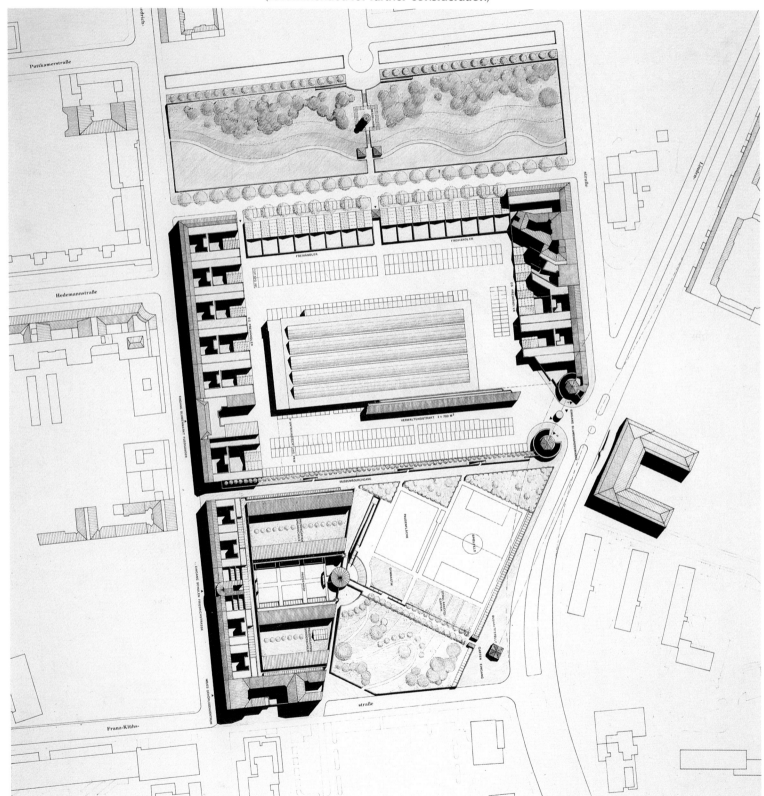

230

Elementary and Special School in urbanistic context with wholesale flower market and planned Bessel Park, Friedrichstrasse 13, Block 606 Planning since 1983

Gino Valle
Mario Broggi
Michael Burckhardt, Milan/Udine

with Renata Murnaghan, Andrea Nulli

377
Lindenstrasse perspective
Coloured blueprint
25 x 40.7 cm

379
Sectional elevations towards west, north and south, and Friedrichstrasse elevation, scale 1:200
Coloured blueprint
60 x 73.6 cm

378
Friedrichstrasse perspective
Coloured blueprint
38.2 x 23.7 cm

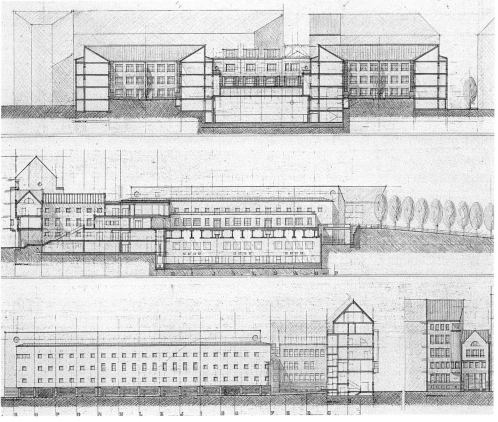

**Centre for the Deaf, Friedrichstrasse 10,
Block 606
Planning since 1984**

Douglas Clelland, London

with Peter Wilson, Mark Dudek,
Lillina Tirone

380
Friedrichstrasse elevation, scale 1:100
Coloured photocopy on yellow paper
36.5 x 36.5 cm
Signed: 2/84, sign. Clelland

381
Courtyard elevation, scale 1:100
Coloured photocopy on green paper
36.5 x 36.5 cm
Signed: 2/83 Clelland

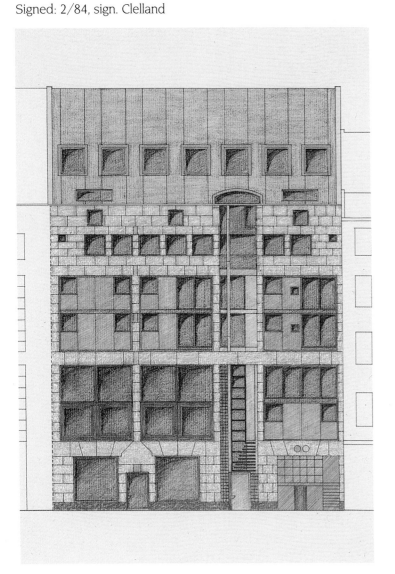

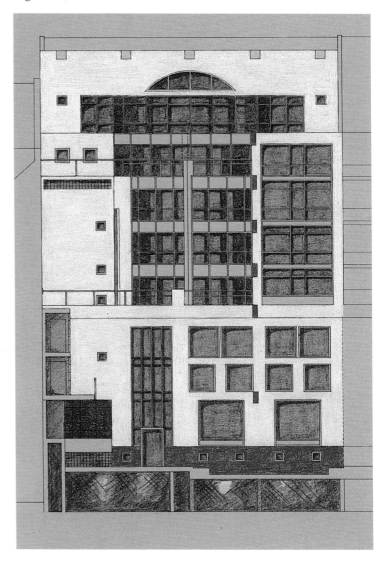

382
Section, scale 1:100
Coloured photocopy on yellow paper
36.5 x 36.5 cm
Dated: 2/84, sign. Clelland

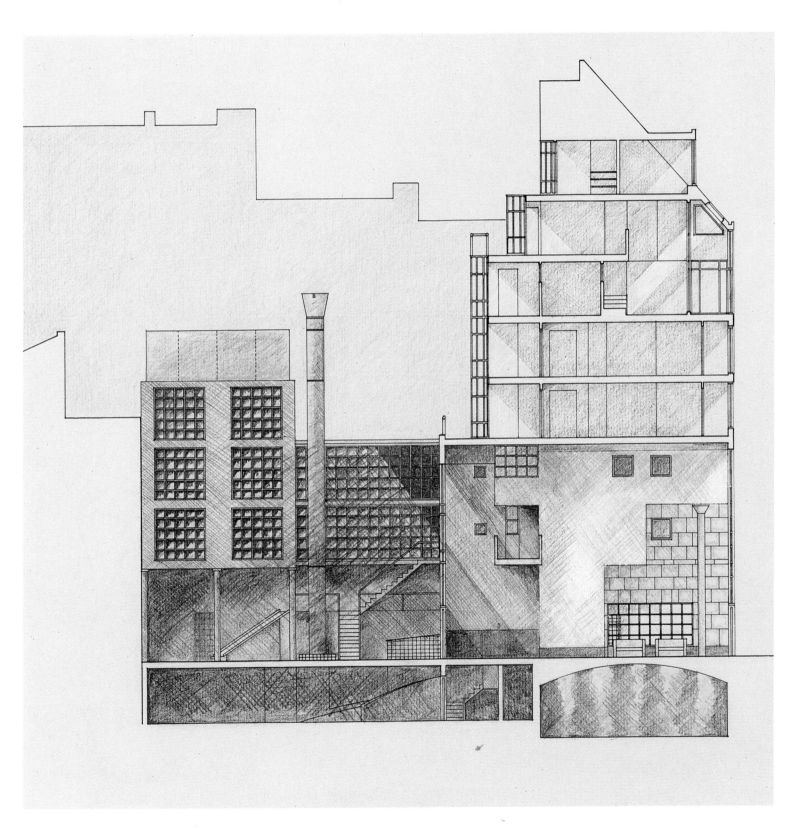

**Residential and Commercial Premises
with Facilities of Cultural and Recreational Centre for the Deaf
Friedrichstrasse 11, Block 606
Planning since 1984**

**Mario Maedebach
Werner Redeleit, Berlin**

383
Street elevation, scale 1:100
Photocopy on kraft paper, coloured
32.3 x 24.4 cm

384
Courtyard elevation, scale 1:100
Photocopy on kraft paper, coloured
31.6 x 24.6 cm

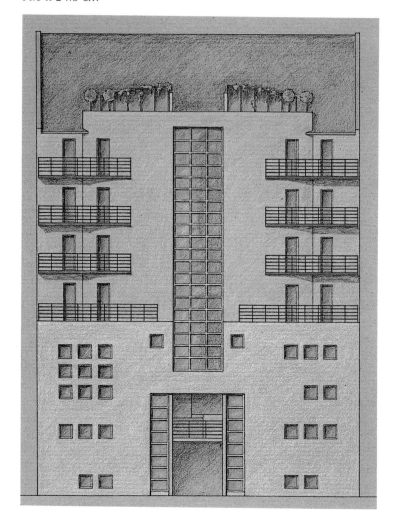

234

**Restricted Landscaping
Competition
Block 20 and Block 606
"Bessel Park", 1985**

**Jasper Halfmann
Klauss Zillich, Berlin**

with Dixon W. Strauss, Josef Metzler
Garden landscaping consultant:
Renate Liefke

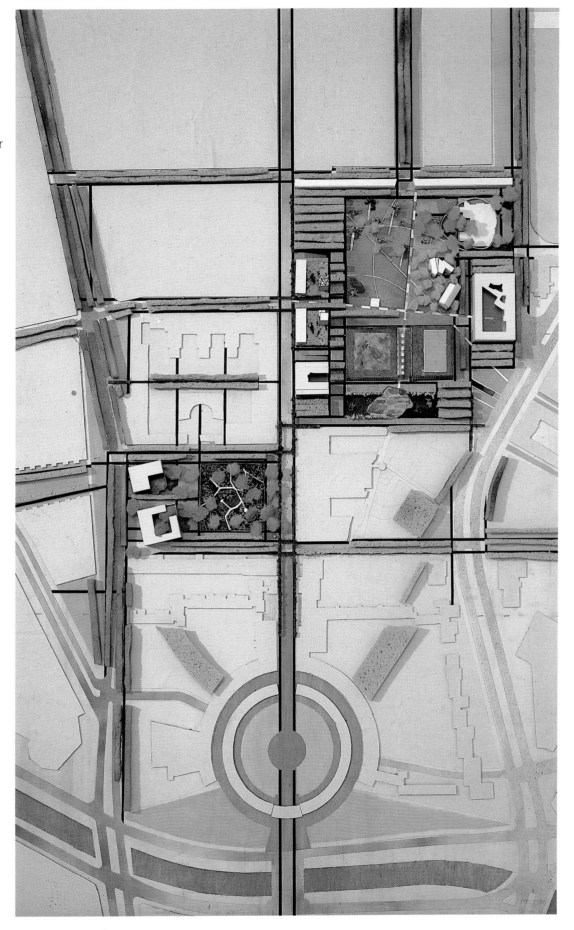

385
Site plan, scale 1:500
Mixed media wood, pasteboard,
artificial sponge, plexiglass
200.3 x 125.3 x 11.5 cm

Bessel Park
Friedrichstrasse/Neue Besselstrasse,
Block 606
2nd Phase of Competition, 1986

Jasper Halfmann
Klaus Zillich, Berlin

with Dixon W. Strauss, Josef Metzler
Garden landscaping consultant:
Renate Liefke
(recommended for further consideration for
Block 606)

386
Site plan, scale 1 : 200
Coloured Xerox copy, transparent
63.6 x 150.5 cm

Bessel Park Kindergarten, Block 606
Planning since 1984

Christoph Langhof
Thomas Hänni
Herbert Meerstein, Berlin

with Ulrike Schröder, Werner Stuckhardt

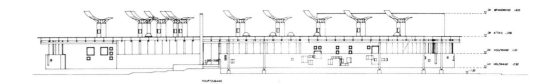

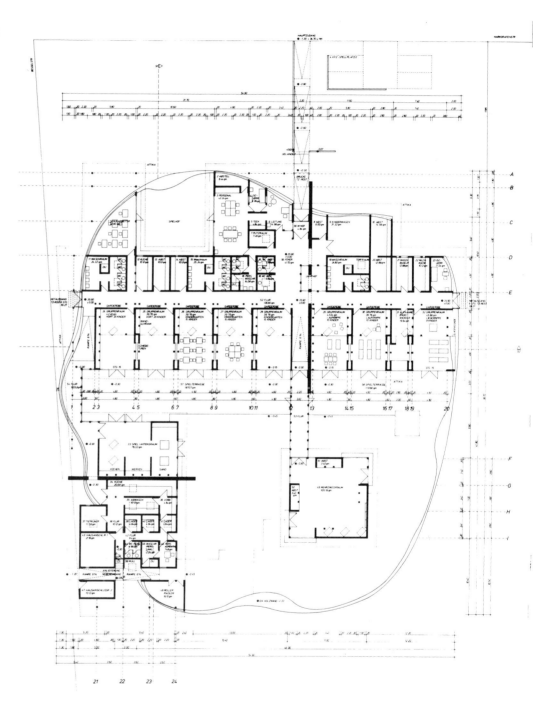

387
East elevation, scale 1:100
India ink on transparent paper,
self-adhesive foil
33.8 x 117.7 cm
Dated: 13.1.86

388
Ground plan, scale 1:100
India ink on transparent paper
Dated: 13.1.86

389
West elevation, scale 1:100
India ink on transparent paper
33.7 x 117.8 cm
Dated: 13.1.86

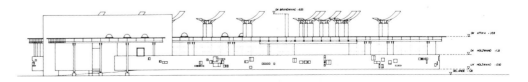

390–392
Alternatives to "Children's Island"
Three structural images, scale 1:500
Balsa wood and coloured paper in
plexiglass box
3.8 x 56 x 34.8 cm

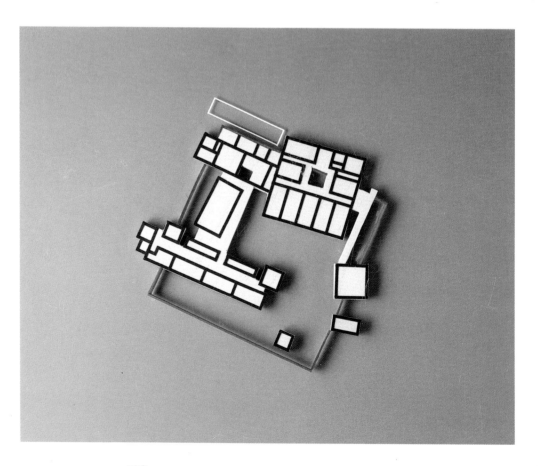

Urban Renewal

"Blue Plan"
Action Concept, April 1981
Retention of existing buildings;
no need for residents to move out

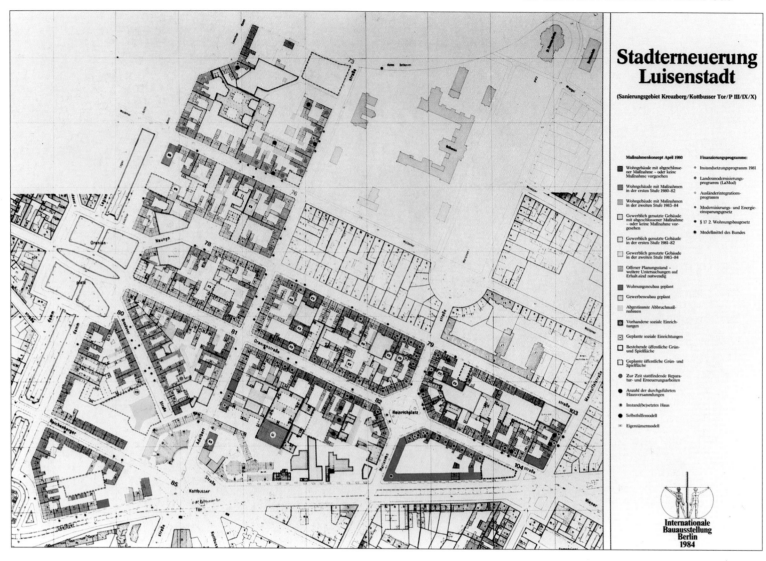

Stadterneuerung Luisenstadt

(Sanierungsgebiet Kreuzberg/Kottbusser Tor/P III/IX/X)

Internationale Bauausstellung Berlin 1984

Urban Renewal

Demonstration Areas
Luisenstadt and Kreuzberg SO 36

The exhibition presents designs drawn up in the course of preparations for the International Building Exhibition Berlin, the IBA 1987. This process of striving for more affection in the way we treat the city concentrates on two distinct spheres: IBA "Old" and IBA "New". The idea was to present, for the moment, only one of these spheres in the German Museum of Architecture.

But our efforts to save the city from despoliation assumed considerably different shapes in the two sectors of the IBA. It was therefore eventually decided to include contributions from the other field of work, the urban renewal in the east of Kreuzberg. In this very busy part of town there is an overly dense agglomeration of buildings; it has been condemned, for decades now they have been knocking buildings down to make way for a new, allegedly rational and ideal structural scheme – the mistakes that have been made, the decisions that have been based on a partial understanding of the issues, can be clearly traced here. In such a situation, if we wish to preserve values and take account of changing times, the traditional idea of artistic freedom must more than ever before be incorporated in the quest for more freedom for as many people as possible, so that in this way peace might be attained – peace as understood by Alfred North Whitehead, for whom nothing could replace the direct perception of the concrete perfection of a thing in its reality. What we need, in his view, are concrete facts, and to this end a powerful light must fall upon that which is relevant for their preciousness. By this he means art and training of the aesthetic sense.

However, since this reality is often distorted by pictures so that it becomes harder and harder to grasp, fragmentary pictures remain ambivalent and also always tend to distort more and more, to push even more of reality out of the picture.

This is all the more true in the light of a very evident trend toward graphics for the sake of graphics: for catalogues and publications.

"The converse tendency is at least equally noticeable; the egoistic desire for fame – 'that last infirmity' – is an inversion of the social impulse, and yet presupposes it. The tendency shows itself in the trivialities of child-life, as .well as in the career of some conqueror before whom mankind trembled. In the widest sense, it is the craving for sympathy. It involves the feeling that each act of experience is a central reality, claiming all things as its own. ... The point, which is here relevant, is that the zest of human adventure presupposes for its material a scheme of things with a worth beyond any single occasion, However perverted, there is required for zest that craving to stand conspicuous in this scheme of things as well as the purely personal pleasure in the exercise of faculties. It is the final contentment aimed at by the soul in its retreat to egoism, as distinct from anæsthesia. In this, it is beyond human analysis to detect exactly where the perversion begins to taint the intuition of Peace. Milton's phrase states the whole conclusion – 'That last infirmity of noble mind'". (Whitehead, "Adventures of Ideas", 1933)

Thus it is to be feared that the idea of a complex system of interrelations being illuminated by way of drawings, as the organizers of this exhibition hope, only applies to a narrow field of specialized interests. The global perils, however, which in the wake of a one-dimensional progress threaten our cities and our whole lives, can only be overcome when each detail is shown as part of an all-embracing scheme. This is what we have tried to do in the microcosmos (or microchaos) of an urban district, in Kreuzberg, Berlin. Here, once again, is the list of principles adopted in consultation with experts who have tackled analogous problems in other cities, but above all in consultation with those affected, those closest to the reality.

The Twelve Principles of careful urban renewal in Kreuzberg, Berlin

1
Careful urban renewal is a factor of the needs and interests of the present residents and businesspeople of the district. Existing structures will be used wherever possible, not destroyed. For economic, political and social reasons there is no alternative to this concept. It admits of developments over a longer term.

2
Careful urban renewal requires a very large degree of agreement on objectives and methods between the residents and businesspeople and the developers or sponsors of projects. Technical and social planning and execution must go hand in hand.

3
The inherent vitality of the quarter, its typical features, the correlations between living and working in a downtown area must be preserved and developed, confidence and optimism must be promoted. The security of residents and businesspeople requires firm, long-term tenancy agreements and leases. The structural safety of the buildings calls for the immediate repair of roof, façade and cellar defects that endanger the fabric.

4
The renewal of houses and apartments will be carried out in progressive phases. The basic phase – repair of all defects, provision of adequate riser mains, installation of inside toilets and in most cases of baths and showers – can be followed up later by further modernization work. Do-it-yourself measures on the part of the residents will also play a role in the programme.

5
The exisiting residential superstructure will be explored for opportunities to create new dwelling forms, for example, by adaptation and reorganization of ground plans.

6
The surroundings of the dwellings will be improved step by step via "minor" strategies, such as provision of greenery in interior courtyards, embellishment of façades and fireproof walls by decorative measures and plantings, and in exceptional cases via the demolition of buildings.

7
Public facilities must be renewed and added to. Streets, squares and parks are to be brought into trim and modified, avoiding drastic measures, so that the area will gain in beauty, usefulness and variety, and one is more easily able to identify with it.

8
A prerequisite for careful urban renewal is the establishment of generally binding principles for social planning. These will define affected persons' rights to be heard and their rights to material compensation.

9

The procedure of discussing and taking decisions on objectives and measures to be taken, programme planning and control should not go on behind closed doors. Delegations of interested parties will have more rights; decision-making commissions will meet locally.

10

A programme of careful urban renewal should enjoy the confidence of all concerned. This necessitates that funding for the district in question be guaranteed for a period of several years. The funds must be made available promptly according to the requirements of each case (programme flexibility).

11

The new working procedures require that the agencies and firms responsible for the renewal programme develop new organizational structures. Advisory and supportive functions (sponsors) need to be kept separate from construction-related functions (operative agents). All involved will have their tasks and functions clearly laid down. All new contracts and modifications of existing ones must conform to this principle.

12

Careful urban renewal is a continuous process. All measures taken must be so designed as to permit further urban renewal on the lines of this concept after a particular date (1987).

In his *City Portraits* Walter Benjamin writes: "Living in Moscow, one gets to know Berlin sooner than one does Moscow itself..."

But then he realizes: "How dead and empty Berlin is...; everywhere in Moscow goods are for sale out of doors. They hang on fences, they are propped against gratings, they lie on the sidewalk. Every fifty meters stand women with cigarettes, women with fruit, women with candy. Beside them, sometimes on a little sledge, is the laundry basket full of goods. A brightly colored woolen shawl protects apples and oranges against the cold, with a couple of showcase specimens on top. Next to them candy figures, nuts, sweets..."
A far-off city, a near-at-hand city. Maybe we can get to know Berlin from a visit to Frankfurt – and vice versa! Maybe we'll get a glimpse of the composite picture that otherwise escapes us.

Hardt-Waltherr Hämer

Survey to Create an Urban Environment for the area north and south of Oranienstrasse, 1986

Kaufmann & Partner, Berlin
Graphic presentation: Wolf Kaufmann

393–397
Analysis of a typical street entity. Example:
Oranienstrasse, perspective drawings
Pencil on transparent paper
Series of 5 drawings, each 30 x 42 cm

Light and shade in street perspective

Primary structure of street delineation

Evolution of alternative reorganization
proposals, Blocks 103/104

398–400
Situation 1985, Blocks 103/104 perspective
Pencil on transparent paper
30 x 42 cm

Reorganization proposal, alternative A,
Blocks 103/104 perspective
Pencil on transparent copy
30 x 42 cm

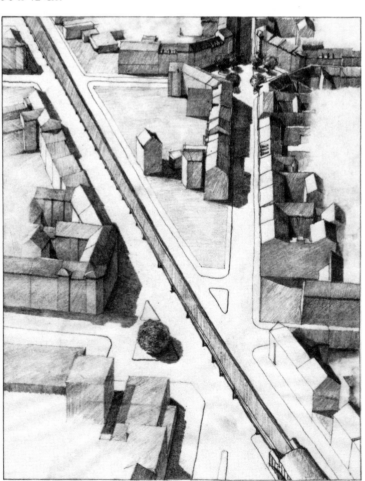

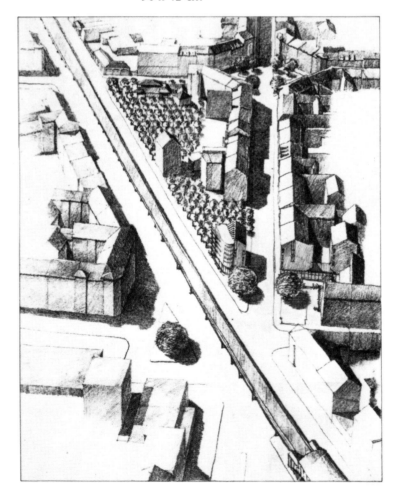

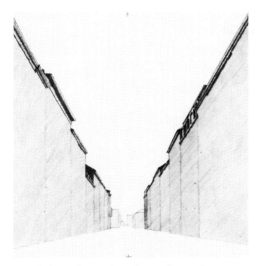

Spatial configuration through varying heights

Relief sketch of street delineation

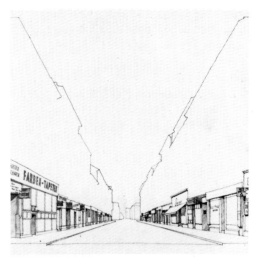

Special zone: street level

Reorganization proposal, alternative A,
Block corner perspective
Pencil on transparent paper
30 x 42 cm

SKALITZER STRASSE /ORANIENSTRASSE / MANTEUFFELSTRASSE
ALTERNATIVE A

WK 85

245

"Bullenwinkel"
Proposals for Function and Layout of
Urban Square in Naunynstrasse
Planning 1985

Peter Jürgen Haug, Berlin

401
Present state of affairs: use of square for
parking, central perspective seen from
above, scale 1 : 200
Chalk on Xerox copy on brown paper
120 x 86 cm

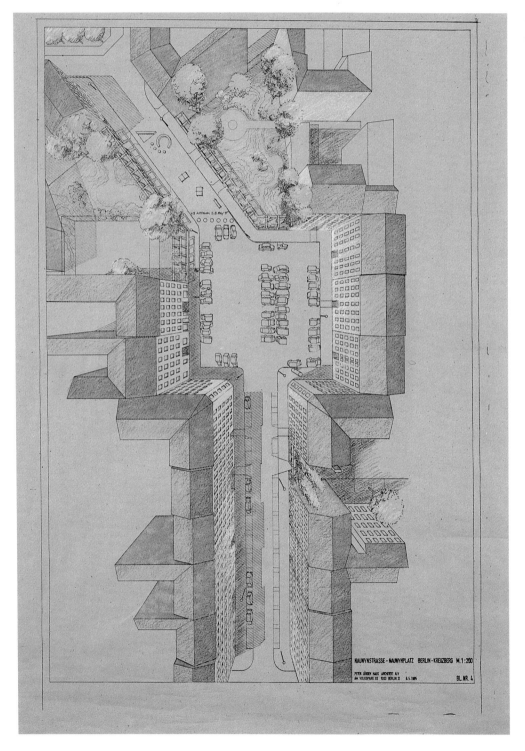

402a–c
Alternatives for utilization of space
(fountain, trees), planning kit for discussion
of projects with residents

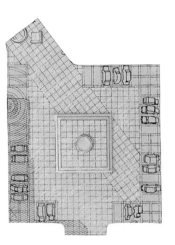

Conversion of Empty Factory into Kindergarten, rear building Oranienstrasse 4
Design 1983

Sedina Buddensieg, Berlin

with Justus Burtin, Berlin

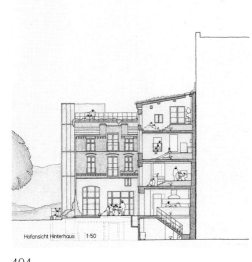

403
Garden elevation of rear building,
scale 1 : 50
Crayon on photocopy
84 x 60 cm

404
Courtyard elevation of rear building,
scale 1 : 50
Crayon on photocopy
84 x 60 cm

405
Lateral wing elevation, scale 1 : 50
Crayon on photocopy
60 x 84 cm

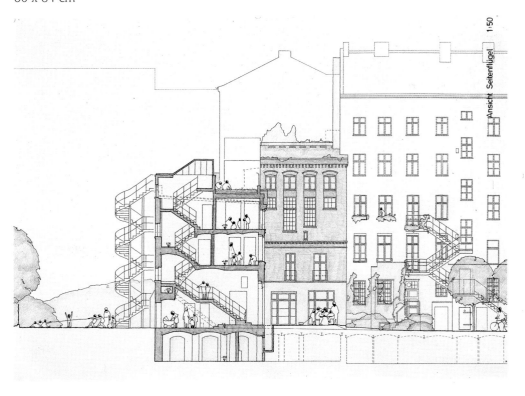

**Establishment of Kindergarten
in former factory premises and
modernization of prewar dwellings,
Naunynstrasse 69
Planning 1985**

Axel Volkmann/IBA, Berlin

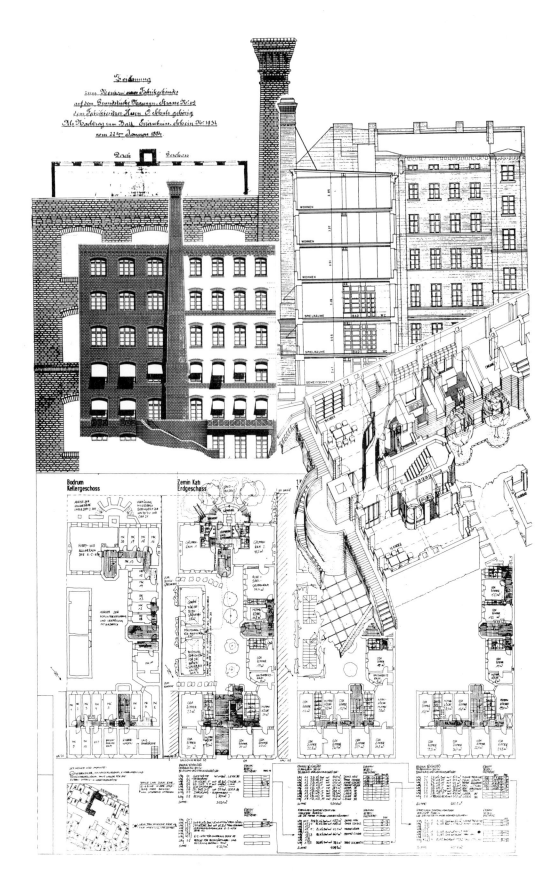

406
Elevations, section, axonometric and
ground plans
Montage from transparent photocopies
161 x 99 cm

**Design for Courtyard and Conversion
of Outbuildings, Block 79
Completed 1986**

Axel Volkmann/IBA, Berlin (planning)

Planungskollektiv Nr. 1, Berlin (execution)

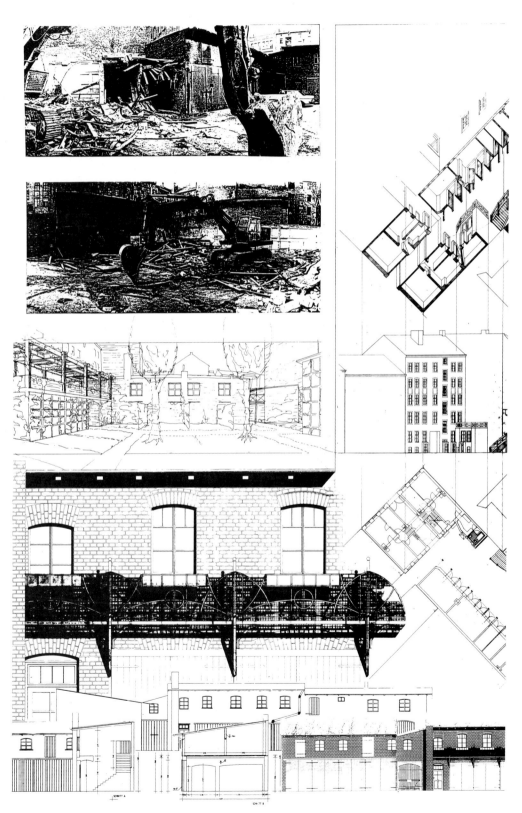

407
Perspectives, elevations, ground plan,
section and axonometric
Montage from transparent photocopies
158 x 98 cm

**Renovation with Occupant Participation
Young People's Residential and Training
Project
Oppelner Strasse 16
Work commenced 1983**

**KreuzWerk, Berlin
Graphic presentation:
Brendan Mac Riabhaigh**

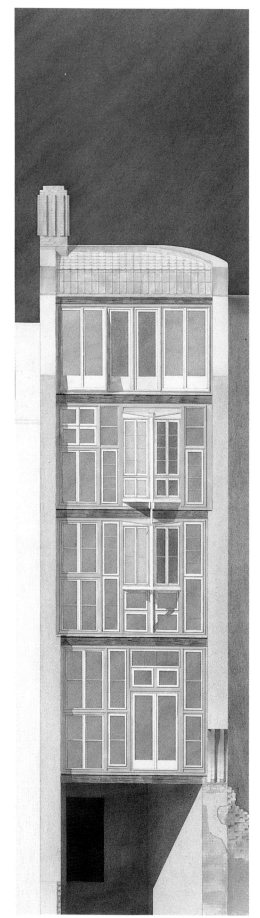

408
Façade elevation of rear building: recycled
window elements from demolished houses
used to fashion aspect facing cleared site,
scale 1 : 33.3
Pencil, pastel chalks and albumin
ultramarine on paper
93 x 54 cm

"The Two Lives of Block 88"
Historical survey of a block in Kreuzberg: planning, architecture, use – 1984

Michael Gies, Felicitas Mossmann, Fiede Rau and Martin Wuttig, Berlin

409–414
Series of six site plans showing diverse stages of development, scale 1:500
Felt pen and pencil on paper
75 x 50 cm

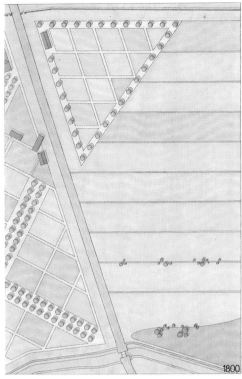

1800, garden land

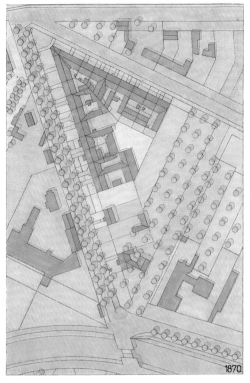

1870, development begins

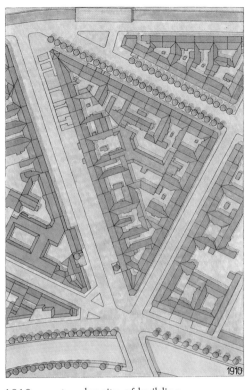

1910, greater density of building

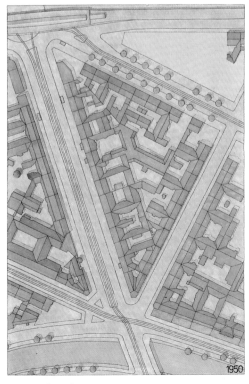

1950, after the war

1979, slum clearance

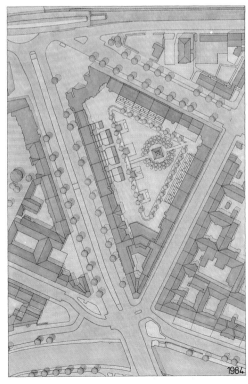

1984, new development

**Residential Development Corner of
Reichenberger Strasse and Mariannen-
strasse, Block 88
Completed 1984/85**

Wilhelm Holzbauer, Vienna

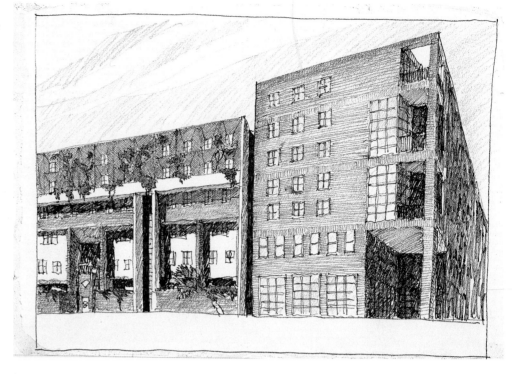

415
Sketch for corner development,
perspective
Felt pen and crayon on paper
34 x 49 cm

416
Axonometric of entire complex, courtyard
side, scale 1 : 200
Crayon on photocopy
85 x 85 cm

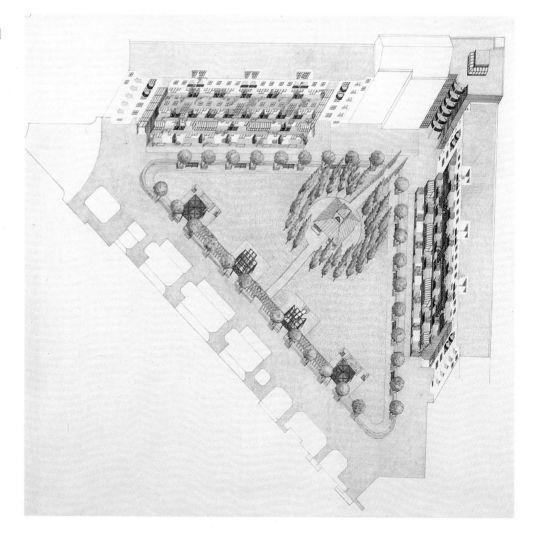

417
Façade elevation (detail), scale 1 : 25
Crayon on photocopy
80 x 49 cm

"From Auto Parking to Kid Parking"
Conversion of empty multi-story
carpark in Dresdener Strasse to kinder-
garten
Provisional design 1981/82
Work commenced 1986

Dieter Frowein and Gerhard Spangen-
berg, Berlin

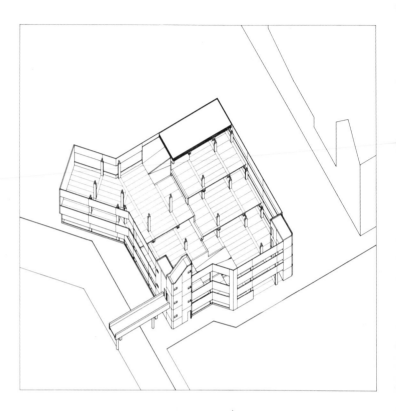

418
Structure of existing building, axonometric
section, scale 1 : 100
India ink on foil
90 x 90 cm

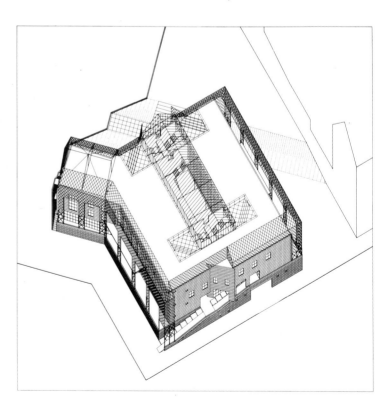

419
Kindergarten, axonometric, scale 1 : 100
India ink on foil
90 x 90 cm

420
Kindergarten, axonometric section,
3.33 m and 4.62 m levels, scale 1:100
India ink on foil
90 x 90 cm

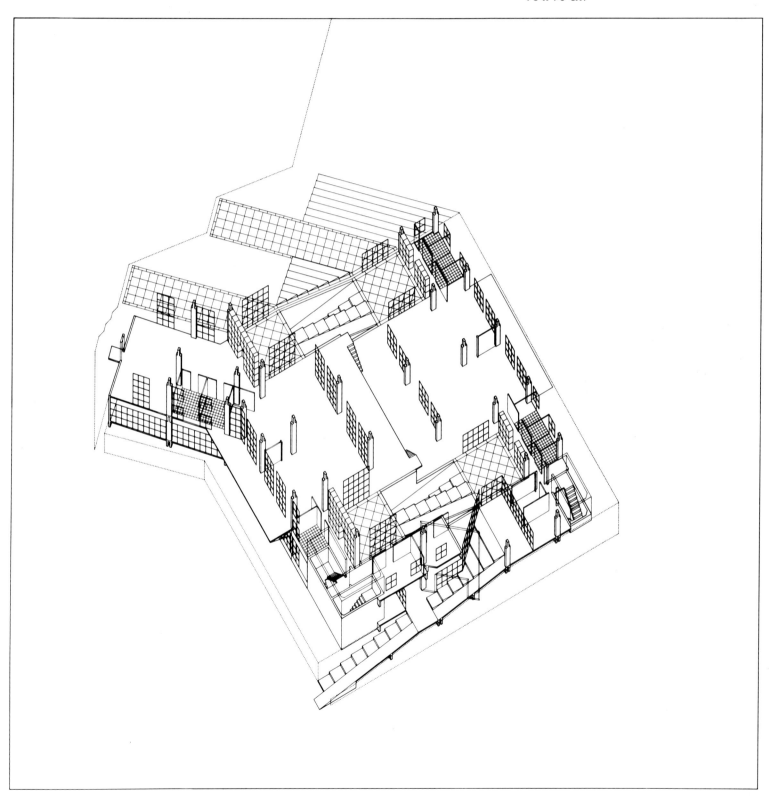

**Urbanistic Reorganization Fraenkel
Embankment, Blocks 70 and 89
Survey 1979**

Alvara Siza Vieira, Porto/Portugal

421 + 422
Site plan street level, scale 1 : 500
Photocopies
2 sheets of set, each 42 x 60 cm

423 + 424
Ground plans and elevations of new
structures planned – six building types,
scale 1 : 500
Photocopies
2 sheets, each 42 x 60 cm

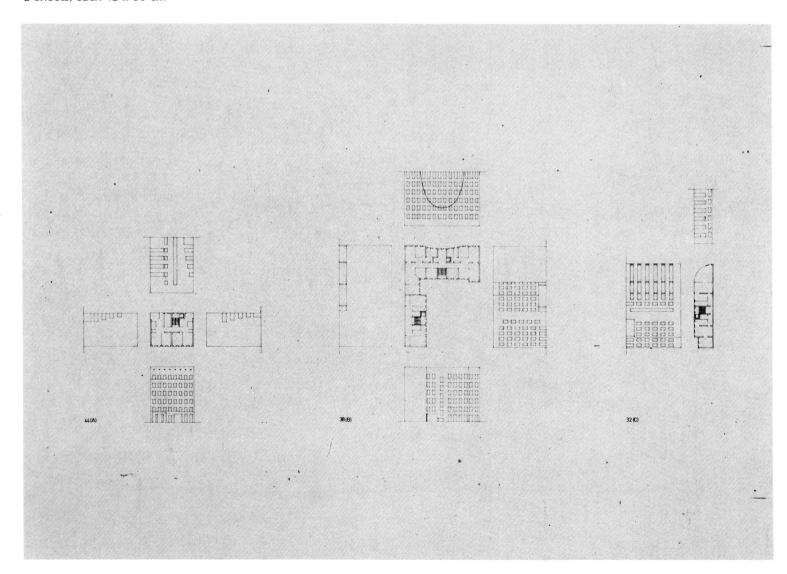

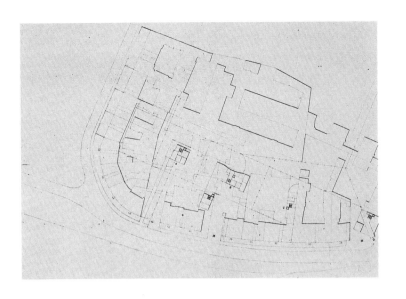

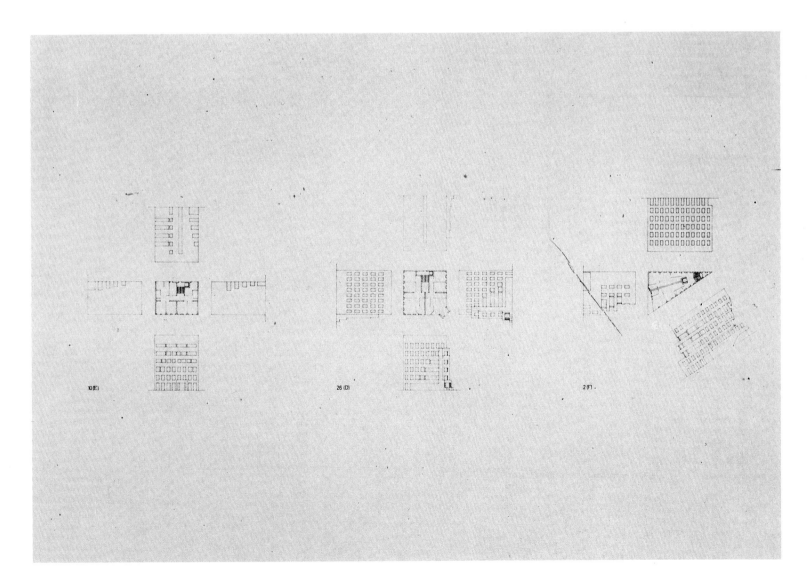

10 (E)   26 (D)   2 (F)

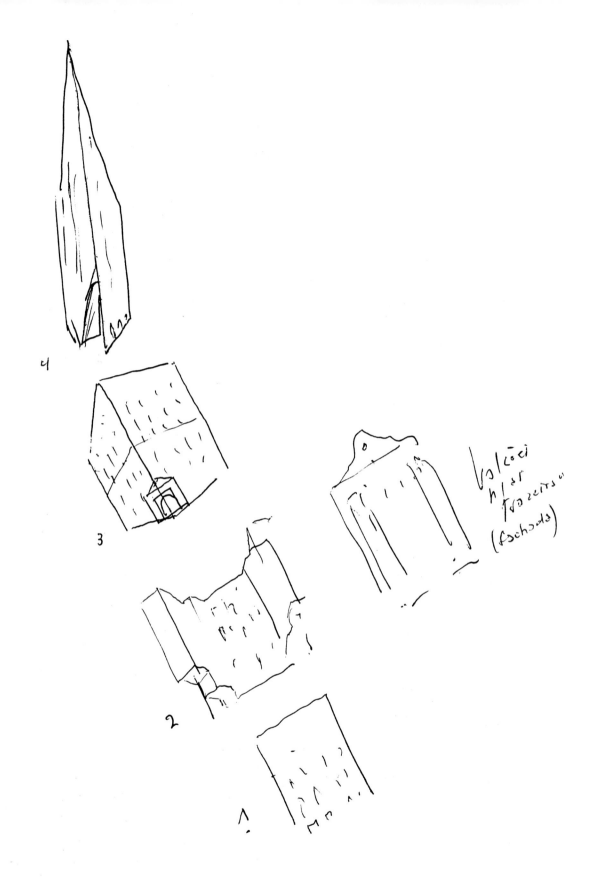

425
Sketches: elevations and perspectives of
the various types of building
Ink on paper
30 x 21 cm

426
Sketches: new development in context of
existing buildings
Ink on paper
30 x 21 cm

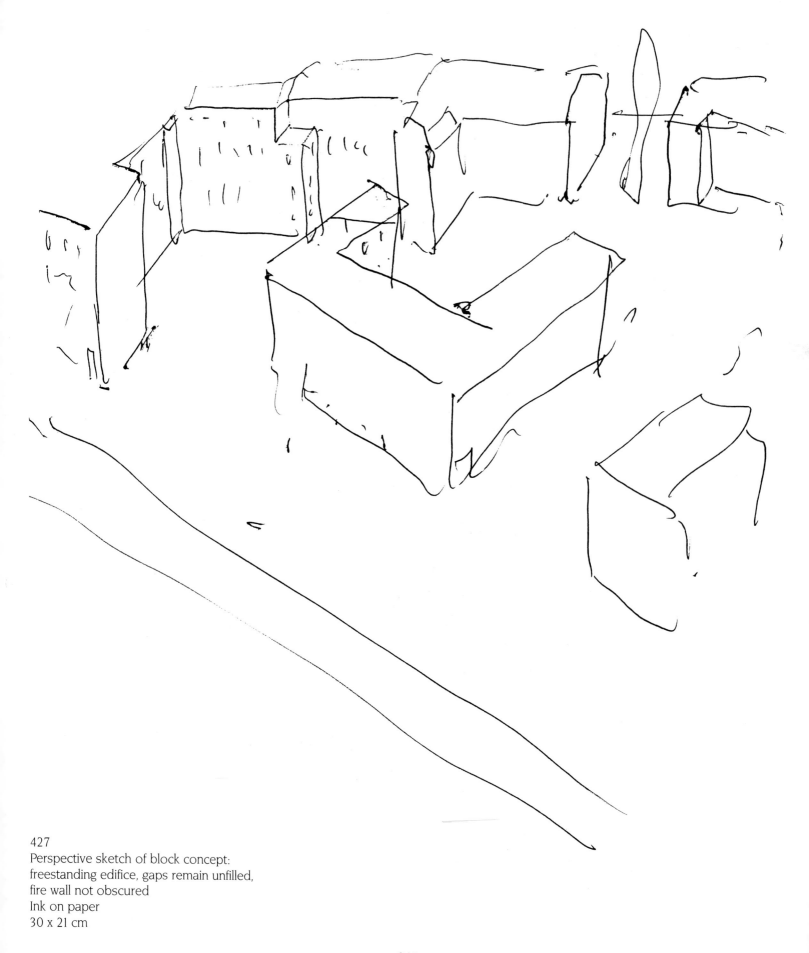

427
Perspective sketch of block concept:
freestanding edifice, gaps remain unfilled,
fire wall not obscured
Ink on paper
30 x 21 cm

**Urbanistic Reorganization Fraenkel
Embankment, Blocks 70 and 89
Survey 1979**

Inken and Hinrich Baller, Berlin

428
Ground plan sketch of urbanistic concept
Ink on transparent paper
33 x 61 cm

429
Perspective sketch of block concept:
closure of block perimeter and new
development adjacent to fire wall
Ink on transparent paper
39 x 44 cm

430
Street and courtyard elevations and
ground plans, scale 1 : 200, sections,
scale 1 : 500, perspectives – later sketches
superimposed
Crayon on photocopy, additions in ink
134 x 136 cm

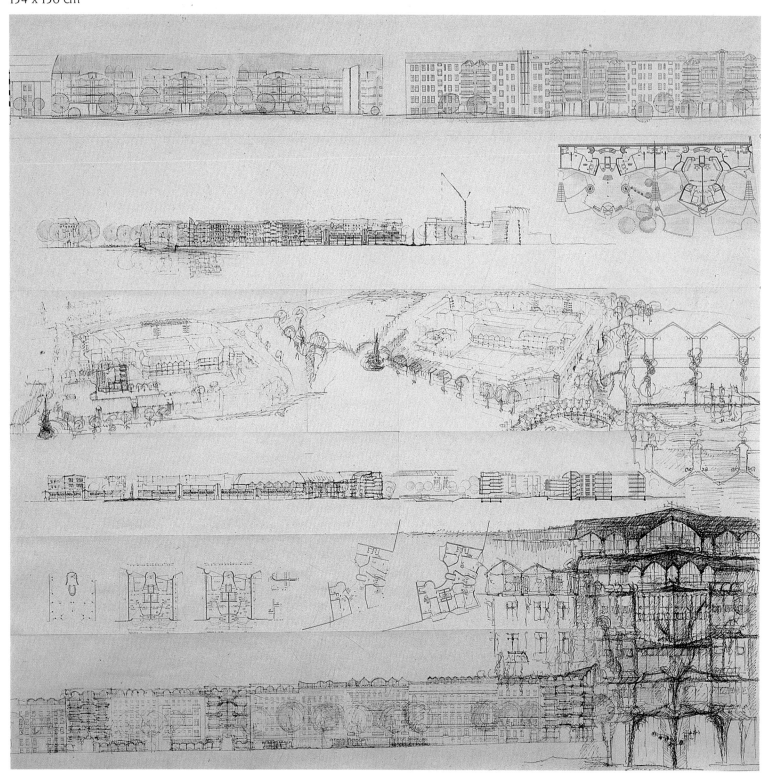

**Residential Development on Fraenkel
Embankment, Block 70
Completed 1984**

Inken and Hinrich Baller, Berlin

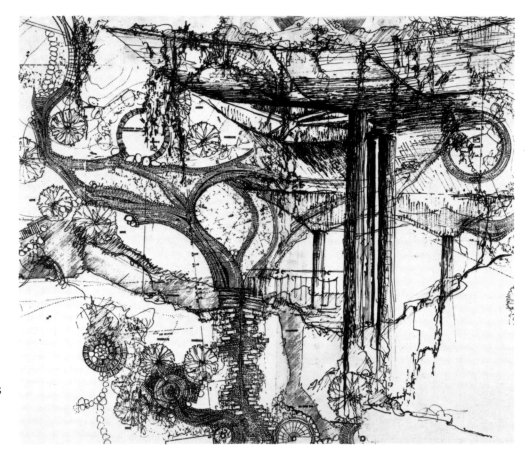

431
Perspective sketch: supports and balconies
in garden plan
Ink on transparent copy
42 x 50 cm

432
Gatehouse and renovated prewar
buildings, elevation sketch, scale 1 : 100
Photocopy and ink drawing, watercoloured
28 x 61 cm

433
"Sheet No. 201"
Working drawing for 1st floor of fire wall
development, ground plan, elevations,
sections, scale 1:20
India ink on transparent paper
80 x 127 cm

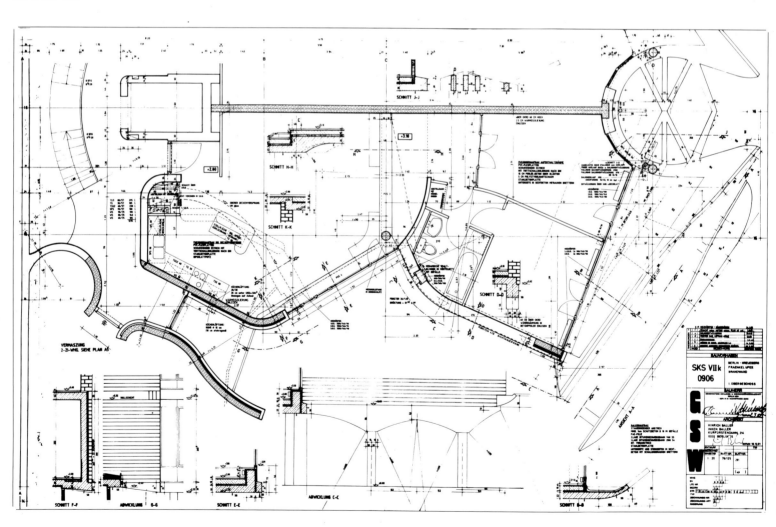

434
Garden layout, scale 1 : 50
India ink on transparent paper
172 x 246 cm (assembled from three
sheets)

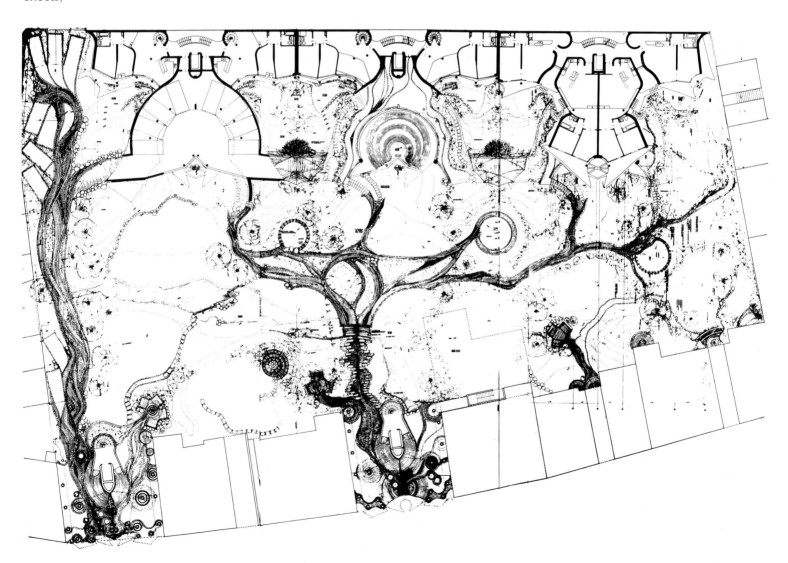

"Residential Shelving"
Do-it-yourself project,
Admiralstrasse 16 site
Completed 1986

Planning and DIY briefing:
Kjell Nylund, Cristof Puttfarken,
Peter Stürzebecher, Berlin

435
Façade axonometric with framework for
climbing plants, greenery and glasshouse
on roof, scale 1 : 100
India ink on transparent paper
42 x 30 cm

**Creche on Ground Floor of Prewar
Apartment Block
Oppelner Strasse 21, 22
Completed 1985**

Werkfabrik, Berlin

437
Ground floor plan, scale 1:50
India ink on transparent paper
80 x 80 cm

438
Prewar buildings penetrated by
new development
Ink on transparent paper
80 x 80 cm

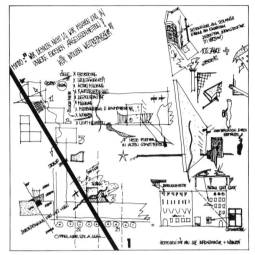

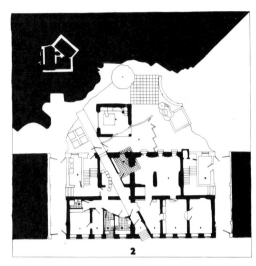

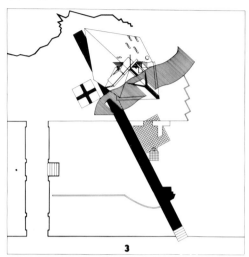

436
Planning sketches
India ink and felt pen on transparent paper
40 x 40 cm

439
Façades of the two 1874 houses, elevation,
scale 1:50
Ink on transparent paper
80 x 80 cm

**Senior Citizens' Apartments
Köpenicker Strasse 190–193
New construction and conversion of
prewar apartments
Restricted competition 1982
Work commenced 1985**

**First Prize and planning:
Otto Steidle and Partner, Berlin/
München – Siegwart Geiger, Peter
Böhm, Roland Sommerer**

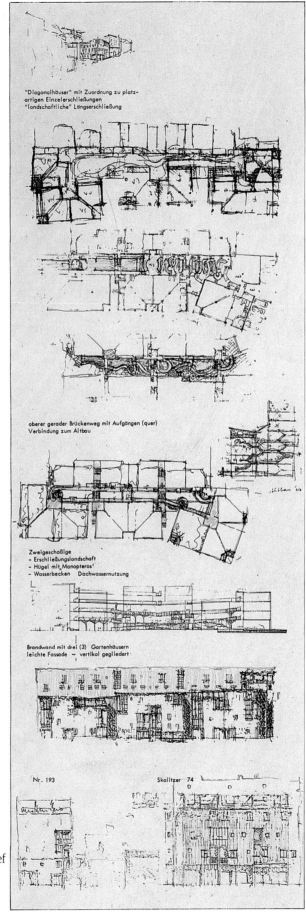

"Diagonalhäuser" mit Zuordnung zu platz-
artigen Einzelerschließungen
"landschaftliche" Längserschließung

oberer gerader Brückenweg mit Aufgängen (quer)
Verbindung zum Altbau

Zweigeschoßige
– Erschließungslandschaft
– Hügel mit Monopteros'
– Wasserbecken Dachwassernutzung

Brandwand mit drei (3) Gartenhäusern
leichte Fassade – vertikal gegliedert

Nr. 193   Skalitzer 74

440
Notes on competition: description of chief
features of design
Crayon on photocopy
69 x 62 cm (detail)

441
Design for competition: elevations and
sections, scale 1 : 200
Crayon and felt pen on photocopy
72 x 83 cm

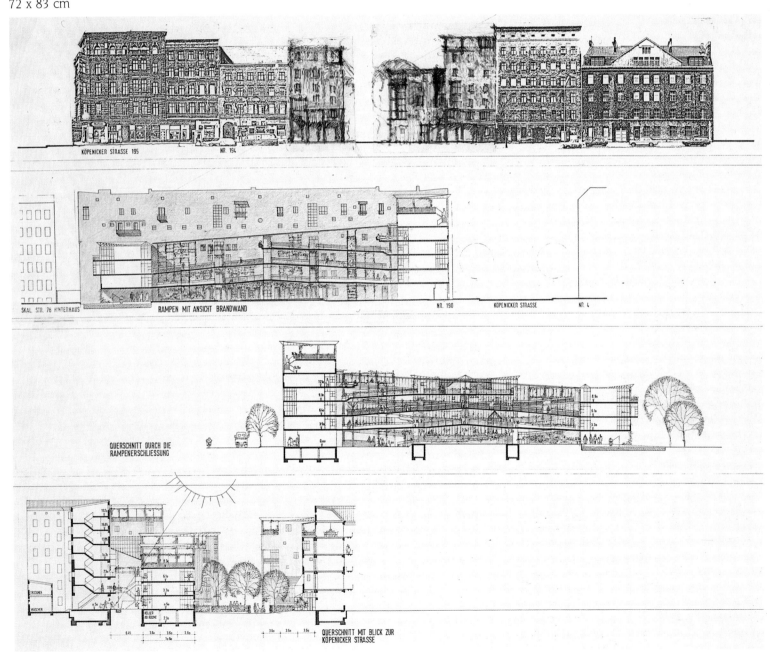

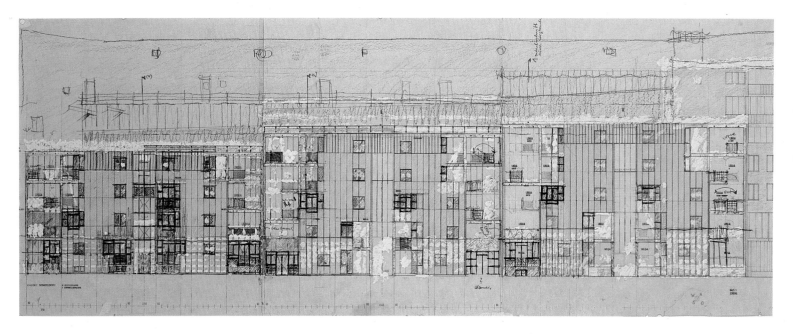

442
Façade elevation of courtyard side,
scale 1:50
Crayon, felt pen and Tipp-Ex
on photocopy
60 x 57 cm

443
Plan of 2nd floor (prewar building) and
2nd/3rd floors (new development) as
in Oct. 84, scale 1:100, with sketches
superimposed

Photocopy with additions in pencil, felt pen
and ball pen
71 x 113 cm

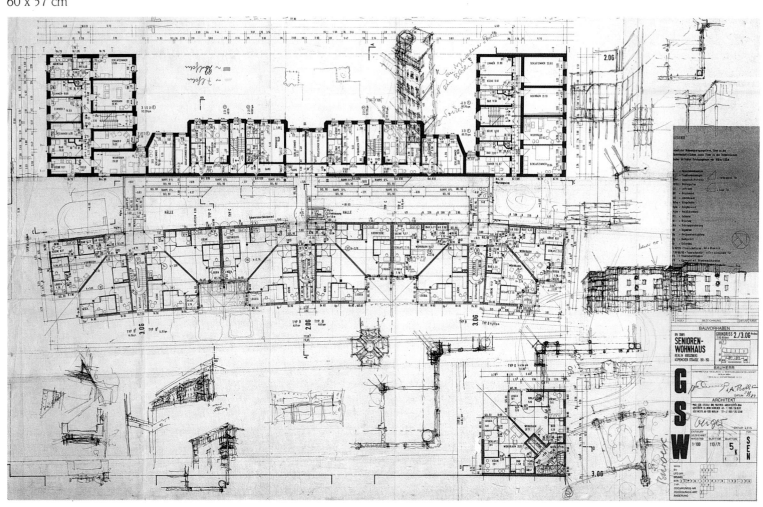

Sports Hall on Lohmühle Island
Open competition 1983/84

Highly commended
Detlef Mallwitz, Berlin

444
Site plan, scale 1 : 500
Ground plans, sections and elevations,
scale 1 : 200
Photocopy
160 x 160 cm (assembled from four sheets)

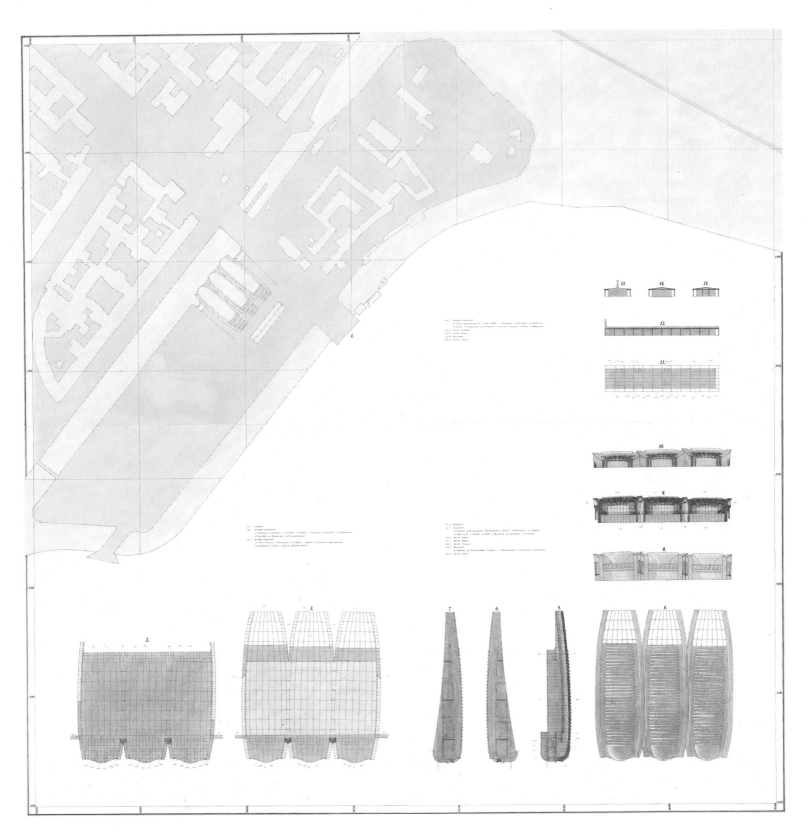

Schlesische Strasse, Block 121
Restricted competition 1980

First Prize
Alvaro Siza Vieira, Porto/Portugal

New Apartments Corner of Schlesische
Strasse and Falckensteinstrasse
Completed 1983
Nursery Schlesische Strasse 3
Work commenced 1986
Elders' club Falckensteinstrasse 6
Planning completed

Alvaro Siza Vieira, Porto Portugal
and Büro Brinkert, Berlin

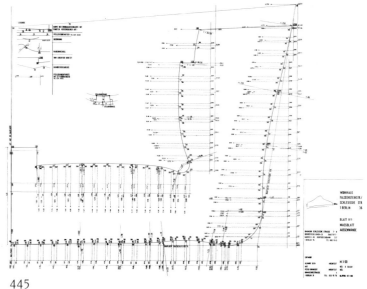

445
Corner building – new apartments
Scale drawing exterior walls, scale 1:50
India ink on transparent paper
90 x 113 cm

446
Competition entry: ground floor plan,
scale 1:500
Crayon on sepia copy under ink
on transparent paper
42 x 60 cm

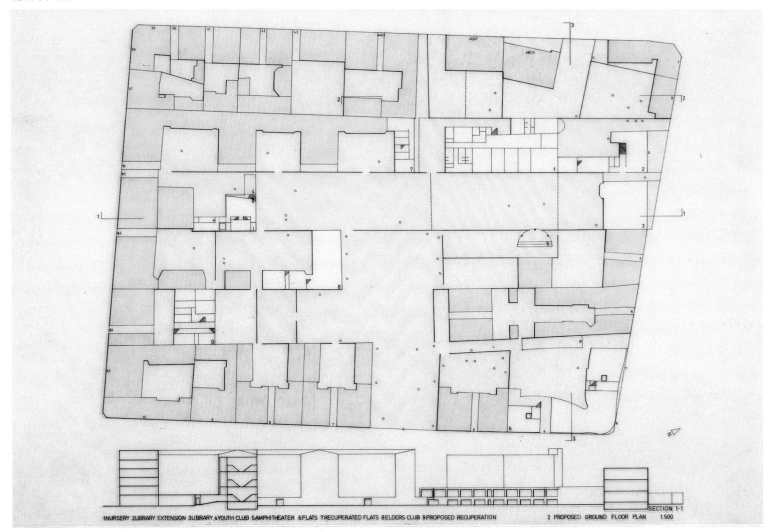

1NURSERY 2LIBRARY EXTENSION 3LIBRARY 4YOUTH CLUB 5AMPHITHEATER 6FLATS 7RECUPERATED FLATS 8ELDERS CLUB 9PROPOSED RECUPERATION   2 PROPOSED GROUND FLOOR PLAN 1:500

447
Design sketches for corner building:
perspectives of street and courtyard side
Ink on paper
30 x 21 cm

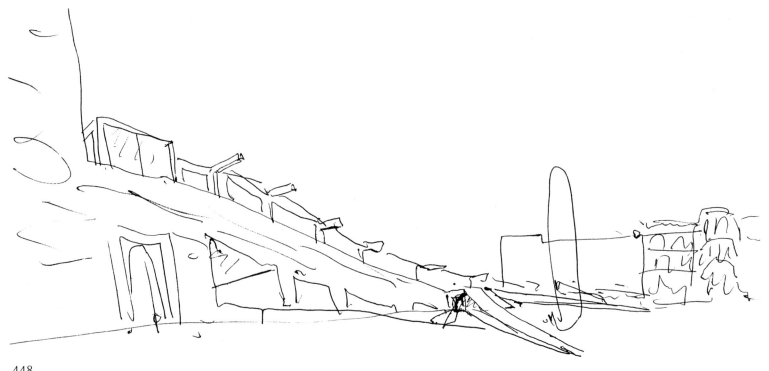

448
Perspective sketch for nursery
Ink on paper
30 x 21 cm

449
Perspective sketch for elders' leisure club
Ink on paper
30 x 21 cm

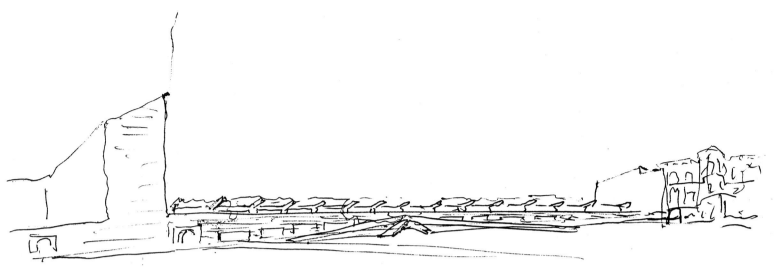

450
Perspective sketch for nursery
Ink on paper
30 x 21 cm

451
Perspective sketches for elders' leisure
club
Ink on paper
30 x 21 cm

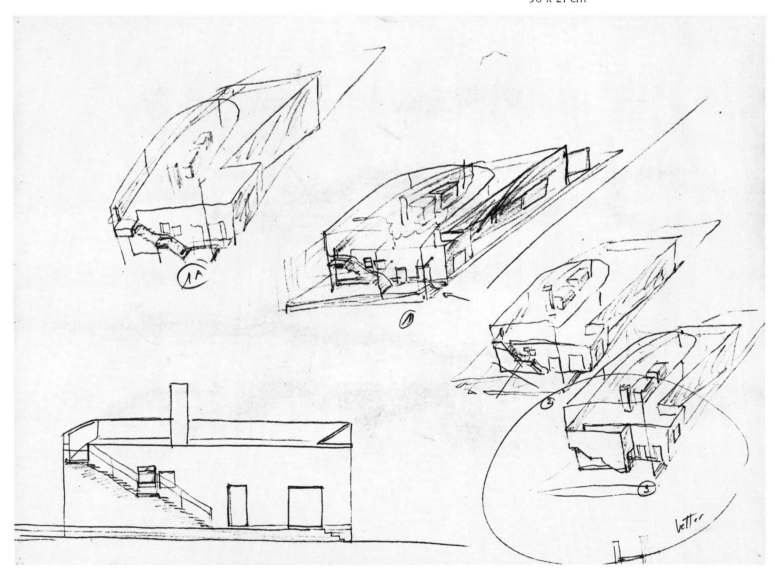

275

454
Revised ground plan for nursery, 2nd floor
Pencil and crayon on transparent paper
78 x 33 cm

452
Design sketch for nursery; perspective of
courtyard side
Ink on paper
30 x 21 cm

453
Breach of garden wall on nursery plot:
elevation, section and perspective
sketches
Pencil and crayon on transparent paper
33 x 88 cm

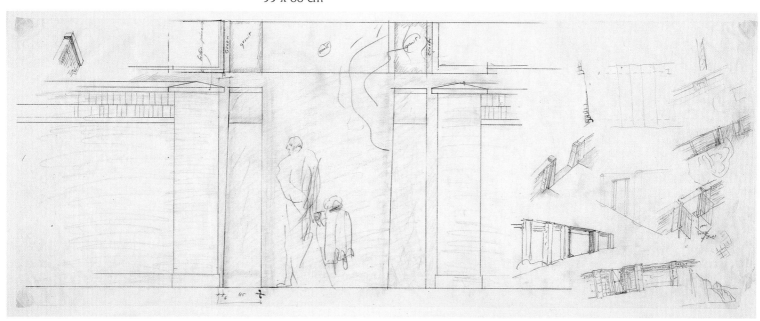

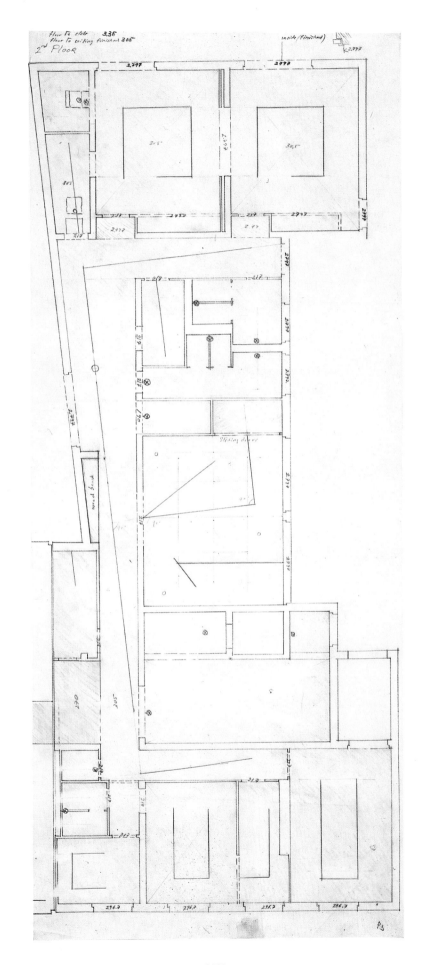

Appendix

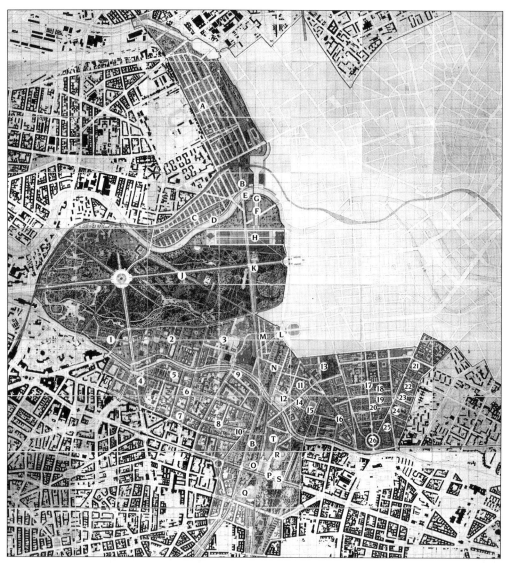

Urban Development Plan for Berlin 1984

Josef Paul Kleihues, Rorup/Berlin

with Mirko Baum, Ludger Brands,
Walther Stepp

70 prints of the Berlin map, scale 1:1000
with additions in ink and felt pen
Single sheet: 60 x 80 cm
Overall dimensions: 6 x 5.6 m

Suggested plans for IBA context areas

Northern sector

A   New urbanistic scheme for northern sector between Shipping Canal and Post Stadium, preserving existing fabric as far as possible. Rehabilitation of historic thoroughfares.

B   Development of north-south connection in the form of a strategic tree-lined boulevard, bordered in parts by green park-like areas.

C   Utilization of site of former Hamburg-Lehrter freight yard as residential area with integrated urban park; dwellings to have river views.

D   Urban configuration for north bank of river to contrast with green bank on Tiergarten side.

E   Bridge across Spree river between Moltke Bridge and Humboldt Docks and continuation of north-south boulevard through Lehrter railway station.

Spree curve and Platz der Republik

F   Reservation of sector within Spree curve for future erection of buildings in connection with Reichstag.

G   New configuration for bank of Spree curve, in keeping with its special topographic and urbanistic situation.

H   Design of an extensive piazza layout between Reichstag and Congress Hall, on both sides of new north-south boulevard throroughfare.

Tiergarten

J   Reconstruction of Tiergarten park after plans of Peter Joseph Lenné. Restoration of principal pathways, visual axes, tree groupings, goldfish pond and other details.

K   Intersection of east-west axis and newly planned north-south thoroughfare, tangential to Soviet memorial.

Potsdamer Platz and site of former Potsdamer railway station

L   New layout for Potsdamer Platz as "forecourt" to Leipziger Platz and geometric component of the stellate street system.

M   Development of areas between Potsdamer Platz and Cultural Forum, Linkstrasse and Bellevuestrasse with retention of existing buildings.

N   Peripheral constructions along Linkstrasse and Köthener Strasse as framework for projected downtown park on site of former Potsdamer station.

Three-point rail junction and site of former Potsdamer and Anhalter freight yard

O   Utilization of this extensive downtown site as second urban park, a counterpart to the Tiergarten park. Reminiscences of earlier function of site via tracings of various building contours, railway tracks and other vestiges of the past.

P   Joining up of main artery between Bülowstrasse and Gneisenaustrasse.

Q   Creation of a sports area with ancillary buildings inside the rail triangle of the urban electric network by Yorckstrasse.

R   Public swimming-bath on ground plan of former engine depot on site of Anhalter freight yard.

S   Creation of a large lake on both sides of main artery.

T   New uses for sheds of rail triangle and/or of parcel post depot in conjunction with long-term extensions to Technical Museum.

Projects and plans for new developments in central urban area

Southern Tiergarten District

1   Terraced "ecology" house and free-standing multi-unit houses (town villas) on perimeter of Tiergarten park.

2   Retention for new uses of former Japanese and Italian embassies. Former diplomatic quarter to be set aside for projects of national and international importance. Site to be used for active leisure pursuits as overspill from Tiergarten park.

3   Cultural Forum to be complemented by Science Centre alongside Landwehr Canal and apartment buildings on Sigismundstrasse. Centre of Cultural Forum to be designed as lavish downtown area between the two hubs of the divided city.

4   "Reconstruction" of Lützowplatz as "gateway to the Tiergarten park" by enclosing square on three sides by new buildings. Recreation of a green urban square, aided by elimination of thoroughfares. Re-erection of a Hercules fountain.

5   "Repair" of the derelict blocks on Lützowplatz by building energy-saving houses along Landwehr Canal, terrace and free-standing urban houses in block interiors, "transparent" peripheral structures. Preservation of former "Pumpe" and rededication as youth centre, erection of new day nursery.

6   New layout for Magdeburger Platz.

7   Creation of another green urban square. New building for day nursery and long-term plans for walkway network in block.

8   Renovation of old structures, provision of green spaces within block, and new buildings to round off picture.

9   Emphatic corner structures will make the opening of Potsdamer Strasse onto the Cultural Forum a sort of "gateway". In the long run, closing off of the quasi-park Am Karlsbad by a crescent.

10   Apartment houses to emphasize perimeter of urban area opposite planned local park on site of former freight yards.

Southern Friedrichstadt

11   Diversified measures for "block repair", creation of green courts, pocket parks and walkways, as the excessive dimensions of the blocks in southern Friedrichstadt are a hindrance to the communicative vitality of the metropolis.

12   Restoration of the former dock basin and utilization as ships' moorings for Technical Museum.

13   Memorial for victims of Nazi regime and utilization of site of former Prinz Albrecht palace as downtown park.

14   Erection of primary school with gymnasium and sportsground on Schöneberger Strasse.

15   Utilization of former Anhalter railway station as local park; ruderal vegetation on the old elevated embankment to be retained and incorporated in the scheme.

16   Creation of a "Schinkel Square" with central greenspread to set off Kreuzberg monument.

17   Revitalization of Friedrichstrasse as shopping centre and central artery of southern Friedrichstadt.

18   Projected park opening onto Friedrich- and Markgrafenstrasse. Integration of a day nursery into this park, to be christened "Bessel Park".

19   Long-term project for demolition of flower market hall and use of site as public green space surrounded by block structures of diversified detail.

20   Development of primary school with play areas and creation of a centre for deaf people.

21   Adjuncts to north Ritterstrasse project.

22   Eventual relocation of a factory, additions to residential block and creation of green areas and playgrounds.

23   Realization of so-called "Victoria Project".

24   Development of an ornamental garden for the Berlin Museum and plans for a southern extension to the building.

25   Degrading of Lindenstrasse and realignment of thoroughfares around Erich Mendelsohn's Metal Trades Union building.

26   Long-term plans to reinsert Wilhelmstrasse and Lindenstrasse into the circle of Mehringplatz, retaining existing structures as far as possible and complementing design with new buildings.

Index of Names